CALL ME GIAMBATTISTA

FOOTPRINTS SERIES
Jane Errington, Editor

The life stories of individual women and men who were participants in interesting events help nuance larger historical narratives, at times reinforcing those narratives, at other times contradicting them. The Footprints series introduces extraordinary Canadians, past and present, who have led fascinating and important lives at home and throughout the world.

The series includes primarily original manuscripts but may consider the English- language translation of works that have already appeared in another language. The editor of the series welcomes inquiries from authors. If you are in the process of completing a manuscript that you think might fit into the series, please contact her, care of McGill-Queen's University Press, 1010 Sherbrooke Street West, Suite 1720, Montreal, QC H3A 2R7.

Call Me Giambattista

A Personal and Political Journey

JOHN CIACCIA

McGill-Queen's University Press

Montreal & Kingston · London · Chicago

© McGill-Queen's University Press 2015

ISBN 978-0-7735-4577-9 (cloth)
ISBN 978-0-7735-9742-6 (ePDF)
ISBN 978-0-7735-9743-3 (ePUB)

Legal deposit third quarter 2015
Bibliothèque nationale du Québec

Printed in Canada on acid-free paper that is 100% ancient forest free
(100% post-consumer recycled), processed chlorine free

McGill-Queen's University Press acknowledges the support of the Canada
Council for the Arts for our publishing program. We also acknowledge the
financial support of the Government of Canada through the Canada Book
Fund for our publishing activities.

Library and Archives Canada Cataloguing in Publication

Ciaccia, John, 1933–, author.
      Call me Giambattista : a personal and political journey
    / John Ciaccia.

    (Footprints series ; 21)
    Includes bibliographical references and index.
    Issued in print and electronic formats.
    ISBN 978-0-7735-4577-9 (bound). – ISBN 978-0-7735-9742-6 (ePDF). –
    ISBN 978-0-7735-9743-3 (ePUB)

    1. Ciaccia, John, 1933–. 2. Québec (Province). Assemblée
    nationale – Officials and employees – Biography. 3. Politicians – Québec
    (Province) – Biography. 4. Lawyers – Québec (Province) – Biography.
    5. Italian Canadians – Québec (Province) – Biography. 6. Québec
    (Province) – Politics and government – 1960–. 7. Québec (Province) –
    Biography. I. Title. II. Series: Footprints series ; 21

    FC2921.1.C52A3   2015 971.4'04092   C2015-903797-2
                                                              C2015-903798-0

To all those who aspire to the political life
in order to bring positive change to the lives of people.

Contents

Acknowledgments

I want to thank Bryan Demchinsky for his help in drafting the text, Philip Cercone who quickly accepted to have McGill-Queen's edit the book, Mark Abley for his advice and patience with my inquiries and for titling the photos, Shelagh Plunkett who did a superb job of editing, Ryan Van Huijstee for coordinating the editing with his colleagues, and Jacqueline Michelle Davis for her work on the marketing copy.

I appreciated the enthusiastic response of Lise Bergevin, who heads Lémeac Éditeur and who also published my first book. It was gratifying to hear her reaction.

Thanks to Marie-Claude Fortin who found the book "passionnant" and who edited the French edition.

I want to express my thanks and gratitude to Suzanne Roch who translated the book to reflect the spirit in which it was written in English.

I want to thank my son Mark for his patience and understanding, for patiently living with a father who spent all of his time writing a book.

I want to thank Norma for all the work she did in keeping the press clippings, which helped me to write this book, for helping me in my early political life and during every election, and for being a good mother to our son Mark.

I want to give special thanks to Martha Ebssa who was my sounding board every day when I was writing, for her research and documentation of the newspaper clippings, for reacting to my reading of the book and offering her opinion which often led to improved changes, and for organizing the photos.

Thanks to Paula Pedicelli, for her contribution to the title and in the early chapters of the manuscript.

To Worku Aberra for his help in the editing.

A book does not get written alone. I was fortunate, and gratified, to have received the help of so many capable and pleasant people.

My father, Pasquale Andrea Ciaccia, as an Italian soldier in 1918.

My father proudly wearing his Italian war medal, the Medaglia e Croce di Guerra al Valor Militare.

At age four with my mother
Angèlina (sitting), my aunt
Carmelina (standing), and my
sister Maria in 1937.

My parents on their wedding
anniversary in 1951.

Graduating from McGill University with a BCL in 1957. My future wife Norma is on the left.

At home with my son, Mark, who was born in July 1962.

Sailing to the Bahamas for a winter vacation with Norma and Mark in 1966.

With Chief Dave Courchene, one of the founders of the National Indian Brotherhood, and Jean Chrétien, minister of Indian Affairs and Northern Development. (The identity of the man on the right is unknown.) In 1971, I had been appointed assistant deputy minister of Indian Affairs at the federal level.

The James Bay and Northern Quebec Agreement of 1975 was a pivotal moment in the history of both Quebec and Canada. Seated, from left: Judd Buchanan (federal minister of Indian Affairs and Northern Development), Charlie Watt (representing the Inuit of northern Quebec), Quebec Premier Robert Bourassa, myself (chief negotiator for the government of Quebec), Jean Chrétien (president of the Treasury Board), Billy Diamond (representing the James Bay Cree).

Campaigning for the "No" side in the 1980 referendum on sovereignty-association.

I wonder now what Prime Minister
Pierre Trudeau was saying into my ear.

A picture from the late 1980s, with Premier Robert Bourassa, Jean Chrétien,
and Quebec Revenue Minister Michel Gratton. I was minister of Energy at
the time.

Jacques Chirac, then prime minister of France, visited the James Bay development in 1987. To Bourassa's disappointment, he showed more interest in the bears than the dams.

Signing an economic development agreement with the State of New York in 1988. New York's governor, Mario Cuomo, is standing at the back right.

An emotional moment in the National Assembly
in December 1988. My friend Clifford Lincoln
(shown with me in this picture) and two other
anglophone ministers resigned from the Bourassa
government because of the language restrictions
in Bill 178. I chose to remain in the cabinet.

Visiting an elementary school in my riding, Mount Royal, during an
election campaign.

In November 1989, a few weeks after I became Quebec's minister of
International Affairs, I met Lech Walesa, the founder of Solidarity and future
president of Poland, on his visit to Montreal. The Berlin Wall had only
just fallen.

As minister of International Affairs, I had the chance to visit more than forty
countries. This picture shows a private audience I had with Pope John Paul II
in Rome, February 1990.

In Prague, in 1990, I met the recently elected president of Czechoslovakia, Vaclav Havel.

From time to time I would show off my skills on the jazz piano. This event was an AIDS fundraiser in 1991, and I was performing with the Preville Big Band.

In the Paris office of Édith Cresson, who from 1991 to 1992 was the first female prime minister of France.

With Russian President Boris Yeltsin, on his brief visit to CAE Electronics in Montreal, 1992.

While on an economic mission to Africa I had a chance to play the drum in a village in Gabon.

Visiting Saudi Arabia on another economic mission.

With Rigoberta Menchú, the Guatemalan activist for indigenous rights.
She gave a speech in Montreal not long after winning the Nobel Peace Prize
in 1992.

With Yitzhak Rabin, the prime minister of Israel, and Sheila Finestone
(federal MP for Mount Royal) in Montreal, 1993.

In January 1994, Daniel Johnson Jr became premier. Here I am being sworn into his cabinet as minister of Immigration and Cultural Communities as well as minister of International Affairs.

With my grandsons Eric and Nicholas in my Beaconsfield home in 1996.

CALL ME GIAMBATTISTA

I

Arrival in a New Land

Baci a I miei figli, ci vediamo in l'altro mondo.
(Kiss my children goodbye; we'll meet in the next world.)

These were the words my father wrote to my mother, who had initially refused to leave Italy and to join him in Canada. Fortunately she later changed her mind, and we arrived in Montreal, via Ellis Island, in 1937, on the eve of World War II.

And so Giambattista Nicola Ciaccia, came to a new country. I was four years old.

We had sailed on the *Rex*, a ship that was the pride of Mussolini's Italy, which had won the blue ribbon for the fastest time in crossing the Atlantic. She was sunk by the British, on the Mediterranean, shortly before the end of World War II. The captain of the British destroyer who was given the order to sink the *Rex* almost apologized for sinking such a beautiful ship.

Having been told that my father had gone to America, I expected to see him when we arrived at Ellis Island. But standing on the dock surrounded by our few possessions, it was obvious that no one was there to greet us.

"Where is *papa*?" I demanded of my mother.

"He's not here," she said.

"Then this is not America," I insisted.

"Yes, Gian," my mother patiently replied. "We are in America."

"Then where is *papa*?" I pressed on asking.

These questions of a curious child and the responses of a patient mother went on for some time. If my father was not on the dock with us, I thought, then we must be somewhere else, and despite my mother's reassuring answers, I could not be convinced otherwise. Even at such an early age, my brain showed a stubborn preference for logical thinking, the rules of which were ingrained in me and stuck with me throughout most of my life. Whether it is my upbringing or an innate capacity, I seem hardwired for logical thinking.

We almost didn't make it to Canada. In those days, because of the US government's health requirements for immigrants, when newcomers arrived they were examined by a doctor. The unfortunate souls who did not meet US health standards, were not admitted and sent back, their dreams shattered, their hopes dashed, and their ambitions frustrated.

I had been very seasick on the voyage from Naples to New York, a trip that took us seven to eight days. To the horror of my mother, the doctor who examined me wouldn't certify my good health because he felt there was something about my eyes – eyes that were sunken by sea-sickness and saddened by my father's absence – that indicated an unhealthy child. We were held over. We slept overnight in the government barracks, where there were people from different ethnic groups and backgrounds, including some black people. My mother, who had never seen black people before, was terrified. The next day, the doctor realized we were not staying in the US, and, despite his reservation about my health, let us go.

This was not the first time that my parents had immigrated to Canada. They had come to this country in 1922, after the birth of my sister Mary, but then returned to Italy in 1929 because, I was told, my father was needed there to support and take care of his father.

My father came from a small town called Ielsi, which was then part of Abruzzi, a region halfway between Rome and Naples, on the Adriatic side. In the early 1960s it separated from Abruzzi and became the new region of Molise. With that regional "separation" as a reference point, during the 1980 referendum on Quebec independence, I would facetiously say that I knew all about separation. My mother, on the other hand, lived in Limosano, a hillside town, some twenty kilometers from my father's hometown. Following an old tradition, after the war, both of my parents' families arranged for them to meet, visit, and eventually marry, a marriage between two reputable families. Later, after the birth of my sister Mary, my parents immigrated to Canada. It was 1922, the year Mussolini came to power.

In his late teens my father suffered the heart-breaking end to a youthful romance. The timing of the breakup was doubly unfortunate for him because World War I, in which Canada and Italy were allies, had just begun. In a fit of anger and frenzy at his loss and out of the desire to get away from the scene of his pain, he joined a cavalry unit, which was much riskier than becoming an ordinary soldier. He fought in the trenches, the brutal hallmark of the Great War, earning many medals, one of which was given only to soldiers involved in trench warfare for at least one year. For his bravery and dedication he was made a Cavalliere (Knight) of the Order of Vittorio Veneto, a town in the Alpine foothills, famous for its history. There, between October and November of 1918, Armando Diaz, the Italian general, won a decisive victory over the Austrians. This ended the war on the Italian front with the unconditional surrender of Austria-Hungary.

The military Order of Vittorio Veneto was founded as a national order by the fifth President of the Italian Republic, Giuseppe Saragat, in 1968, "to express the gratitude of the nation" to those who had been decorated with the War Cross for Military Valour (Medaglia e Croce di Guerra al Valor Militare). As a young boy, to seek popularity, I shared my father's medals with my friends on St Denis Street, not knowing the importance they signified.

When my father enlisted in the army and went to the war front, his mother was gravely ill, but she prayed to stay alive until his safe return. Her prayers were answered; my father did return home safe and sound, and she died shortly after.

After we arrived in Montreal, my father worked as a tailor. We first lived in a triplex on St Denis Street in a mostly French-speaking area of the city. It was on the fringe of Montreal's "Little Italy," one block north of the Casa d'Italia, built in 1936 as a centre of the city's Italian community.

A vivid recollection from that time: one winter, while walking down the sloping, snow-covered back steps, I slipped through a broken railing and fell two-and-a-half storeys. Miraculously I was not hurt. I picked myself up and howled all the way back up to my home on the third floor. Today, people would sue the landlord for neglect and damages; then, we just kept paying the rent.

My mother was a remarkable woman in many respects. She immigrated to Canada at a young age without knowing either French or English but managed to lead a successful life. Her endeavour, desire, and determination to succeed in life, and her hopes for her two children to have the best that life could offer, were her utmost goals.

She was an excellent money manager, who was skilful at saving and wise in spending. Besides intelligently managing my father's earnings for household expenses, she was able to put enough money aside, in five years, to buy our first home in NDG, a middle class neighbourhood.

When it came to our education, she placed equal emphasis on academic studies, art, and music for both my sister and me, making sure that we had properly qualified teachers for all our education. She made all of the important household decisions, with my father taking a secondary role. Driven by success, inspired by her devout dedication to her children, she had a will of iron.

Despite her modest background, she had an extraordinary aptitude for solving problems, handling people, and managing a business, the benefits of which she generously shared with her friends. Many of them bought fine properties at her urging. My mother was adept at handling unexpected situations, even crises. For example, when I was still in law school, a partner and I made an offer on a building, but after the offer was made and as we were about to sign the deed of sale, my partner reneged on our agreement. I was shocked. I was confused. I didn't know what to do, but luckily my mother took over. She negotiated a new deal with the owner, Mr Michael Hornstein of Federal Construction, and we completed the transaction. I still own the building, a monument to my mother's adept negotiation skills, business acumen, and stubborn determination.

My mother had elegant tastes, always looking for and obtaining the best furnishings and decorations. When I moved into my present home, she arranged for a Persian carpet, a Kerman, to be brought from Vancouver for my living room. Some years later, when I went to Tehran on an official mission, I saw a similar carpet in the Shah's palace.

Although Canada is a country of immigrants, it did not mean that all immigrants were universally accepted, especially by the youth. Attitudes toward each other, especially between French-speaking youth and immigrant children, were often brutal. St Denis Street was no different. As a reminder, I still have a scar under my nose from a rock thrown at me.

During my primary education, I attended Holy Family, an Irish Catholic elementary school with many immigrant children, mostly of Italian origin. It was located two streets over and directly to the rear of where we were living. During the early part of my third year, I was told I was "too smart" to be in third grade and was placed in fourth grade. Although grade four was initially challenging, I soon adjusted and excelled in my schoolwork.

We left our rented home on St Denis Street when my mother bought a duplex on Draper Avenue north of Monkland, in NDG, a mainly English-speaking area. (I say "my mother" advisedly because she made all the important decisions.) How we were able to buy such a property, in a relatively prosperous neighbourhood, just five years after arriving in Canada, is one of her many remarkable achievements.

In the meantime, Canada declared war on Germany at the beginning of my first school year and then, just prior to the end of that year, before the summer break, on Italy. Canada's declaration of war did not in itself affect the attitude of the French-speaking community toward the immigrant communities of the district, especially among the youth, but we had our own private wars.

But the attitude of the English community was different. The war created a particularly hostile atmosphere and resulted in personal battles between myself, then ten years old, and other children in NDG. In any group, outsiders are harassed. However, at my age these persistent torments were cruel and hard to bear. They turned what should have been a joyous and carefree time of life into a time of fear and misery. It was not only physical (as with the incident on St Denis Street). There were more vicious methods of rejection and humiliation. Rock throwing has physical effects that are quickly overcome. Emotional hurts endure.

I remember ringing the doorbell of someone I knew to ask him to come out to play, only to have the door slammed in my face. On another occasion, I screamed and refused to kiss the foot of one of my tormentors who had wrestled me to the ground in front of his friends. I was the enemy. Although I come from a rich culture, history, and civilization, I was made to feel ashamed of my culture. And so "John" Ciaccia was born, and "Giambattista Nicola" Ciaccia became a memory.

In later years, my attitude towards the negative treatment I was subjected to changed, but going through it at the time, during my formative years, was painful. The experience had profound effects on my behaviour, my work, and the career that I pursued.

My mother, ever eager to help me develop intellectually and artistically, decided that I should take piano lessons when I was seven years old. It was obvious to her that, for Giambattista, the piano teacher had to be a good one, if not the best. And that excellent piano teacher, Mrs Fleuritte Huppé happened to live some distance, a few kilometers, away from our home. So, every Saturday, I would take, alone, a fifteen-minute tram ride to St Joseph Boulevard, where the teacher lived. (In those days, electric tramways were still the principal part of Montreal's public transportation system.)

When we moved to NDG, my mother found another reputable piano teacher, Mr Arthur Letondal, whose son was a well-known musician. He lived even farther away from our home. Again, every Saturday I would take two busses, from NDG to Pine Avenue, for my piano lessons. To my mother my musical education seemed to be important, no less significant than my academic education.

At home, my mother decided that I should practice playing the piano one hour every day. I had no choice but to accept her decision, sometimes even when I really didn't feel like practicing. Occasionally, when I desperately did not feel like playing, I would mischievously advance the clock to show that I had done my one hour of piano playing, and my mother would say, "is it already one hour?" To which I would answer, "yes, mama."

After we moved to NDG, I spent the rest of my mostly uneventful elementary school years at Daniel O'Connell. My memories of those years are not so pleasant, one of which I clearly recall to this day. I had only one worn-out sweater that my mother continued to patch; it tore often, particularly at the elbows, and every time she would stitch up the holes. I was embarrassed wearing day-in and day-out that worn out sweater with its clearly visible stitches.

One of my classmates, Paul Lamothe, who was obviously from a well-to-do family, used to look away embarrassedly every time he saw me wearing that sweater with those patches. Eventually when I got a new sweater, to my ultimate delight, he looked at me and smiled. I can still see his smiling face.

At Daniel O'Connell elementary school, an inspector from the School Commission would periodically visit the classroom and ask the students questions. One day, a Mr Dansereau came to our class and afterward spoke to one of my classmates who had been rude to him. I remember that the student's last name was Ranger, but I am not sure of his first name. The inspector said to him, "You must be Italian," as if only Italian students were rude. I was shocked and angry by the inspector's remarks, and to this day I regret and am upset that I didn't stand up and say, "No sir, he is not. I am Italian." Even today, I can still see that man's face with its small round mouth, his round glasses perched on his nose, and the blank face of Ranger, the stunned student.

From Daniel O'Connell Elementary School in NDG, I went to Thomas D'Arcy McGee High School on Pine Avenue next to Bleury Street, a fair distance from my house. It was run by the Presentation Brothers, an Irish order, with a number of lay teachers.

I enjoyed my years at the new high school and became active in a number of extra-curricular activities. I became the piano accompanist to the Glee Club (the high school choir), participated in arts activities, sang a brief solo (with a deep bass voice) in the choir, and wrote a regular column in *Student Prints*, the school paper. I remember one of the teachers, Mr Sbraggio, talking about me to one of his colleagues and saying, "John is a good writer."

At Thomas D'Arcy McGee, not surprisingly, different teachers were responsible for different extracurricular activities. Brother Matthias was in charge of all entertainment events. He was bouncy and vivacious, always busy with some activity, rushing through the corridors or the auditorium, preparing some event or other, urging the students on. His enthusiasm was contagious. He was also my form teacher in first year high school.

Although most of the teachers at the high school were careful, one semester I discovered a major error in my marks. That semester, after we wrote the exams and were assigned marks, I looked over those in my various subjects, and to my great surprise I found that many of the teachers had erred in calculating the marks. I pointed out their errors and requested that the marks be corrected. Corrected they were. After I asked every teacher to correct the grades they had given me, I ended up with the highest marks of all first-year students. I was awarded a special prize for my outstanding academic achievement. I still have the prize I was given: *A Tale of Two Cities* by Charles Dickens.

The school organized a few plays performed by students and directed by teachers. Auditioning to be part of the cast was always an exciting moment for students interested in acting. In one play, the role of a particular character had to be performed by a relatively short person. When Mr Nolan, the teacher in charge of casting, asked for students to act the character, I was ready to jump at the opportunity. During the audition, I was so anxious to be chosen that I volunteered to be the first to read the assigned part.

After my performance, Mr Nolan said, "Well you can't do any better than that, but let's give Forcillo a chance," raising my hopes high. Forcillo, who was no fool, read the part exactly as I had and because he was shorter than me Mr Nolan gave him the part. I was hurt, upset, and devastated, and I still think about it. I was attracted to acting – I thought actors might have the opportunity to get out of their own skin, to enjoy the freedom of being someone else – but was stopped from realizing that dream. And so my acting aspirations came to an abrupt halt thanks to Mr Nolan. I sometimes wonder if my deeply held desire for acting led me to my career that some cynics (like Arthur Miller in *On Politics and the Art of Acting*) call a form of acting: politics.

The school had some eccentric teachers. One of them was Mr Leo O'Connell who would often call me to his desk and ask me all kinds of inane questions that had nothing to do with my schoolwork. Did I play hockey? What did I do last week? I would stand there in front of the classroom by his desk dutifully answering all of his questions. A few times he would sing quietly to me, keeping rhythm with his ruler, looking at the class, while singing, "Bongo, bongo, bongo. I don't want to leave the jungle. No, no, no, I don't." It was one of the popular songs of the time, and it was quite amusing to hear it out of the mouth of my teacher. But imagine how surprised and amused I was when, some forty-five years later, I went to Gabon and was introduced to a president whose name was Bongo.

Parents always wish the best for their children, often charting career paths that mirror their own. At fourteen, my father took me aside, sat with me in the kitchen, and told me that I had an important decision to make. I had not been close to my father and didn't know what to expect, not having had a discussion with him on important matters before, but was curious as to what decision I would have to make. This was the time, he said, to decide whether I wanted to take up his trade, tailoring, or continue with my studies. I had a choice to make, a career path to pursue.

His question brought to my mind the winter clothes he used to sew for me when I was younger, including the memory of a black winter coat with a hat that covered my forehead and part of my face and which had holes for my eyes. It protected me from the cold but made me look like Batman.

I chose to continue with my studies, but this gesture, his desire to discuss my future with me instead of telling me what was good for me, was very unusual for immigrant families at that time. Among immigrant families, most children went to work after finishing high school, sometimes even before finishing, becoming wage earners in the family. This act of love by my father, his decision to respect my choice, allowed me to pursue academic studies, eventually graduating from McGill University with two degrees – a bachelor of arts and a law degree. I appreciate his consultation about my future, but I deeply regret not having had a proper relationship with my father. It has affected my whole life.

High school, despite some minor disappointments, was overall a happy experience for me. On graduating, I received the prize for music. I met the girl I would marry and I made two lasting friendships, with

Bob Burns and Cliff Tooker, which I renewed, maintained, and enjoyed later in life. (As well, they received the prizes for drama and for journalism, respectively.)

In the yearbook showing the Thomas D'Arcy McGee graduates of 1947, each student gave a quote, reflecting his interests, state of mind, or ambitions. The quote under my picture read, "I go to seek a great perhaps." I was sixteen years old.

Curiously, all of the schools that I attended have been closed, most probably due to demographic changes in the city of Montreal and in the educational policy of the government. When it was announced that D'Arcy McGee would close (some years after I was first elected as the representative of Mount Royal) *Le Devoir* headlined "L'école de John Ciaccia ferme ses portes." ("John Ciaccia's school closes its doors.")

In high school, I met Norma Murphy who later became my wife. Among Italians those days, you had to get the approval of your family, especially of your mother, for the girl you were going out with. When I brought Norma home to meet my mother, my mother approved of her. We were married after I graduated from law school in 1957.

2

The Law Beckons

After obtaining my bachelor of arts from McGill, the Faculty of Law was the next stop in my life's journey. Even though the academic demands of attending law school were substantial, I became the managing editor of the *McGill Law Journal*. At the Faculty of Law in the 1950s, there were a few great, dedicated professors and scholars who not only imparted the substance of their subjects but also conveyed the spirit of the law to their students. Those legal scholars included Professor Frank Scott, a great constitutional lawyer, with socialist views, who later became dean of the Faculty of Law. Professor Gazdik, was another, a legal expert on Roman law who spoke English with a European accent but captivated his students with his immense knowledge.

Professor Cohen expounded the philosophy of jurisprudence, although we had a difficult time understanding his abstruse reasoning. Professor Louis Beaudouin compiled a comparative legal study of the entire Quebec civil code, Le Droit Civil de la province de Québec, a monumental 1,300-page explanation of every article and section of the Quebec civil code, drawing comparisons with the French civil code. (I still have the book in my library.) Perhaps because he was a professor from France and because in the early '50s the Second World War was still fresh in everyone's mind, some students imputed dishonourable motives to him, spreading the rumour that "he was a collaborator of the Vichy regime," a totally unfair allegation, but that's what students sometimes do.

Then came the young professor of commercial law, Professor Gerald Le Dain who the class loved because of his youth and depth of knowledge. In the early 1970s he chaired the famed Commission of Inquiry into the Non-Medical Use of Drugs. Often, when he entered the classroom, we would burst into singing: "Good morning to you, good morning to you. We're all in our places with sunshiny faces, good morning to you, good morning to you." He would shake his head with incredulity, smile, and proceed with his lecture.

We had a few memorable events in his class. One day, we decided to have ice cream during his class. While the professor lectured, we casually licked our ice cream while listening inattentively to the lecture. When Michael Awada, the student who had organized the event, raised his hand during the presentation, Professor Le Dain, who thought he wanted to ask a question on the subject that was being discussed, said, "Yes, Michael?" Michael turned to the students and asked, "Does anyone want any more ice cream?" The entire class burst into laughter, and the good professor took the whole incident lightheartedly.

We had other mischiefs with other professors as well. One snowy day in March, right after lunch and just before Professor Gazdik's class began, Marvin Gameroff (with the full support of his classmates) threw some snowballs on the ceiling right above the professor's chair. We all sat in our seats and studiously looked at our Roman law textbooks while waiting for the professor to enter the room. By the time Professor Gazdik sat down in his chair the snow began to melt and drip on his head. He looked up, looked at us, and said in his distinct accent "Gent'lemen, vat have I done to you?"

Some of our pranks were not always that innocent, as was the case in an incident involving five students from Ethiopia. The Quebec legal system is a mixture of both English common law (the criminal code aspect) and French civil code (first created by Napoleon). Aside from the cultural benefits of exposing lawyers to the thinking and approaches of two great cultures, the two systems provide great training for the mind in terms of legal formation and analytical process. It widens horizons and expands possibilities.

It is perhaps for these reasons that the Ethiopian emperor, Haile Selassie, sent five students from his country to study at the McGill law faculty. One day I was with one of my friends, Godefroy Marin, a bit of a prankster but with an intellectual bent, sitting in the lunchroom. The Ethiopian students were sitting at the next table. We knew that fascist Italy had invaded and occupied Ethiopia, then known as Abyssinia, in 1935, and that the League of Nations had refused to condemn the invasion. Godefroy looked at me and mischievously suggested that we sing the fascist national anthem: "Giovinezza" (Youth). He obviously knew the words. So we sang:

Giovinezza, Giovinezza, primavera di bellezza
E Benito Mussolini e la nostra liberta

Youth, youth, spring of beauty
And Benito Mussolini is our liberty

And then we let out a whoop – "Hai!"

Naturally, the Ethiopian students looked at us in stupefaction with indignation, outrage, and shock. I hadn't thought it was possible to see blood drain from black faces. They were not amused at all.

I made many lasting friends in law school – Alex Paterson, who became a prominent leader of the English community; John Gomery, who was named to the bench and led the Gomery Commission into questionable federal government contracts; Trammy Malcolm, who was proud to wear his kilt whenever an occasion arose; John Hannen, who was also named to the bench; John Lawrence, who went into the federal civil service; Michael Awada, who became a prominent member of the Lebanese community. They all brought their own particular contribution to law school and to life.

After graduation, most of us proceeded to various Montreal law firms, but a firm's decision to hire did not entirely depend on that graduate's academic performance. Generally speaking, students of English origin went to the well-established English firms, while students of French origin went to the French firms. The one exception was a large prominent firm whose members were mostly Jewish and which represented the wealthy Bronfman family who had amassed a fortune with their distillery located on the south shore, across from Montreal. Another firm had only Jewish lawyers and was mainly active in real estate and construction. (Several years after my graduation, I became the first gentile lawyer to join that firm.) The rest of us had to make do with what we could get. This was Montreal in the 1950s with its law ghettoes.

I went to Malouf and Shorteno. Albert Malouf was of Lebanese origin and later became a judge who granted the James Bay Natives an injunction against the government of Quebec, thus halting work on the James Bay hydroelectric project. Peter Shorteno was the first jurist of Italian origin to have been nominated to the bench. He was well respected (the *Montreal Gazette* ran an editorial on his accession – a most unusual gesture). I not only worked with Peter Shorteno but was also close to his family. He had a warm, welcoming wife and three children. We often got together on weekends and holidays. They were more like a second family to us than friends.

But I did not enjoy the kind of general law that was the mainstay of Malouf and Shorteno. Perhaps I was not cut out to go to court, to persuade someone who happened to be on the bench that day and did not have the patience to listen (especially in the lower courts), who had other thoughts going through his mind, and was probably anxious to go back to whatever he had been doing before he had to come in to hear you. I didn't have the patience either.

I decided to try working for a corporation to spare myself the tedium of court work. I answered several ads. They were all from English-speaking companies – all my training had been in English schools and I did not feel sufficiently competent to do legal work in French. The reactions from the companies that I applied to brought me back to my early days in NDG when I was shunned and rejected because of my origins. In one interview, I was actually asked, "What made you think that with your name you would be hired for this position?"

My early experiences cushioned the blow, and this reaction did not destroy me. Nor did I give up. One of my classmates, Jacques Ducros, knew that I was unhappy working at Malouf and Shorteno; he would later be the crown prosecutor who obtained the conviction of Paul Rose, the FLQ member accused in the death of Pierre Laporte. He told me that he was leaving the position he had in the legal department of Steinberg's, the supermarket chain, and suggested that perhaps I could try and take his place.

Steinberg's was the most successful grocery chain in the province. It had been started by Sam Steinberg and his mother Ida and then was everywhere in Montreal and various regions of Quebec. I applied, was hired, and thus began another formative period in my life as I encountered the Steinberg family and others who worked for them.

3

Working for Mr Sam

The 1960s was a decade of activity, enthusiasm, movement, and creativity. There was excitement in the air. Montreal hosted Expo 67 – one of the most successful and attractive world exhibitions and one that became a model for others – and that summer, the world converged on the city and discovered what Canada had to offer. Montreal was the financial hub of Canada at the time and offered opportunities for everyone, irrespective of background. Those years were good economic times when almost everyone had the chance to participate and prosper. Not only did individuals succeed, but communities thrived too. Italian, Jewish, and other communities, with their colourful and active leaders, became vibrant. The French Canadians (as they were known before being called Québécois) have an expression for this kind of economic opportunity: "Au coureur la poche," meaning, "to the runner belongs the bag." In other words, if you were active and you tried, you would make it and enjoy the rewards.

It was at that time that I joined Steinberg's. Before I started work, I was given, a psychological test, by Sidney Caplan, vice-president of personnel, and when I passed the test I began working in the real estate department of Steinberg's. Although James Doyle, an experienced lawyer, was the secretary and legal counsel for the company, I handled all the legal aspects of the company's real estate operations. At first I spent a good part of my time on leases for the twelve new stores that would be opened each year, one store every month. At that time Steinberg's was the fastest growing chain in Quebec. My immediate boss was Leo Goldfarb, the director of real estate. Married to Rita, one of Sam Steinberg's daughters, he was a friendly and shrewd man, with an attractive smile.

At Steinberg's, there were people from all backgrounds. The company hired individuals from different communities – Jewish, French, English, Italian, and other Europeans – making it then Montreal's most inclusive company. There was only one criterion for employment: could you do the job?

In the course of my work, I would come into contact with other members of the Steinberg family – Max, Nathan, Morris, and, of course, as we called him, Mr Sam. I learned more from my days at Steinberg's than in all my years at university. What I learned not only marked me but also helped me meet work challenges for the rest of my life. Dedication, business ethics, decency, confidence, trust, persistence, foresightedness, and even humour, took on new meaning.

The work environment, ethic, and management style at Steinberg's were unique. Of course, the company applied all the professional management tools available at the time. To acquire the latest skills, I was often sent to seminars with the American Management Association (AMA) in New York. I still have the embossed, framed certificate given to me "in appreciation of the contribution of his services to AMA seminars and to the philosophy of education for management by management on which they are founded."

Management gurus were often invited to train us. At one time, a group of us was sent to Toronto, to attend a seminar designed to let down barriers and expose true feelings and personality. We discovered traits about each other that we normally kept well hidden. It was rough. It was also amazing how differently individuals reacted to revealing their innermost selves. Afterwards, for several days, we were almost embarrassed to speak to one another. This was all done with the supposed purpose of improving our management skills. Whew!

But there was more, much more. And that was what made Steinberg's such a unique place not only to work but to experience different facets of life – indeed, to learn how to enjoy life. Steinberg's taught me that work should always have a human side, that serious moments can be tempered by humour, that there are emotions associated with what we do and we can express them; that there is a time to be serious and a time to be humorous, and that all these can be mixed spontaneously at times. At Steinberg's, sometimes people were humorous without intending to be or being aware of it, and this made those moments even funnier.

I started working at the head office, located at 5400 Hochelaga Street, in east end Montreal. Since my office was on the "executive" floor (first door to the left as you entered the building), I came into contact with the senior executives regularly and with Max, Nathan, and Mr Sam. Morris, who took care of odd assignments, (for example, the baseball team) was in another part of the building. There were many managers, but there was only one undisputed boss: Mr Sam, who, with his mother, had founded the company. He was respected and loved by all employees. He was involved in the operations of the company and, of course, in all major decisions related to it. He was meticulous and knew all the details of the company's operations, the locations of its new stores, its real estate investment, and its development plans. He was involved in everything. We all looked up to him.

He knew what had to be done, and he made it happen. Under his leadership, Steinberg's became more than a household word; it became an expression, a shopping experience. Instead of saying, "I'm going to do my shopping," people would say, "I'm going to do my Steinberg's" and this in both languages – "Je vais aller faire mon Steinberg."

Because of Mr Sam's far-sighted planning, Steinberg's was one of the most successful companies of its time – and also the most colourful. I remember an interesting incident. The Development Committee was responsible for the future expansion of stores and shopping centers but one day, at the committee's meeting, after Leo Goldfarb suggested the acquisition of a particular site, Jack Levine, who was in charge of store operations, disagreed and, when Leo insisted, told Leo he was crazy. The heated conversation between them went like this:

"I'm crazy?" exclaimed Leo. "Yah, you're crazy," replied Jack.

"No, you're crazy," retorted Leo.

Jack didn't budge.

"Well, ok, we'll see who is crazier than who," Leo said forcefully. "All those who think I'm crazier than Jack, raise your hands."
Dutifully, Jack and those who worked for him raised their hands. Leo counted three individuals.

"All those who think Jack is crazier than me, raise your hands," said Leo. Leo and the four members of the committee who worked for him raised their hands. Leo turned to Jack. "See, you're crazier than me." (Irving Ludmer, a member of the committee, who went on to successfully develop his own retail and real estate business, remembers that day and that vote.)

There were many meetings, of various committees or to discuss particular problems, but discipline was not the primary rule during the deliberations of those meetings; it was far down the list of committee rules. At one particular meeting, above noise and chatter, Nathan piped up, "Everybody's talking, who is listening?"

Nathan was the executive vice-president and was in charge of the company when Mr Sam was away. His brothers accepted his authority without question, but it was when Mr Sam wasn't there that strange things sometimes happened. One day, Tower's Discount Stores, a competitor with a location on Viau Street close to Steinberg's head office and one of its stores, decided to have a sale on turkeys. Tower's sold them at half the usual price, a maximum of one turkey per customer. Nathan decided that he was going to teach Tower's a lesson. Not only would he meet the Tower's price in the nearby Steinberg's store but he also arranged for Steinberg's employees to buy the turkeys at Tower's. There were so many employees involved and all had to line up at the Tower's cash registers to pay for the single turkey they bought.

After a few hours, the Tower's store was still full of turkeys and Nathan had run out of money to give to his employees to buy turkeys with, and so he called in the comptroller, Jim Kearney, and arranged for more cash to be available. Much later, there were still turkeys available at Tower's. Their supply seemed to be inexhaustible.

What Nathan didn't realize was that Tower's soon figured out what was happening, and, to counteract Steinberg's plan, arranged for its own employees to buy the turkeys that were on sale at Steinberg's and return them to the shelves in Tower's. Unbeknownst to him, Nathan was buying back his own turkeys. When Sam returned and found out what had happened, he gave Nathan a tongue-lashing.

Nathan was involved in other amusing incidents.

One day, Mr Sam Gerstel, who worked in the research department, came to me and said, with a grin on his face, "You don't know what happened to me on the weekend." Apparently, the decision had been made to reduce the space between aisles in Steinberg's stores. This would create more shelf space, allowing the display of more goods. However, the narrower aisles didn't allow for two customer carriages to pass side by side. So, overhead signs were posted at the end of each aisle indicating the direction that customers were to take, to avoid a blockage.

"I was doing my shopping at the Queen Mary store, pushing my cart when all of a sudden Nathan came up to me and shrieked, 'Sam, you're going the wrong way.' I had forgotten to pay attention to the signs."

There was the executive vice-president of the company acting as a traffic director in the stores. It was amusing. But it also shows the interest that people like Nathan, a senior member of management, took in the company, even in its day-to-day operations – amusing and heartwarming.

Leo Goldfarb, one of Mr Sam's son-in-laws and head of the Development Committee, could ask for a vote on who is crazier than whom but could also dispense sound advice. One day, after I had an argument with one of the developers who was trying to build premises for Steinberg's and who was critical of what I had been doing, Leo said to me, "Johnny, you don't get into a pissing contest with a skunk." Sound lesson.

For all the toughness they showed in their business dealings, these men all had a soft spot in their hearts. At one point, Leo redecorated his office and ordered a bright blue desk chair to go with the new look. After several months, the chair was delivered to the new offices on Cote de Liesse, in Montreal. When I saw the delivery people pushing the chair down the hall, I instantly liked it and led them to my office where I had them install the chair behind my desk. When Leo came into my office, I jokingly said, "Leo, look how good this chair looks behind my desk." The colour of the chair matched the back wall of my office, deep blue. He looked at me, incredulously but resignedly, probably thinking of the several months that he had to wait to get that chair. He went back to his office without saying much, and in the end let me keep the chair. I don't know why I didn't send it back.

Sometimes Leo gave the impression that he had forgotten his humble background and expected all his colleagues to be well off. One day one of my fellow workers, Gus Dubinsky, bought a used car. When Leo found about it, he told him, "Gus, you should have bought a new car!" Gus, surprised and discouraged at Leo's statement, remarked after Leo left, "Johnny, does he really think that if I could afford a new car I would have bought a used one?"

After working for some years with Steinberg's, I felt I wanted to move on. At the time, Place Ville Marie, which became a Montreal landmark, was being developed by a well-known American company, Webb and Knapp, headed by William Zeckendorf. The company was looking for an experienced lawyer to work on the legal aspect of the project. When Jim Soden, a respected lawyer who headed the project, offered me the job, I accepted and submitted my letter of resignation to Steinberg's.

The next two weeks were unbearable. Sam Steinberg sent emissaries to persuade me not to leave. The company solicitor, Jonathan Robinson, sheepishly admitted that he was sent by Mr Sam to persuade me to stay. I was also summoned by Jack Rosenbloom, a wealthy man and good friend of Mr Sam, who supplied Steinberg's with all of its paper bags. When I went to see him at his office, he gave me every possible argument to stay. Finally, he warned me with what he thought would be the coup de grace. "Johnny, I've been buying shares most of my life. You know which company never went up in the market? Webb and Knapp."

Despite the pleas, imploring, and cajoling, and with a great deal of willpower on my part, I continued to tell everyone I had to go to Webb and Knapp as I had given them my word! I prepared notes and instructions on the hundreds of files that I had been working on, gave them to Leo Goldfarb, and left. I was shell-shocked.

During the first week at Webb and Knapp, compared to the frenzy at Steinberg's, I found that I had little to do. Leo called me to ask how I was feeling, and I said, "Leo, I have so little to do here that I get headaches every day."

"Oh yeah? Why don't you come back, then," he replied. "You'd take me back?" I asked incredulously.

"Sure."

"OK, I'm coming back."

Soon after the talk with Leo, I gave my notice of termination to Jim Soden, and one week later I was back at Steinberg's. I was welcomed with open arms.

Among all the people I worked with Sam Steinberg was the person who had the most impact on me not because of the position he held but because of the genuine person that he was and because of what he did and how he did it. He trusted me, valued my work, and inspired confidence. One day he sent me to Toronto, alone, with a cheque for one million dollars to negotiate and finalize a transaction, the only instructions being, "Johnny, I don't want any lawsuits." I was only twenty-nine years old.

He had his own, sometimes amusing or at least different, way of making his point. He would often pass by my office and have impromptu meetings on a variety of subjects. One day, he dropped in at our Wilderton shopping center offices (where the real estate department had recently moved). At one point during the discussion, in response to something I had said earlier, he asked, "Johnny, is there a barber shop in this shopping center?" "Yes," I replied innocently. "Good, I'm gonna get a razor and slit your throat." This was his affectionate way of admonishing me.

Once, when Leo Goldfarb was on holidays, Mr Sam came to see me ostensibly to talk about various projects but really to chitchat.

He would often complain about his son-in-law Leo, my immediate superior and ask me embarrassing questions. That day he asked, "Tell me, Johnny, if Leo were working for Woolworth's [another successful chain], do you think he would keep his job? " Of course," I defended Leo. "He's ok; he's not as bad as you think." My response must have sounded like a backhanded compliment to him.

Mr Sam was thinking of expanding into New Brunswick, and he took me to Moncton to look at a new site. After he announced that a particular site was good, I asked him how he could make such a decision without any market research or other relevant data. "Johnny," he said to me, touching his nose, "I can smell it."

Mr Sam was a devoted husband. At the opening of the Beaconsfield shopping center, he came to my nearby house and immediately asked to use the phone. (This was before the cellular age.) He called his wife and sheepishly told her that he was sorry that he would be late for supper. Here was the head of a multimillion-dollar company, with dictatorial powers over thousands of employees, apologizing to his wife for being late. I was impressed by his devotion, love, and respect for her.

He also gave me insight into the meaning of business ethics. He was about to build a shopping center at Sources and the Trans-Canada Highway, in Pointe Claire. Earlier, he had tried to build one on Saint Jean Blvd, across from the Fairview Shopping Center, but the Bronfman interests that owned Fairview succeeded in blocking the proposed changes in zoning. A senior member of Morgan Trust wanted to invest in Mr Sam's new center. The Morgan's had owned a department store in downtown Montreal, which they later sold to the Hudson's Bay Company. Mr Sam refused the offer from Morgan Trust. I was shocked and asked him why. "Because I don't know if the shopping center will be successful." He was, prophetically, right. The center was not successful and it took many years before it made any profit. He did not want to induce a partner to invest in a potentially unprofitable project.

I can say without any reservation that my true education, especially in the business world, began at Steinberg's. In the late 1960s, Steinberg's decided to expand into Ontario. By then, since I had become the director of real estate, I had to travel to Toronto to supervise the acquisition of new sites. With a permanent office in Toronto, it soon became known that Steinberg's was looking for new locations, but we got absolutely nowhere. The moment that the name "Steinberg's" was mentioned, all discussions ceased. I got the distinct impression that there was a hint of anti-Semitism in the air. This was the Toronto of the 1960s, with its rather closed business community. Later, in 1976, things changed when the city expanded as a result of those leaving Montreal's English and Jewish communities following the election of a Quebec separatist government. Sam Steinberg finally expanded into Ontario by purchasing Grand Union, an existing chain of stores.

Discussions among the employees were not always limited to work topics. One day, in the lunchroom, we were talking about the treatment of Jewish people by the Nazis (the Second World War was still relatively recent), when someone said this could not happen in our country. To this day I still remember Ed Wallen, the red-haired, heavy-lipped veteran who had fought in Europe, disagreeing. He said, "It could happen anywhere. Just scratch the surface and it can be there." I never forgot what he said.

I had been working at Steinberg's for five years, minus the two weeks at Webb and Knapp, when I received a call from Nahum Gelber, a senior partner at Chait Aronovitch, the largest legal firm in Montreal specializing in real estate law, inviting me for lunch. During lunch with him and Sam Chait, I was asked to join their law firm. Remembering what had happened the last time I tried to leave Steinberg's, I answered, "I don't say yes, but I don't say no. Let me get back to you."

I thought this was a great opportunity to get back into my profession – the practice of law in a field that I knew and enjoyed. I went to see Mr Sam. I told him I had received an offer to work in a law firm and that I wanted to accept it. I said, "I want to leave. Please let me go."

"What's the law firm?" he asked.

I was almost afraid to tell him because Chait's office had often taken legal action against Steinberg's. "Chait Aronivitch," I said quietly, in almost a murmur.

"Ok Johnny, you can go." Then he added, "Johnny, you're the best little negotiator I ever knew."

I thanked him. And so ended my days at Steinberg's.

But I never left Mr Sam. And Mr Sam never let me go.

After I went to Chait's office, even though that law firm had taken actions against Steinberg's, I continued to receive mandates from Steinberg's and represented the company.

4

The View from Place Ville Marie

I returned to the practice of law, at Chait Aronovitch, but in a manner that I had never known or imagined. By coincidence or fate – depending on how you look at life – I had an office on the 36th floor of Place Ville Marie, the building developed by Webb and Knapp, the company for which I had very briefly worked.

It was an elegant, spacious office in a uniquely shaped cruciform building, the pride of Montreal. It had rich mahogany panelled walls and one all of glass, giving me a magnificent view of the St Lawrence River. The company that furnished desks to American presidents at the White House sculpted my oak desk. I brought it to my home when I left the firm.

At the new firm, I met colourful characters who had equally colourful stories to tell. *Plus ca change, plus c'est la même chose.* (The more things change, the more they remain the same.) There was Shulim Krauthammer, who used to regale me with fascinating stories of Leon Blum, the first Jewish president of France (and who he claimed had been his friend) who resisted the Vichy regime, was imprisoned by the Nazis, and miraculously survived. Shulim was having problems with one of the firm's clients, Peter Issenman, regarding land that Shulim had sold him in St Bruno, a short distance from downtown Montreal. "Johnny," he told me in his thick accent one day, "if I had an atom bomb, I would drop it on St Bruno." "Mr Krauthammer," I replied, "if you dropped an atom bomb on St Bruno, it would also destroy this office building where I'm working." "Don't worry," he reassured me. "If I had the power to have an atom bomb, I would also have the power it shouldn't affect you in Place Ville Marie."

One day, Richard Solomon, a commercial real estate agent who I knew, came to see me. He was angry and wanted to sue William

Zeckendorf, whose book about the development of Place Ville Marie included a discussion of the underground section of the building with its passageway to the Metro and myriad of attractive shops. Richard Solomon said, "I was involved in the leasing of the shopping area, and he didn't mention my name in his book. I want to sue him." I had to explain to Richard Solomon that the law cannot remedy all mishaps.

Soon after I joined the firm, I was called by Ralph Esposito, a prominent notary in the Italian community. He was an active organizer of the Union Nationale party, which had long ruled Quebec under Maurice Duplessis, in an era described as *la grande noirceur* (the big darkness). Following the Quiet Revolution of 1960, during which the province was lead by Jean Lesage and his Liberal government, the Union Nationale had surprisingly come back to power under a new leader. When I went to meet Ralph and his partner Mario Beaulieu, the Union Nationale government was preparing for another election.

At that meeting, I was offered a judgeship in the criminal court, a provincial jurisdiction. When I showed reticence at being a criminal judge, they offered the social welfare court, another area of provincial control. That was very enticing; imagine being one of the youngest judges ever to be named to a lifetime appointment. They also mentioned that the Union Nationale government would publicize my nomination, to gain political benefit from it, particularly in the Italian community. I said that I would think about it.

And for a while I did think about it. I even drove to the attractive and relatively new courthouse building on St Denis Street, the same street where I had lived when I first arrived in Montreal. But, the more I thought of the offer, the less it appealed to me. I was in my early thirties. Sure, I would never have to worry about my paycheck, but I was too young. The prospect of burying myself in a courthouse at such an age and for the rest of my life did not attract me. As well, I did not relish the idea of being used to promote the objectives of a political party. I called Ralph, thanked him, but declined the appointment. Sam Chait was surprised that I had been offered a judgeship but was happy I had declined.

I had many real estate clients, rich and not so rich, who I negotiated and wrote contracts for. Although the firm had a dining room, with a chef, where members usually had their lunch (the only law firm, to my knowledge, to do this) I became a regular patron of Altitude 737 – a restaurant-bar atop Place Ville Marie, where, after several years in my new practice, I often had two-martini lunches – not a sign of a man at peace with himself. I was drifting.

Then, two events occurred that changed the direction of my life. I received a call from Jean-Baptiste Bergevin, the assistant deputy minister of the Department of Indian Affairs and Northern Development in Ottawa. I had known him when he worked at Steinberg's. Apparently he was trying to initiate new programs for Native people but was constantly told by the Department of Justice, that they did not conform to the Indian Act. He asked me to find a way that would enable him to implement his programs legally and so they didn't derogate from the Act.

That is how the federal Department of Indian Affairs and Northern Development became a client of my law firm and how I began to get involved in the legal problems of Native communities.

Working with the Department of Indian Affairs and Northern Development was interesting and the problems I was called upon to resolve were fascinating. However, I found myself taking more than a legal interest in the problems I was asked to resolve. While representing the department I became aware of Native people and their plight. I saw their misery and their frustrations and the possibilities that existed to help them. To this day, the problems they face strike a deep part of my being. I approached each situation with dedication and enthusiasm. I wanted to apply all of my mind and heart to my work and became personally and emotionally involved in the problems, issues, and challenges facing the Native people of Canada.

One of my first interesting experiences took place in British Columbia. Native reserves are under the jurisdiction of the federal government. One particular band in British Columbia had been in discussion with the provincial government to become a municipality, but it didn't want to exclude federal authority on the reserve.

I went to Vancouver and met with the band, representatives of the provincial government, officials from Indian Affairs, and members of the federal Department of Justice. I made a few proposals, but none of the solutions that I proposed were acceptable to the federal lawyers. I became frustrated and emotional. After unsuccessful negotiations, some of us (not the federal lawyers) adjourned to one of the lounges in a Vancouver hotel. I vented my frustrations. I got emotional. I said, "When I go back to Quebec, I'm going to join the separatist party. I've had it with the federal government." And then I took another sip of my drink. Just then I saw Queen Elizabeth and Prince Philip walking down the hallway of the hotel. (Security measures were less strict in those days.) They were on an official visit to British Columbia. I froze, wide-eyed, then relaxed. The presence of the smiling queen had a calming effect. I announced, "Ok then, I won't become a separatist. We'll keep Canada together. " Wide smiles beamed from those who were with me.

One day, Denis Chatain, an oblate of the religious order that worked with Natives in Alberta, came to see me at home. He showed me an agreement signed by the Alberta Blood Band and an Alberta company, which had been acquired by the Wickes Corporation of Saginaw Michigan, to build on the reserve a plant to produce prefabricated houses. He asked for my help in getting the agreement implemented. I told Denis that the agreement was one-sidedly in favour of the company, giving it total control of the operations – no rights for the Band were included. "Yes, but it's signed," he replied. I was adamant. The company was taking advantage of the Band. I pointed out that the project needed financing and federal approval and insisted that the agreement had to be renegotiated.

Some weeks later, I went to Alberta for a preliminary meeting with the Band and company representatives. Another meeting was scheduled in Ottawa. When I arrived a little late, some thirty people were sitting around a long, oblong table – company representatives and a slew of Department of Indian Affairs members. I sat at the head, in the seat reserved for me, with a bunch of faces staring at me wondering what I would do. I was introduced to the president of Wickes Corporation, who had come in his private jet. With his stiff crew cut and blank face, he looked like a captain in the Vietnam War.

I proposed a series of changes to the agreement that effectively gave more protection and control to the Band. For example, I asked that the Band be entitled initially to 40 per cent of the annual profits with, over the years, an increase to 75 per cent. I noticed that every so often during the discussion of various changes, a member of the department would leave and then return. The company was reticent to accept many of the changes that I proposed. Finally, to get their approval, I went out on a limb. "If you approve all of the changes, I will guarantee you all the financing for the project," I suggested. There were audible gasps from the department members, many of whom left the room.

I knew that the government had a development fund for Native Bands in each province. I was convinced that the government wouldn't refuse to use the fund if a proper agreement were signed. So I took a chance and made that commitment.

I learned, later, that the department members who were going back and forth from the room were calling the minister, telling him to get me out of the negotiations. The minister then called Bergevin who told him not to interfere.

After the agreement was signed with the changes that I had proposed, a senior member of the Alberta company, Haico Industries, told me that I was tough but fair. I was pleased. The plant was built and Prime Minister Pierre Elliott Trudeau attended the opening ceremonies, dressed in Trudeauesque fashion – open shirt and a ten-gallon hat – accompanied by Chief Jim Shot Both Sides. Trudeau was surprised to see me and asked what was I doing there.

Bergevin was so pleased with my work that he asked me to replace him as assistant deputy minister (ADM) since he was moving to the Department of Health and Welfare. As much as I enjoyed dealing with Native problems, I ridiculed the idea of becoming ADM, pointing out that my annual income was four times the salary of a civil servant. Looking back, it is clear that I rejected this too quickly, not paying attention to myself, to my deep needs, and only to superficial considerations.

During this time, while working for the federal government, I continued to service my other clients. I had become a partner, the only non-Jewish member, of a firm of some sixteen lawyers then called Chait, Salomon, Gelber, Ciaccia, Reis, and Bronstein.

Sometimes there are events in life that present you with alternatives and that force you to make decisions to be true to yourself. Fate? Coincidence? Opportunity? Such an event took place in my life. Just prior to Expo 67, my clients had built two apartment houses in the rear of the Sheraton hotel on Sherbrooke Street in the east end of Montreal. The hotel owner, who expected a bonanza from the world exhibition, leased both buildings at considerable rent, using the hotel as collateral. The enforcement provisions of the agreement that I prepared were completed in my office. But the expected bonanza did not occur. The hotel owner incurred a big loss and, consistent with the agreement I had prepared, lost his hotel. He was a dejected, sad, and desperate man when he left my office long after midnight. The next day, the hotel owner's agent, Robert Vinet, whom I knew, called. "John, do you know what my client did after he left your office? He cried all the way to his car."

That situation provoked me into thinking: did I go to university for eight years to do this, to act for those who inflict suffering on others, who ruin them? Was I to be the instrument of human vultures profiting from the sweat and tears of others? Concerned only with the superficial and not paying attention to my real calling, I had rejected Bergevin's offer too quickly. It seemed it had taken a bolt to jar me, to wake me up, to make me aware of what I was doing and who I really was, to question my heart and save my soul. This event forced me to face myself.

I called Bergevin and told him I was prepared to accept the position of assistant deputy minister of Indian Affairs and Northern Development in Ottawa.

5

On to Indian Affairs

My partners were stunned. Sam Chait told me that if I wanted to help people, there were ways of doing it that wouldn't mean abandoning a law practice. I felt they didn't understand and that it would be difficult and even inappropriate to try and explain it to them.

Before my appointment became official, I still had to complete two formalities – meeting with the three members of the Civil Service Commission who were courteous and direct in their discussions with me and then seeing the minister of Indian Affairs, Jean Chrétien. He came from the Shawinigan region of Quebec and spoke English with a very pronounced French Canadian accent. The first thing he said to me was that this job had never been given to someone of Italian origin. I thought, "Here we go again, echoes of my youth," but said nothing. However, I later worked very well with him and we developed a close relationship. He was a very good minister of Indian Affairs. He listened to sound advice.

I was very enthusiastic. I was in a new world – full of ideals, hopes, and dreams. I thought that by properly identifying problems we could form solutions, that they would be accepted and applied – that people would understand once the solutions were explained to them, that the possibilities were beautiful and endless, that all was possible. It was utopian. It was innocent.

I did not move my family to Ottawa. I decided that I would go back to Beaconsfield every Wednesday after office hours and return to Ottawa the following Thursday morning. This would reduce my absences from my son. Or so I thought. Since I also would be traveling extensively across Canada, I thought it was better for my family to endure those absences in Beaconsfield, where they had friends, than alone in Ottawa. My intentions were good. I also did not believe, for some reason, that I would spend the rest of my life as a civil servant in Ottawa. I did not have a definite plan; it was just a feeling. I did not know what I would do or when I would leave Ottawa.

Officially, I was the assistant deputy minister in charge of the Indian and Eskimo Program. My title reflected accepted social norms. It was 1971. The change from Eskimo (eaters of raw flesh) to Inuit (the people) only came later.

One of the first things I did in my new position was address a group of Native people at an Ottawa gathering organized by the National Indian Brotherhood. I told them the problems that we didn't see were more important than those, such as poverty, unemployment, and housing, which were visible. I saw the basic problem affecting any proposed solution as a *cultural* one.

We had to accept that Native people had a different culture – the sum of all transmitted values we hold. Quoting from my speech:

> These values, ideas, and attitudes come to us from one generation to another, modified and changed but carrying a constant thrust that is part of our heritage. It has taken thousands of years to produce you. It has taken thousands of years to produce me – and we have been produced with different sets of values and ideas. And what has taken so long to produce cannot, and should not, be changed overnight. Unless we accept this, any government proposals, rather than help the situation, might even make it worse. Moreover, since the Native people are the best interpreters of their own culture, they are the ones who must find the solutions or make the proposals to solve the existing visible problems. The government should only have a supportive role.

I undertook to involve Native people at every level – from organization to implementation.

To resolve the challenges facing Native people, I felt that the non-Native community also had to recognize and respect that Natives had different customs. "We have heard the phrase 'the last frontier,'" I told the audience. "Perhaps you are the last frontier where the battles against bigotry and prejudice will be fought." I concluded,

> In the land of *my* ancestors, in the fourteenth century, there began a new era that must have seemed as unlikely as anything could to the people at the time. After the dark ages, after years of misery and stagnation, a new time began with the Renaissance – a rebirth of

hope for man. That time saw the flowering of culture, an outburst of activity, and an up swelling of creative energy, which carried the world forward. It was a time of material bounty and spiritual wealth, and the benefits were felt by everyone from the poorest peasant to the richest ruler. I am sure that you have begun a rebirth of the Indian people, and I want to work with you with all the resources available to me so that this new era will see *your* people given *their* place in the sun.

This was pretty heady stuff in 1971.

The official recognition of the importance of their cultures came as a surprise to Canada's Native people. In the April 1972 edition of *Agenutemagen* – published by the Union of New Brunswick Indians – an editorial titled "Godsend?" echoed the general reaction of Indian communities. The editorial commented:

> There appears to be a whole new direction in Indian Affairs administration in Canada under the new Assistant Deputy Minister. Recently the ADM at various public functions, has repeated over and over again that culture of the Native people is going to be looked at in relation to programs of the Department ... He has stated in very plain understandable English to his employees of the Department that Indians have different values, because they have different aims and aspirations and that they think differently. The Indian people have been saying the very same thing for years and years. For a while everyone thought that our pleas had been in vain, but all of a sudden, here comes a new man, who at long last has seen the light ... If the Assistant Deputy Minister is sincere, and all indications are that he is, the Indian people should support him in his new "direction." All eyes will be on him to see how well he carries out his ideas and his preaching and how well he weathers the storm.

Yes, and storms there were in my department, in the regions, in the Native communities, and in the reactions of some non-Native educators.

NEW DIRECTIONS

The government had issued a white paper in 1969 calling for the abolition of the Indian Act and placing Indians on the same footing as other Canadians. It was so vehemently opposed by Natives that in Alberta the minister, Jean Chrétien, was burned in effigy. Harold Cardinal, a young, fiery, dedicated Indian leader from the Sucker Creek reserve in Alberta, who had studied at Carleton University in Ottawa, led the Indian communities in their fight.

I responded to Native people with my feelings and beliefs. I prepared a document, signed by the minister and submitted to cabinet, which would not only change the 1969 white paper but also provide a new government approach to problems facing Native people. It was time to break with the past, time to listen to Indian people, time to get rid of the old bureaucratic mind-set of civil servants. New directions were needed. We needed to show more respect for Natives. We had to listen to Natives.

I was at the cabinet meeting when the document I prepared was discussed. At the time, senior civil servants could attend cabinet meetings for such presentations. The prime minister, Pierre Elliott Trudeau, presided. Other leading personalities of the time, Gerard Pelletier, Jean Marchand – the two other members of the "three wise men from Quebec," – and Otto Lang, the minister of justice, sat around the cabinet table. I answered the objections raised with my usual logic and devotion to a cause. Trudeau was very diplomatic. He did not wish to embarrass anyone, especially his ministers, when I had better arguments. At the end of the discussion, rather than make a decision that would contradict his ministers, he deftly referred questions to Gordon Robertson, the cabinet secretary, to look into and report on later. Afterwards in his office, Jean Chrétien said to me, "You know what Trudeau said after you left? He turned to me and said, 'Who is that guy?'"

Following the discussion of the document I had prepared, the old policy was abandoned and new groundbreaking approaches were accepted. Cultural differences, education, Indian participation in all decisions affecting them, land claims, and aboriginal rights were discussed and clarified. The government reversed its position in many key areas.

The document took the concept of Native cultural differences beyond mere recognition and urged that such recognition be applied in the government's approach and in its programs. The document I prepared read, in part,

Probably the greatest challenge in the next few years will be to
adapt programs to take account of Indian cultural aspirations.
In some areas cultural traits are so pronounced that to ignore
them risks negating any endeavour. Indian traditions are radically

different from the European heritage in respect to land ownership and use, in the role of the majority in determining policy as well as in interpersonal relationships.

In the day-to-day relationships of a schoolroom or playground these and like differences can have an important role in creating or destroying self-respect and a sense of identity.

Growing up as an Italian Canadian, I had been denied my culture. I knew all about the hurts and torments of the playground. Was I expressing my needs and projecting them on to Natives? Since I represented the government, I *was* the government. I wouldn't allow similar injustices to happen to Natives.

One of the major areas where cultural differences became important was in the education system. There was an admission that the residential schools, located away from the reserve, had imposed severe handicaps on Indian children. There was not yet the awareness, which came many years later, of the tremendous harm and traumatic effects caused to Indian children who were denied their identity and their language in the residential schools. This system had to change. Clear new directions, until now ignored or denied, were openly stated and accepted.

The document continued:

There will be no transfer of the federal education program to a provincial system without the clear consent of the Indian people involved. The department will seek ways to fully involve Indian people in all aspects of the school system through local committees, developing school boards and through establishing local societies to operate the local school with necessary funding.

Adaptation of the school curriculum to meet Indian needs, a concerted effort to recruit teaching aids fluent in the Indian languages spoken in each community and special emphasis on pre-school classes using the native language and where possible, operated by Indian people themselves with federal financing.

Furthermore, the Indian Act was not drafted with the purpose of facilitating the economic development of the reserves but to protect the reserves, that is to make sure that the Indians would stay set apart and left alone.

The document I prepared for submission to cabinet was a landmark in the approach to Indian affairs. It was also, effectively an indictment of past government action. Education was a key area that required drastic changes. The dropout rate began in first grade for Indian children. First grade! I thought that the curriculum discouraged and even antagonized Indian children. There was almost a "cowboy and Indian" content in the teaching aids. "What do you expect?" I once told the director of education, George Cromb. "Do you think an Indian child relates to Sesame Street?" Those were the kind of programs used in the schools.

My proposal might have appeared too radical for some officials, but after I left the department I received a letter from George Cromb the director of education telling me that initially he had opposed my approach but eventually realized I was right. I was touched. Thank you George.

The new approach to education had not been easy to implement. I remember going with the minister to Regina where he was to speak on Native education to a meeting of provincial teachers from all parts of Canada. I purposely waited to be on the government jet with him before giving him a copy of his speech. He read it and was astute enough to realize the speech had not been written by members of the department. He then turned to me and said, "This speech was not written by the department." (Ministerial speeches were always written either by the department or by the staff in his cabinet.)

I said, "No it wasn't."

"Who wrote it?" he asked.

"The National Indian Brotherhood," I replied. That association represented Native people across Canada and had been forcefully critical of government policies.

The minister paused for a moment and then said, "Ok, I'll give it."

Harold Cardinal, in his book *The Rebirth of Canada's Indians*, relates how the Indian position paper on education was accepted by the federal government. He wrote,

It is extremely unlikely that the department's response to the Brotherhood's policy paper would have been as positive, had it not been for the presence in the department of a new deputy minister, John Ciaccia. If credit is due for the turnabout in department policy, it must go to Ciaccia. The new policy was diametrically opposed to the position so long and so fiercely held by the old guard.

I remember certain provincial teachers opposing the new education policy. I was in the Yukon meeting with them, when they accused me of creating apartheid through the new policy of allowing Indians to build and operate their own schools. I looked out the window where I could see in the distance a Native reserve with dilapidated buildings. It was totally separated from and in sharp contrast to the neighbouring white community. I pointed, "Apartheid? You have it now."

The government had opposed Native aboriginal rights and land claims, and this too changed. We would begin by fulfilling our obligations under existing treaties and agreed to negotiate land claims, particularly in northern British Columbia and the Territories. Although it took time, this opened the door to the Nisga'a settlement and the establishment of Nunavik.

I was also concerned about the Natives of James Bay who were facing the development of the James Bay hydroelectric project in northern Quebec. Canada had transferred the territory to the province in 1923 with the obligation that Quebec settle Native claims. The Natives of the area now asked for our help in getting the Quebec government to protect their interests and fulfill their obligations. I later funded the Cree to help them in their claims against the province.

The optimist that I was then, I even tried to change the attitudes and methods of the Department of Justice. My conflict with the department lawyers, which had begun when I was a consultant to Indian Affairs, continued. Now, I went beyond my disagreement with their interpretation of the Indian Act. I went to the core of their approach to the law. My views on Native people and the law were expressed in a letter I wrote on 26 January 1972 to the assistant deputy attorney general of the Department of Justice some months after I joined Indian Affairs. The Department of Justice wanted to be the sole purveyor of legal advice in Indian matters, but Natives wanted the right to hire their own lawyers to represent them, believing that the justice department was too categorical and restrictive in defining Indian rights. I had to refuse the signature by my Minister of many letters prepared by Justice, which often referred to a conflict of interest between Indian people and the government. I didn't believe that our relationship was a conflictive one.

The opinions and behaviour of the justice department seemed to reflect the belief that law was a science. My letter of 26 January was addressed to C.R.O. Munro, the assistant deputy attorney general at the Department of Justice. In it I wrote, "If law were a science, if our legal interpretation consisted solely of reading the words of a statute and basing ourselves on precedent, segregation would still be legal in the United States. I firmly believe that one cannot separate the legal rules from social conditions." It continued:

> In effect, the principle of the Brandeis brief has been applied by our courts. If the legality of a statute is attacked, the Court should allow the evidence from the social sciences, which would show the probable results of the legislation in question. In other words I believe that you must look at the social needs of the people in the interpretation of statutes. We are not dealing with the laws of the marketplace.

I then expressed my true feelings, almost hoping that they would react in the same way. "How can anyone adequately represent the Indian people unless he can get into their hearts and minds and feel and think as they do? A knowledge of 'the law,' of the statutes and precedents, I submit, is insufficient ... We must let the Indian people and their representatives put forth their own views to the Court."

I was fortunate in that I had a legal background and could stand up to the Department of Justice. Now I understood more fully the situation Jean Bergevin, my predecessor, had faced when he first came to me when the Department of justice had restricted his actions.

YOUTH PROGRAM

My decisions and methods sometimes provoked strong reactions from people. Part of that was due to my impatience, part was due to my inexperience as a civil servant, and part was due to my exuberance in the pursuit of my goals.

In 1971, I observed that out of a budget of $350 million allocated for Indian Affairs, nothing was directed to Native youth even though they formed a large part, if not a majority, of the Aboriginal population. As there were always programs that didn't spend their complete budget, I instructed the comptroller, Dom Nigra, to "find" me a million dollars. He found the funds, and, without informing the minister, I created a youth program. I didn't ask for new legislation. I just did it. We hired a group of young Native people headed by a non-activist. They came to work in the department with their briefcases but wearing feathers in their hair. It caused quite a commotion.

At the same time I hired Kahn-Tineta Horn, an outspoken activist from Kahnawake, the Mohawk community on the South Shore, near

Montreal. Not unexpectedly, the hiring created an uproar. I received calls from various members of parliament including Len March- and, a member from British Columbia, who came to see me. He was Native. "John," he complained, "do they have to call themselves 'Free- dom Fighters'?" Each youth who was hired by the department had a business card with his name over the words "Freedom Fighters" and "The rotten shall not be forgotten." Precious. Although I under- stood his concerns, I did not think the words on the business cards were too odious.

There was also a backlash from employees in the department who were stupefied by my hiring of those youths. They knew they couldn't complain to me directly, and so they complained to the press. I was asked for my reaction, and my response was drastic. I told the Cana- dian Press, "I get the backlash from idiots in the department who hate Indians," adding that I had employees who were more afraid of los- ing their jobs than seeing a transfer of power to the Natives and others who "simply don't have the mental capacity to deal with people of a different culture."*

The Public Service Alliance (PSAC) entered the fray and took up the battle.

"These blanket references to mental incompetents and idiots are made by the man responsible for the recruitment and use of staff at the Department of Indian and Northern Affairs. The low attack on his own people in the columns of the press is unprecedented by federal government executives of Mr Ciaccia's rank," Claude Edwards, the PSAC president, told the *Ottawa Journal*.

The PSAC did admit that employees were afraid that they could lose their jobs if the department turned over the administration of programs to Natives. But the PSAC severely criticized the youth program, which seemed "to involve $800,000 for taking on 33 youth workers at sala- ries of between $10,000 and $11,000 on one-year contracts ... What is the purpose of the program?" it asked.

The PSAC wanted a full retraction of my "slurs on [Edwards]" and other employees. Otherwise "Mr Ciaccia would be branded as irre- sponsible and unfit to head up the branches under his charges at Indian Affairs."

Of course, the minister became involved. During a parliamenta- ry Indian Affairs Committee meeting, he was asked by Conservative

---

* The Canadian Press story was picked up by the *Montreal Star*, the *Toronto Sun* and the *Ottawa Journal* among other newspapers.

Joe Clark, who later was briefly prime minister, whether the people I referred to were being removed or had resigned. Joe Clark felt that such remarks impeded department work. "Not so," said Chrétien. "They were a good stimulant, especially to those who felt the cap fitted." The headline in the next day's *Ottawa Journal* read, "Ciaccia's 'idiots' show marked improvement."

That wasn't all. I also took a strong position with some of the representatives of Native people. The National Indian Brotherhood, whose members were elected by and represented all of the Indian bands across Canada, got into the act. They saw money, and they wanted to control the money going directly to Indian communities. I gave them an earful, too. I called them "power-hungry politicians" who were trying to sabotage a department program aimed at helping young people on reserves. The National Indian Brotherhood pressured Flora MacDonald, the opposition Conservative Party spokesperson for Indian Affairs. She rose during question period and asked first if my statement had ministerial approval and then requested my immediate resignation. The minister answered in vintage Chrétien style:

> Mr Speaker, first of all I should like to make a remark concerning the first part of the question. There are people who are power hungry even in this House and who do not have it. The phenomenon is quite natural. With regard to the second part of the question, I would say, Mr Speaker, that I trust the assistant deputy minister wholeheartedly. I do not deplore the fact of having someone who can express his views and discuss them. It is extremely difficult to be assistant deputy minister of Indian Affairs and Northern Development, but I am pleased to have a very good one."*

Next time I saw Chrétien he said to me, "God loves me." "Why?" I wanted to know. "Because they asked for your resignation, not mine."

The official opposition in Ottawa had not asked for my resignation when I had called the employees of the department idiots, but they did so when I attacked "power-hungry politicians." Interesting. I now know that I went too far. Perhaps it was an uncontrolled reaction to all that I had seen, the frustrations, the lack of understanding and sensitivity, and the reaction of the department, which almost behaved like an army in occupied territory. Indeed, there were many former members of the military in the higher echelons of the department.

* House of Commons debate, Hansard, 29 June 1973, 5198.

The job of assistant deputy minister in Indian Affairs involved quite a lot of travel, which for me was an eye-opening experience. I went to a reserve in Alberta, with its frigid winters, to see government-built houses that had no heating systems. The district supervisor told me the savings resulting from having no heating were invested in building an additional room on each house to accommodate the large families dwelling in the buildings. I responded, "Yes and you could have saved more and built more rooms by not building a roof!"

Later, when investigating accusations of malfeasance against a departmental district supervisor, I had an adventurous flight in a DC-3 airplane landing at a remote reserve in northern Alberta near the border with the Northwest Territories. The plane started to land and then rose again. After this had happened a few times, I asked why and was told the pilot did it to scare away horses grazing on the landing strip. Later I found out we had landed on the wrong field and that there was a mountain directly in front of the runway where we were to take off. My staff refused to get back on the plane, and I was left travelling with a journalist who had accompanied us. On takeoff, the pilot revved the plane's motors to full throttle and skirted and cleared the mountain by just a few feet. The strain of revving the motors caused a rubber hose to break and oil was squirted on the window beside me. The copilot took out his watch, measured the flow, and said, "It's okay. We'll make it to Edmonton." When we arrived, one side of the plane was covered in oil.

After that visit, I became even more convinced that Native people should manage the funds allocated to them, but changing government policy to give the bands the power to administer their own funds was challenging. I was also concerned that district supervisors might not adequately explain the program, so, with my Ottawa directors, had a video made to explain the department's aims, and it was sent to supervisors across Canada. All they had to do was show it to the bands.

All of this work took a toll, and I sometimes vented my frustrations in public. But it could have been worse.

6

Entering the Political Arena

I wondered ... whether one was ever justified in neglecting the welfare
of one's family in order to fight for the welfare of others ... Is politics merely
a pretext for shirking one's responsibilities?
  Nelson Mandela, *Long Walk to Freedom*

When I was working as an assistant deputy minister, without realizing
it, I was behaving as a politician. When members of parliament asked
me to resign, when the media reported my actions and took notice of
my differences of opinion with people in authority, government or otherwise, I was not behaving as a civil servant. It became clear to me that
I was moving beyond the territory of the civil service. Inevitability, my
instincts led me into the political arena.

I did not choose politics. It chose me.

My entry into politics began with a phone call from Quebec Premier
Robert Bourassa. When my secretary announced that a Mr Robert
Bourassa was on the line, I didn't even think of the premier of Quebec. I was so engrossed in my work with Native people that I thought
he was probably a person calling to inquire about some business or
about some issues dealing with Native people. I was startled when he
announced himself as "le premier ministre."

He said he needed someone to represent minorities in the next
Quebec election, to be held in October 1973. I wasn't too sure that he
wanted me to only represent the minorities. He asked me if I would
agree to be a candidate, and I was given forty-eight hours to answer.
I was a little confused at the offer. I had given the James Bay Natives
$750,000 to pursue their claims against Quebec. Surely, Bourassa must
have known about that. I'm sure that he also spoke to Chrétien, but I
was never able to confirm this.

The offer to run for the Liberals was totally unexpected, and I
did not know what to do. I sought the advice of Basil Robinson, the
deputy minister of the Department of Indian Affairs and Northern

Development, a wise, calm, and gentle person, who had been counselling politicians for many years. Among those who had sought his advice were Lester B. Pearson, a recipient of the Nobel Peace Prize and former prime minister, and Jean Chrétien, who was to become a prime minister. Basil Robinson encouraged me to accept. "John," he said, "This is an honour and a privilege that very few people get."

And so I accepted and was in the running, facetiously giving as a reason to whoever asked me that I had only gone to Ottawa temporarily and that this was a good way for me to get back home.

The late 1960s was a momentous time to enter politics in Quebec, and the social and political background to my candidacy was unique. Nationalism and the protection of the French language were on the rise, with consequences for cultural communities. In 1969, a school board in the heavily Italian east end municipality of St Léonard had decided that all immigrant children should be admitted only to French schools. The Italian community reacted vociferously. There was an uproar that culminated in a riot on the streets of St Léonard.

Perhaps drawn by my Italians roots, I went to see the commotion on Jean Talon Street where it formed a border between St Léonard and Montreal. On the St Léonard side, the local police were trying to contain a raging crowd, but on the Montreal side, there were no police.* The scene was ugly. It was sad. I was profoundly affected by what I witnessed. The Union Nationale government immediately passed Bill 63, effectively overturning the decision of the school board and giving everyone the freedom to choose between schooling in French or in English. This added fuel to the burning desire of those who wanted to limit access to English schools, of those who feared for the survival of the French language. The Italian community had been stalwart in its defense of English language rights. The decision to grant freedom of choice sealed the fate of the Union Nationale in the election of 1973.

Also still fresh in Quebecers' memories were the events of 1970 when the October Crisis saw the kidnapping and murder of Pierre Laporte, a provincial cabinet minister, and the kidnapping of British diplomat James Cross. These violent events, which followed a series of mailbox bombings in Westmount, the bastion of English-speaking Quebec and at the Montreal Stock Exchange, the symbol of big business "controlled" by the English, shook a normally quiet and peaceful Quebec

---

* This was before the unification of all police forces on the island of Montreal in 1972.

society to its foundations. Prime Minister Trudeau invoked the War Measures Act, and, at the request of Premier Bourassa and the mayor of Montreal Jean Drapeau, sent the Canadian army into the streets of Montreal. Hundreds of people were taken into custody. There were human rights violation charges and countercharges. Most people were later released. The atmosphere was tense and fearful, and, because of the political turmoil, an exodus of people, especially the young, from Quebec. It was the beginning of the shift in economic power from Montreal to Toronto. Property values plummeted. People were terrified. It was a dark moment in the history of Quebec.

Out of this upheaval emerged a stronger Parti Québécois, which went on to change Quebec's political dynamics. A social democratic march toward independence became the Parti Québécois chosen path, the rationale for independence being that the federal government did not protect or promote the interests of Quebec.

THE CAMPAIGN

This was the political environment into which I stepped. But before I could officially become a candidate, a few obstacles had to be overcome. I was informed that I would be running for the Liberal Party in the district of Mount Royal, but the district's riding association had already chosen a candidate – Jean Charbonneau – who lived in the Town of Mount Royal (TMR), an upscale enclave of the electoral district where anglophones were predominant. I lived in Beaconsfield. However, Charbonneau graciously stepped aside in my favour. He could have objected and caused difficulties for my nomination but he didn't. Considerate and sincere, a good party loyalist, he became my official agent and worked tirelessly for my election.

The Town of Mount Royal had formerly been part of the riding of Outremont and had only been created as a separate district in a 1973 redrawing of the electoral map. I was its first Liberal candidate. The new riding included Côte-des-Neiges, a densely inhabited immigrant and working-class neighbourhood. With decisions for the riding being made in the Town, it needed its own organizational structure.

But, first I had to get the approval of Isobel Schofield – the "first lady" of TMR and widow of Richard Schofield who had been a mayor of the Town in the 1940s. No decisions affecting the Town were made without her approval. I went to see her at her home on Graham Boulevard to seek her support. She was a gracious, cordial, but imposing woman. We chatted a bit and then talked about politics. To my surprise, she continuously mispronounced the premier's name, calling him Mr *Bourasso*. When we finished the conversation, she gave me her blessing. In recognition of her contribution to the Town, a park near her home was renamed in her honour in 1992, having previously been accorded its name in memory of her husband.

I had never participated in an election campaign before. But, I had seen movies about political campaigns where there was always a parade, so I decided to organize a parade. I hired musicians – a quartet to play on the back of a truck. They were Jamaicans. Remember that this was the early 1970s and having Jamaican musicians play music in a neighbourhood of upper-class conservative anglophones was most unusual. I wasn't trying to show that I wasn't prejudiced nor did I expect the surprised reaction of the staid people of TMR.

Denis Chatain, a former Oblate priest, who had been my right-hand man in Ottawa, followed me to the Town Mount Royal. He decided that I should have a campaign song and wrote the words, to be sung to the tune of "The Happy Wanderer."

> Dans le comté de Mont-Royal
> Nous votons Liberal,
> Néo-Canadiens et Québécois
> Ti-Jean, c'est l'homme pour moi.
> Bourassa–Ciaccia
> Ti-Jean, c'est l'homme pour moi
> Arrivederci Ottawa,
> He's coming home, Hurrah!
> Experience and energy,
> Progress and liberty
> Bourassa–Ciaccia
> Progress and Liberty

We went up and down the streets of Côte-des-Neiges and the Town of Mount Royal. My son's English sheep dog, Garibaldi, was also part of the parade. He was a lovable creature, with black and white hair covering his eyes, making you wonder how he could see. We had placed a large bow – Liberal red – around his neck, to the amusement of many. As we went by, a very young boy, obviously excited by the sight of the prancing Garibaldi, pointed to him and yelled excitedly, "I'm going to vote for the dog!"

My Parti Québécois opponent was André Normandeau, a young professor of criminal law at the Université de Montréal. He was very polite and went through the motions of campaigning, knowing that a member of a party that wanted the political independence of Quebec did not stand a chance of winning in Mount Royal. But that fact did not lessen my effort at campaigning. I took nothing for granted; I tried to reach as many voters as I could to convince them to vote for me. Every morning, from 6:30 to 9 a.m., I would be at the commuter train station on Canora Avenue, introducing myself to commuters, shaking their hands, handing them my campaign leaflets. I was never snubbed, but I think they were surprised to see me campaigning, as Outremont–Mount Royal had always voted Liberal. Previous candidates did not think it necessary to do this. But I wasn't a previous candidate.

I was accepted and well supported by the Liberal Association of the riding. Members of the Association, especially Rolande Handfield, Eleanor Coté, and Pat Cohen, worked for my election with enthusiasm. We did the rounds of the shopping centres, and I would speak with shoppers and occasionally get into animated discussions with some of them. On a few occasions, the exchanges became too heated and I had to be restrained by my organizers. At one point, I remember Jean Charbonneau calming me down.

My son Mark was very active during the campaign, especially on election day. He would help to make sure that people voted, and drove many elderly people to voting stations. He was also responsible for his dog Garibaldi during the parade. Mark was always very supportive, working on elections and being patient with my absences.

To reach as many voters as I could, coffee parties were organized in people's homes (electoral law specifically forbade the drinking of liquor during these sorts of gatherings). I don't remember the exact issue being discussed on one occasion, but recall that the opinions expressed were, to my mind, obtuse, limited, and prejudiced. I lost patience. A ten-foot high wire fence had been built all along the eastern border of the Town, barring direct access to the neighbouring district of Park Extension, which had, let us say, more modest dwellings than those of TMR. I pointed in the general direction of the fence and said, "You know that fence you have along l'Acadie Boulevard? All you need now is a roof over the Town and then you can be completely isolated from the rest of the world."

Ed Tobin, one of the leaders of my riding association, who was with me, kicked me under the table. "John, you can't talk like that to the people whom you're asking to vote for you." His remarks reminded me that I was using the same approach as I had at Indian Affairs: expressing what I thought unreservedly. The people in the room were surprised, to say the least.

Voting took place in October 1973. Bourassa had tacitly reminded voters of the upheaval of the past several years, backing his message with the slogan "No to Separatism." His strategy helped bury his opponents. The Liberals won 102 of the 110 seats in the National Assembly. The Parti Québécois took just six seats. Two others went to the Creditistes, who elected Camille Samson and Fabien Roy in northern Quebec. The Union Nationale, which had beaten the Liberals in 1966, lost the election decisively, disappeared from the Quebec electoral map and political scene, as will be shown later, for reasons that had entirely nothing to do with nationalism and language. But the election would prove to be a victory containing the seeds of failure.

The election was also a personal triumph for me. I had won my riding with 23,779 votes, a plurality of 83 per cent. But my first disappointment was not long in coming. I wasn't named to cabinet. Although the premier had not formally promised me a cabinet post, he led me to believe that I would receive one. A front-page article in the *Montreal Gazette* reported that I spoke to the reporter in "acid tones" on being elected and not named a minister. The French expression *un mal pour un bien* – literally a bad for a good – fit this situation. However, events during the next few months were to show that staying out of cabinet actually turned out to my advantage.

7

Bill 22 Stirs Up a Hornet's Nest

Two events highlighted my first term in office. The first was my nomination as the special representative of Premier Bourassa in negotiations with the Cree and Inuit over the massive James Bay hydroelectric development project. The other was Bill 22, a fateful piece of language legislation.

On 21 May 1974, Bourassa tabled Bill 22 in the National Assembly. The bill made French the official language of Quebec. It also introduced measures to make French the everyday language of the province. Official texts and documents pertaining to public administration had to be written in French. They could be drawn up in English, but only the French version would be legally required. The internal language of public administration would be French. However, if 10 per cent or more of the population of a municipality or school district were English and if it had been the practice to draw up official documents in English, the practice could continue.

Public utilities and professional bodies (for example the Quebec Bar) had to offer their services in French and had to write in French when communicating with government. The bill not only dealt with the language of business but also with the names of businesses. "Juridical personality shall not be conferred unless the adopted firm name is in the French language." In other words, new business names had to be in French. The bill also provided that the French firm name had to stand out as prominently as the English version. Consumer contracts had to be written in French. However, one could ask that a contract also be drawn up in English. All products had to be labelled in French, and billboards had to be in French. A period of five years was given to implement this change.

The provisions of the bill that raised the greatest concern, both in the English-speaking community and among ultra-nationalists and the Parti Québécois, dealt with the language of instruction and admission to English schools. The bill provided that enrolment in English schools was limited to those who had a sufficient knowledge of the English language, to be determined by tests, beginning with kindergarten. Those who did not pass would be obliged to attend French schools. English schools were obliged to make sure that their students acquired a knowledge of French, both spoken and written. English instruction was also allowed, with the proviso that the minister's approval was required either to begin or cease teaching in English. This was meant to ensure that existing English schools would continue teaching in English. The school boards of northern Quebec could provide instruction to Natives and the Inuit in their own languages.*

The bill had far-reaching consequences. Municipal Affairs Minister Victor Goldbloom, as reported in the *Montreal Star*, summed it up by saying, "It will no longer be possible to live only in English in this province."

The reaction to the legislation tore the social fabric of Quebec, pitted communities against each other, created unholy alliances between separatists and anglophones, who opposed the bill for different reasons, split the ranks of the Liberal caucus, and gave the press an opportunity for rabble-rousing articles and inflammatory headlines. It created an unhealthy, volatile situation.

Once again, the Italian community, in part because of its status as one of the largest and oldest immigrant communities in Montreal and in part because its children were enrolled, primarily, in English schools, became the staunch defender of English rights. To try and placate the Italian community, Education Minister François Cloutier met with representatives of the community and told them that this was really a "political bill," meaning that it would create an impression of action by the government but that it would not prevent Italian children from having access to English schools. His statement confirmed the PQ argument that the bill was not sufficient.

Other ministers were prone to making excessive claims. For example, Jean Bienvenue, the minister of immigration, was quoted as saying that "Bill 22 will strangle separatism."

* New Quebec, as the far northern region was called, included James Bay, which had been part of the Northwest Territories and only became part of Quebec in 1923 when Ottawa transferred the area to the province subject to the settlement of the land claims of Natives living in the area.

Bill Tetley, the minister of revenue, representing the mainly English-speaking NDG, tried to reason with his voters about the plight of the French-speaking community in North America, outlining the reasonable aspects of the legislation. For his trouble he was shouted down and threatened before a crowd of thousands at Loyola College. Reason and emotions clashed and reason lost.

Six Liberal members of the National Assembly, of whom I was one, criticized the bill, threatening to vote against it, a drastic step that could have led to our being ejected from the Liberal caucus. Kenneth Fraser, the Liberal member from Huntingdon, accused the government of acting like Nazis who had stopped Jews from going to school in Germany. "That was their first oppressive act, and you wouldn't call the Nazi regime a democratic regime." In a reaction to his hyperbole, someone in the French-speaking community noted that Quebec had not yet sent anyone to the ovens.

Parti Québécois leader René Lévesque, whom the English community viewed as a dangerous leader, announced that the PQ would join forces with the English community. "The bill is unacceptable because it gives arbitrary and discretionary powers to the government, which is potentially dangerous to democracy," he argued. The call to democracy was always a tactic that appealed to the English-speaking community. It was useful to stoke the fears of your enemies to bring them to your side.

Claude Charron, one of the six PQ members of the National Assembly, young, competent, and aggressive, said that the six Liberal backbenchers who opposed the bill were "perfectly right," churning dissension.

Bourassa warned the English-speaking community that if the PQ were elected, their legislation would be worse than Bill 22. No one listened. Accusations, counter-accusations, nonsense, and outlandish statements ruled the day.

It was clear that I could not support the legislation as it was written, but I tried to be cautious in how I expressed my opposition, though less so after I was suspended from caucus for voting against Bill 22. I was disappointed with the bill and I told a reporter that now people were going to see what John Ciaccia's temper was all about. Still, I did not want to throw gasoline onto an already burning building. While I criticized the legislation as having "alienated and disenchanted many English-speaking voters," others were far less temperate, calling the bill the betrayal of the English-speaking community.

I also warned against contesting the legislation in the courts. "It would be too divisive," I pointed out in the assembly and it "provides civil servants with too many discretionary powers, and with this you're making abuse of power inevitable. It's only human nature." Given my experience at Indian Affairs, I knew all about the discretionary powers of a civil servant. I trusted my own judgment while I was an assistant deputy minister but was leery of what others would do with such powers. Referring to Native people and what I had seen in Ottawa, I said in a speech in the National Assembly, "I have seen how a bureaucracy can strangle a sector of the population, and I wouldn't want to encourage the same phenomenon in Quebec."

I also thought that Bill 22 fostered a spirit of suspicion and ambiguity; it was clearly discriminatory and illegal to give the French version of documents precedence over the English version. Here my legal training was speaking. As it turned out, I was right. Many years later, the Supreme Court of Canada struck down such a provision in Bill 101, the language legislation of the Parti Québécois government.

Premier Bourassa thought that Bill 22 would assuage nationalists and those who feared for the future of the French language. He was wrong. He did not go far enough to satisfy nationalist demands but went well beyond what many in the English-speaking community could tolerate. He got the worst of both worlds. He provoked his opponents and increased their opposition while alienating two groups that had been staunch Liberal supporters, the English community and cultural minorities. With Bill 22, not only did he not hit a home run – he struck out.

Perhaps it was a time in the evolution of Quebec during which no one could be satisfied; the needs of one group provoked and overwhelmed the fears of the others. Nonetheless, Bill 22 caused an upheaval in the legislative process and in society. Later, the Liberal Party of Quebec would pay dearly for this legislation and for the reactions that it provoked.

A SPEECH IN THE NATIONAL ASSEMBLY

On 15 July 1974, I gave my views of Bill 22 in a speech in the National Assembly. It was a day that I had to decide whether to vote "yes" and be loyal to my party or vote "no" and be loyal to my conscience, my electors, and my culture. Voting "no" might result in my being ejected from the Liberal Party.

I began my speech by pointing out two fears that exist in Quebec. Francophones feared that demographic forces and immigration threatened the viability of their culture and the English-speaking community feared their rights were threatened. Quebec was evolving and the evolution was the result of new forces, new aspirations, which contributed to the establishment of new relations between the different groups in our society. These groups react, making their demands known. They claim not only their identity but also the rights that a society offers its citizens on intellectual, cultural, social, and economic levels. When a society undertakes to modify or change certain relationships between the different groups through legislation, such as Bill 22 attempted to do, I believe that it is essential that this be done legally, respecting human dignity.

I did not share the opinion of those who argued that the English-speaking community had no language or educational rights. "I do not subscribe to the theory that they have only 'privileges.' This theory is too dangerous. They have been here before Confederation. If they don't have rights after 100 years, when will they?" I asked.

I supported declaring French the official language of the province:

Let there not be any doubt on this point. I also agree with the provision of programs to encourage businesses to develop and promote French. I agree with the provisions to oblige anglophones to learn French by teaching that language in the English schools. Why? Because the objective is to assure that all Quebecers learn French and that all francophones could work in French at all levels of a business enterprise. These are articles in favor of French but not against the English.

I am against the discretionary powers given to the bureaucracy. I have seen how a bureaucracy can strangle a sector of the population of this country. I do not want to encourage the same phenomenon in Quebec.* A bureaucracy must reflect the major ethnic groups of a community in order that citizens can be served by public servants who, because of the same cultural background, will be able to be more understanding and responsive to the needs of those they serve.

Unfortunately, this situation does not exist at the present time in Quebec. The bureaucracy, for one reason or another, does not reflect the major ethnic composition of the province. This is all the more reason why the power of the bureaucracy must be limited and must not be as stipulated in Bill 22.

* I was referring to the Department of Indian Affairs in Ottawa and the control it had had over the Native population.

> I am against *a régie* [government board] making the final
> decisions on essential rights and taking away any legal recourse by
> the individual when his rights would be affected. I uphold the rule
> of law.

I suggested that the law contravened a section of the British North
America Act, which was the Canadian constitution at the time. I even
accepted a derogation from the principle of free choice in the selection
of schools, with proper safeguards, providing that the existence of English schools was guaranteed and providing that everyone would learn
both French and English; this could be done by obliging French schools
to teach English courses.

I spoke about culture – the values transmitted to us from the past –
and the need to protect our heritage but not at the expense of others
and certainly not by enacting laws that displayed hostility toward others. I warned against those who maintained *on va les avoir les Anglais*
(we're going to get the English). That kind of attitude should not become a value among French-speaking Quebecers. Quoting John F. Kennedy, I exhorted,

> "Let us not fix the blame for the past but fix a course for the
> future." It is this spirit that must inspire the law on the official
> language. What is the spirit of this law? I wish that the wording
> of this law would reflect the goodwill and the assurances that the
> various members of the government have been giving to the citizens
> of the province and more especially to the members of the English
> community. I wish that this law would reflect *la paix et la fraternité*
> that the member from D'Arcy McGee [Victor Goldbloom] so
> eloquently and fervently hoped for in a speech to this Assembly.
> But, unfortunately, one gets the impression that this law is designed
> to restrict the English community and other minorities, to be
> enforced by a bureaucracy which will not answer to the electorate
> and whose membership does not represent the community; a law
> that places certain officials above the law, removes the courts from
> the protection of the citizens and abrogates the rule of law; a law
> that fosters a spirit of suspicion and ambiguity. If such principles
> are embodied in our laws, then we must ask what is the direction
> that we are giving to our society.

I am aware of my duties as a member of the Liberal Party and of
the government. I am also aware that I have not only the obligation

to represent my electors but also the duty to support all legislation, which would be in the interest of all Quebecers. That is why I am using a moderate approach and proposing changes that would not suppress in any way the principle of the protection of the French language, which I support, and that I favour, but changes that would facilitate the application of the law and render it more acceptable.

I made three proposals: (1) Withdraw those articles in the bill that are not constitutional; (2) eliminate the discretionary powers given to the bureaucrats; (3) guarantee the existence of English schools and assure that English will be taught as a second language in French schools. "It is possible," I said, "to protect the French language and have a spirit of harmony in the law." It was not a vociferous attack on the legislation – more of an accommodation and a demand for clarification and protection of certain rights.

In closing I reminded the Assembly of the words of the Speaker's prayer at the beginning of each daily session asking: "Dieu la grâce d'adopter des measures destinées à faire le bien et la prosperité du Québec."* I reminded the Speaker that his words were particularly applicable to Bill 22. Then I sat down.

Three minutes before midnight, the president of the Assembly called for a vote.

I stood up and voted, "No."

SUSPENSION

Although even the French press† applauded my courage in voting against the legislation, the premier immediately suspended me from the Liberal caucus, but the suspension was lifted at the next caucus meeting a few days later. The suspension had been perfunctory because Bourassa knew he couldn't let my straying from party discipline go unnoticed. Not having levied a suspension could have indicated that he did not attach much importance to his language law. I was upset. I had represented my constituents. I didn't appreciate these shenanigans by a premier who felt he had to send the message that elected members must follow the party line.

* "By the grace of God, let us adopt measures that further the wellbeing and prosperity of Quebec."

† *La Presse*, 18 July 1974.

Despite my disappointment with the suspension, I carried on. Throughout these turbulent times, I continued to meet with the James Bay Natives as a special representative of Bourassa. The ongoing negotiations were critical for the success of the "project of the century" as the James Bay hydroelectric development was being called.

The editor of *The Weekly Post*, a local paper in my riding, had suggested in an editorial that I withdraw from the negotiations as the government's representative. After all, if I didn't agree with the government, how could I be its representative? The paper published my response on the front page. I explained my objectives with Natives and why I could not withdraw from negotiations that were crucial to their future: the need to recognize and protect their way of life, their language, their customs. If my position looked like a crusade on behalf of the Cree and Inuit, so much the better. I could not abandon them. My differences with the government over Bill 22 legislation were secondary to my objective of finding a just agreement for the Inuit and Cree.

The editor said he understood, adding that he had asked me to withdraw with "tongue in cheek."

8

The James Bay Challenge

In April 1971, Premier Bourassa announced a massive hydroelectric development that came to be known as the James Bay Project. The announcement was a shock to the Natives who lived in the territory, as there had been no prior notice or consultation about the project. At the time, I was still the assistant deputy minister of Indian Affairs in Ottawa. Part of my mandate was to help the James Bay Natives, who were alarmed and feared for their way of life and rights, get their fair share of the project. To defend their interests, they needed lawyers and researchers. They needed to be prepared to defend themselves against the possible negative consequences of the project. I obtained the necessary funding for them. And I did more than that. I got involved with the Quebec government.

When I was working for Indian Affairs, I met with one of Premier Bourassa's strong, influential, and competent assistants, Paul Desrochers. Actually, he was more of a decider than an assistant. He had the reputation of getting things done. When you wanted something from the government, you went to see "mon oncle" Paul. I explained to him the plight of the Cree and Inuit and the need to settle their claims. Surprisingly, he did not take the position – as some other advisors to the premier did – that Natives had no rights. He even suggested settling all outstanding issues for the sum of $20 million dollars – an abysmally low amount, but at least it a starting point for the negotiations. I felt a little encouraged by the initial offer.

But a resolution at that time was not to be. At my last meeting with Desrochers, he sadly told me that he was no longer involved with the dossier – it had been taken out of his hands. He apologized and told me that the premier's chief of staff was now handling the portfolio. His name was Jean Prieur. I, too, was discouraged, but I didn't give up. I called Prieur and made an appointment to see him. I met him in his office, next to the premier's, in the Hydro-Québec building on what was then Dorchester Boulevard (now René Lévesque Boulevard) in Montreal. I'll never forget that meeting. It lasted less than ten minutes during which I was told that the Quebec government did not recognize Natives land rights. I had driven two hours from Ottawa for this?

I returned to Ottawa and immediately went to see Jean Chrétien, the Indian Affairs minister. I was fuming. "Look at my parking receipt," I said to Chrétien. "It only cost two dollars. You know how short a time you have to be on a downtown parking lot to pay only two dollars? That's how long Prieur met with me."

This happened in the summer of 1973. In September, Bourassa asked me to become a Liberal candidate in the forthcoming provincial election. After my election to the National Assembly in October, the premier asked me to take over negotiations with the Natives. On 12 November 1973 I went to Ottawa to meet with Chrétien to discuss an approach to the Native claims and to determine what the federal government's participation in the negotiations would be. I came back to Montreal the same day to brief Premier Bourassa.

A ROCKY START

The situation was delicate and difficult. Two large companies had been newly created by the Quebec government to oversee the project: the James Bay Energy Corporation, responsible for all of its aspects – what the project would be and where it would be built – and the James Bay Development Corporation, which was responsible for executing the work according to the Energy Corp's specifications. The development company was also responsible for managing all resources in the project area. Construction of the first phase of the project had begun the year before. Meanwhile, the Northern Quebec Inuit Association had joined with the Quebec Association of Indians to seek an injunction to halt the project. The threat of the injunction hung over the government like a sword of Damocles. The legal proceedings, before Justice Albert Malouf, were hampering my attempts at negotiations. What would be the decision of the court? On 15 November, Malouf ruled to grant an injunction to the Cree and the Inuit, halting all work on James Bay. The workers employed by the project were sent home.

You can imagine the shock that the injunction caused to a government that had been led to believe that Natives had no land rights. I thought of the "nonmeeting" that I had with Jean Prieur. From "no rights" to an injunction is quite a jump. It was also a total repudiation of the advice that Bourassa's legal advisors had provided, suggesting injunction proceedings would last just a few days and then be rejected. The process had in fact taken six months and an injunction had been granted.

Four days later, on 19 November, I was officially appointed special representative of Premier Bourassa to negotiate with the James Bay Natives. Meanwhile, the government appealed the injunction, asking that it be lifted pending the final determination of the rights of Quebec's Native Indians. The government claimed that the balance of inconvenience (the determining factor in the granting of an injunction) was in its favour. In other words, stopping the work would be more damaging to the government than to the Natives. The nature of Native rights, or whether they existed at all, would be determined later.

The fact that Bourassa had such confidence in me that he gave me full latitude – an illustration of his character – was a big help in my negotiations. He did not set limits in regard to my commitment to the James Bay Cree and Inuit. I had a free hand.

One can understand the reluctance of the Natives to negotiate while the injunction proceedings were ongoing. In spite of this, on 20 November, with the injunction still in effect, I had an all-day meeting with representatives from the Cree, Inuit, and federal government at the Queen Elizabeth Hotel in Montreal. I wanted to outline and discuss with them the basic elements of a possible settlement. With the Native representatives was their able attorney James O'Reilly. I had known him when I was assistant deputy minister in Ottawa and was funding the James Bay Natives. O'Reilly chose to leave a very reputable firm in Montreal, which also represented Hydro-Québec, to avoid a possible conflict of interest. O'Reilly was a man of integrity. He was committed to the Native cause.

We began discussing the conditions of a possible agreement. Obviously, the Natives were noncommittal. They were still before the courts and had Justice Malouf on their side. However, I managed to outline the basic principles and some particular details that both parties could agree to.

MY APPROACH TO A SETTLEMENT

I looked at the Alaska Native Settlement Act as a model for my negotiation. In December 1971, President Richard Nixon had signed the Act, making it the largest (peaceful) land claims settlement in the history of the United States. It provided land and money to the 80,000 indigenous people involved. Here was the precedent for a similar deal in Quebec. But my work with Native people until then had convinced me that any settlement on James Bay would have to include more than land and money. The government would also have to fulfill the needs and concerns of the Cree and Inuit in this vast territory. We had to go beyond the terms of the Alaska deal.

That evening I met with Chrétien at the Beaver Club, the dining room of the Queen Elizabeth Hotel, to review the discussions held that day. There were numerous phone calls to the legal representatives of the Cree and Inuit and even to Bourassa. The next evening, on 21 November, I had another meeting with Chrétien and the Cree and Inuit at the Airport Hilton in Dorval.

During this time I was also in contact with representatives of Hydro-Québec and with Armand Couture, an engineer with the James Bay Energy Corporation I needed their consent. I wanted to put the final touches to the revisions to the project that the Natives desired before I presented my settlement proposals, and I needed the government to be on side with what I was doing. Couture saw the potential problems if the changes were not made.

Initially, the Natives did not want the colossal project to go ahead, but when the injunction was lifted, they sensed it was inevitable. If it was to go ahead, they had to be heard, they reasoned. There were significant changes that could be made to the agreement, not only to protect certain communities but also to reduce the impact of the project on the entire region. There would be no changes if the work continued without their input. The goals became flood less land, divert fewer rivers, reduce the number of reservoirs that could affect hunting, trapping, and fishing, and eliminate work that would disrupt a community. These required changes to the government's plans and that meant more Native involvement in the negotiations. The meetings multiplied, but they became more productive. Not all of these changes were easily accepted, and the government agreed to some only after much bickering and insistence from Native representatives that the changes were essential.

The government agreed to stop its plans to construct a seaport at Fort George, home to a Cree community and now known as Chisasibi. The construction of the new airport at Fort George was to be suspended and would not continue without the consent of the Fort George community. Frankly, it is hard to imagine that the government could have arbitrarily decided to build an airport in a Native community that depended on hunting, fishing, and trapping for its livelihood.

A change to the diversion of the Caniapiscau River meant two reservoirs could be eliminated. This was important because it meant that not only would less hunting and trapping territory be taken from the Natives but also that there would be less mercury contamination in the water. Mercury leaches from rotting vegetation when it is submerged and is hazardous to both wildlife and people.

The diversion of the upper basin of the Grande Rivière de la Baleine (Great Whale River) would be eliminated, thus also eliminating the construction of another reservoir. It meant the Caniapiscau River would not be affected. The level of Lake Mistassini would not change. There were also numerous meetings between the experts working for the Natives and the people working for the James Bay Development Corp that contributed to changes in the agreement.

At the request of the Native advisors, the spillway at LG-2, one of the huge dams to be built, was relocated. When a reservoir is in danger of overflowing, a spillway is opened to allow the water to flow out. This opening of the spillway can affect the areas where the overflow takes place.

I recall that in the mid-1980s, while negotiations were still ongoing, Bourassa took Jacques Chirac (then mayor of Paris and not yet president of France) to visit James Bay. Wanting to impress Chirac with the workings of the "project of the century," Bourassa had a spillway opened – a huge, impressive mechanical operation that sent out a tremendous gush of water. It also disgorged fish from the reservoir and that, in turn, attracted bears. The sight of the bears mesmerized Chirac – it may have been the first time he saw a bear in the wild – and he totally disregarded the marvels of modern engineering to the disappointment of Premier Bourassa. Years later, when I had finalized the agreement and went to see Bourassa before it was signed, he asked me one question. "John, is it true that you gave the bears to the Natives?" Was he joking, or is this all he wanted to know? Or was he referring to Chirac's fascination with bears? Whichever it was, I was flabbergasted and never found out his meaning.

On 22 November, the Appeal Court lifted the injunction. The Natives appealed the decision, but then, realizing the project would proceed and rather than wait for the next ruling, they decided to begin serious negotiations and quickly suspended their appeal. They believed, and rightly so, that if the appeal failed, they would be in a worse position.

At least this way there was motivation for the government to settle on more favourable terms.

A week later, I presented the Natives with an eleven-point proposal for the settlement of their claims. The proposal assumed that the James Bay Project would proceed. One had to be realistic.* However, it was possible to make significant changes to the project so as to address some of the objections raised by the Natives, who, by the way, were advised by very competent experts.

One cannot give enough credit to the Native leadership in defending the interest of their communities and in engaging top experts to help them in their fight against the government. They were led by the young Billy Diamond for the Cree and Charlie Watt for the Inuit. In addition to the capable legal representation of James O'Reilly, they engaged the help of various experts including the engineer Einar Skinnarland, who had extensive knowledge of hydro-electric projects and the building of dams. Many of these people were engaged by the Natives with the funds provided by the Federal Department of Indian Affairs when I was its assistant deputy minister. This cohort held its own in the face of the expertise hired by the James Bay Development Corporation and Hydro-Québec.

Throughout the negotiations my sympathies were with the Natives. Being named Bourassa's special representative reinforced the reason I left my law practice to work for the Department of Indian Affairs and Northern Development. Even though I represented the Quebec government and Bourassa, who Natives regarded as the enemy and who had run roughshod over their rights and dignity, I wanted them to know I was aware of their fears and concerned for their future.

I had worked furiously hard to come up with a proposal that would be acceptable to both Natives and government, that would accommodate Native rights and government needs. There were some who pointed out that Natives were here long before white men and that this, therefore, was their land, meaning they were entitled to everything they demanded. As I testily told a reporter, however, "The white man is not going back to Europe."

At first, I could not get the Natives to negotiate. I had several meetings with them, while their consultants met with the James Bay Energy

---

* There had been talk of a nuclear alternative to James Bay, and it had some supporters, but it was evident the Quebec government was not about to replace the project by building the eighteen nuclear plants that would be required to produce an equivalent amount of electricity.

Corporation. They listened to my proposal, but they wouldn't budge. Without a settlement, there would be uncertainty as the project went forward. The lack of an agreement raised all sorts of questions. What would the courts finally determine? What would be the reaction of the financial institutions that were buying Hydro-Quéphbec bonds? Would financing be held back; would interest rates increase because of the higher risks? Billions of dollars were in play and much was at stake for the government.

But the Natives also had much to lose. The injunction had been lifted and work had restarted. Without an agreement, the project would go ahead without any changes in their favour. There would be no remedial work and greater destruction of the habitat. And my biggest concern: no recognition of Native culture or protection for their way of life.

In January 1974, Bourassa made another of his media moves. After two months of waiting for a negotiated agreement, he held a press conference with me by his side, in which he made public my proposal of 29 November 1973 and explained the philosophy behind it. An energy crisis was engulfing the Western world, and he spoke, in that context, of the energy needs of the country. As production lagged behind demand, gas shortages gripped the US, producing lineups across the country. Bourassa warned of a subsequent shortage of electric power in the 1980s if the project did not proceed. And he spoke in words that I had suggested in order for the world to hear of the needs of Native people:

> It is not our intention to proceed with the project without respecting and preserving the cultural heritage of those who have lived for so long in this territory. On the contrary, we wish to make sure that these people and their cultural values will flourish with the changing world of today. We wish to assist them in maintaining their traditional pursuits and in preserving their cultural heritage but also wish to help them adapt, at their own pace, to the changing world around them – to changes which are taking place inevitably, even without major projects.

He then spelled out the eleven points of the proposal I had presented to the Natives on 29 November. He knew that public opinion is a powerful force, and he was trying to mould it to put pressure on the Natives. And it worked. The Native representatives knew what Bourassa was doing and that it would weaken their bargaining power; they were furious, indignant and protested. The premier was accused of breaking an understanding that the proposal was not to be made public until an agreement had been reached.

But finally cooler heads prevailed. Only in his early twenties, Billy Diamond, who was the Grand Chief of the James Bay Cree Nation, had wisdom beyond his years. When he spoke in his deep booming voice, you listened. He had a sense of duty and a vision for the future. He was, I believe, a strong voice in the decision to negotiate with the government.

Many people were involved in the negotiations. Billy Diamond, Ted Moses, and others were the spokespersons for the Cree, with James O'Reilly as their lawyer. Charlie Watt, Zebedee Nunquak, and other distinguished members of the Inuit community represented their people. Robert Litvack and lawyers from the law firm that I had left to go to Ottawa represented the Inuit. And there was the government, with some twenty departments directly affected by my proposal to the Natives.

THE AGREEMENT IN PRINCIPLE

The question then was, how to proceed in order to resolve the myriad issues raised by both sides? An agreement involving only land and money would have been simple – sit all the parties together and work out acceptable amounts – but the eleven points of our proposal were much more comprehensive. Yes, they surely dealt with land and money issues, but also with intangibles such as values and traditions.

I might have been a neophyte to politics but I had gained important experience with civil servants from my time in Ottawa. An agreement would be difficult to reach with a group of them sitting with me around a table. For that reason, initially, I did not involve civil servants from the Quebec government – their presence would have led to a dead end at that stage of the negotiations, but eventually government departments had to be involved.

The Native representatives and I agreed on a plan. I would negotiate an agreement in principle with them and their lawyers. This would include the outlines of a settlement – the topics and their broad content that we could agree upon. The details would be worked out in a subsequent final agreement. None of us wanted these agreements to drag on forever. Legal proceedings were still pending before the courts, and so avoiding delays was important.

Under the terms of the Quebec Boundaries Extension Act of 1912, the federal government transferred the James Bay territory to the province with the obligation that Quebec would settle with the Natives. At that time, governments did not recognize Native land claims but did acknowledge that they had exclusive rights to use the land. The Natives had to give up those rights in exchange for certain agreed-upon socio-economic benefits.

In November of 1973, we decided to sign an agreement in principle no later than 15 November 1974. After the delays in starting the negotiations, mainly because of the court proceedings, this didn't give us much time. Meanwhile all legal proceedings would be suspended. If a final agreement was not signed by 15 November 1975 – one year after the initial agreement – the agreement in principle would be considered annulled, all negotiations would come to an end, and the parties could resume their legal options. Clearly, there was much at stake for everybody.

Agreeing to sign a final agreement in one year was an objective that all participants thought could not be achieved. I was determined that we would meet that date. The agreement in principle contained twenty-eight pages plus two appendices of another twenty pages. The final agreement had thirty-one chapters and 455 pages.

To give a sense of the complexity of the agreement in principle, here are the topics it covered:

- Changes to the project
- Remedial work
- Land
- Hunting, fishing, and trapping
- Future development
- Environmental protection
- Compensation
- Native development and economic measures
- Local and regional government
- Burial sites
- Negotiations with other Natives of Quebec
- Eligibility
- Continuation of negotiations
- Cost of negotiations
- Other benefits
- Interpretative clause

There were also two appendices:

- The proposals of 29 November 1973
- General principles concerning a hunting, fishing, and trapping regime with a list of species in the territory reserved exclusively for the Natives

The changes to the project and the remedial work, some of which I have already outlined, were difficult to obtain. I went back and forth between meetings at Hydro-Québec and the James Bay Development Corporation. The mentality of certain people in lofty corporate positions, especially when combined with government proprietorship, exhibits a sense of entitlement. Negotiations of this kind seem to bring out the worst of both the corporate and the bureaucratic worlds. Their orders become the law and there is no room for dissension. On many occasions, I had to be assertive and sometimes indelicate.

A representative of Hydro-Québec, who had previously been the vice-president of a bank, came into one meeting and systematically opposed all of my suggestions. I became so exasperated that I finally said to him, "If you're so sure of everything, why don't you negotiate with the Natives? Go ahead, take over!" He backed off while his colleagues smiled. This person eventually ran for office and became one of my colleagues in cabinet. We became good friends too.

Another incident was even more unpleasant, and perhaps I went too far. The president of the James Bay Development Corporation, who was originally from Belgium, objected to every proposal I made. He really had a negative attitude towards the Natives. After keeping my feelings under control, I finally lost my cool and told him, "You're not in the Congo here." I was referring to the brutal colonial rule Belgium had imposed in that country, and I felt badly the minute I uttered the words. He was not pleased with the remark.

Changes were made to the original project:

- We did not obtain the elimination of LG-1 reservoir and power station, but Energy Corp. agreed those would be moved a distance of thirty-two miles (51.5 kilometres) – from Mile 22 to Mile 54.
- There would be further negotiations to attempt to reduce flooding, especially the impact of flooding on Native harvesting, if the costs to the James Bay Energy Corporation were the same.
- To compensate for some flooding, the government would allocate the Eastmain Band twenty square miles (thirty-two square kilometres) of reserve lands and additional thirty square

miles (forty-eight square kilometres) of Category 2 lands and would provide a further 175 square miles of land (282 square kilometres) – seventy-five miles of Category 1 and one hundred of Category 2 – unless flooding indicated in the existing plans was substantially reduced.*

- The Fort Chimo (today Kuujjuaq) people would be guaranteed the same harvest of fish for equal effort and Energy Corp. would take the necessary steps to do this at its expense. A joint study would be made to determine the average catch in the previous five years.
- To efficiently manage precious timber, it was agreed that a substantial portion of the timber of the Eastmain–Opinaca diversion reservoirs and the LG-1 reservoir would be cut prior to or during the flooding.
- There would be general remedial work carried out and paid for by Energy Corp. to minimize all possible damages of the project on the Native people or to the animals, birds, and fish upon which they depend.
- The Quebec government or Energy Corp. would pay for the cost of changes and remedial work. (Compensatory and remedial work was also listed.)
- The Quebec Government agreed to install a water intake system for the Eastmain and Fort George (Chisasibi) settlement.
- The government agreed that no permanent non-Native town would be built in the Eastmain–Opinaca area (the location of EM-1, another reservoir) during the construction of the project.
- The settlements at Eastmain, Paint Hills, and Rupert House were isolated from each other. The government agreed to continue the negotiations to construct access roads to join those settlements.
- The terrestrial fauna (caribou, moose, beaver, and bear) would be captured and relocated prior to flooding. The Natives could perform this work if they so wished.
- Water level fluctuations would be managed, taking into account environmental considerations.
- A mechanism would be established whereby any individual trapper whose equipment had been damaged would receive personal compensation.

* Category 1, 2, and 3 lands are described below.

- The government or Energy Corp. would subsidize the reorganization of any trap lines laid by the Eastmain and Paint Hills people which were affected by the hydro project. All justifiable costs needed to attain the same level of subsistence harvesting, based on the last five years, and would be covered. The programs to be set up by government would include fur-bearing and big game animals. The programs would also include salaried Cree workers and the possibility of establishing cooperatives.

The transfer of lands to the Native communities presented a political problem. There were no "reserves" in the territory. The creation of reserves would effectively transfer such lands to the federal government under the terms of the British North America Act (the Canadian constitution) since it had jurisdiction over Indians and Indian lands. I had to be mindful of the nationalistic, anti-Ottawa sentiment from the Quebec side, and I did not want to give ammunition to the Parti Québécois. But we still wanted to expand the settlements. We, therefore, limited the area of land to be set aside as reserves and gave the bands ownership of additional areas adjacent to those reserves. This effectively expanded the reserves but limited the area of federal jurisdiction and allowed me to give more land – under provincial jurisdiction – to the Cree. The creation of all these different categories over such an immense territory was the inspiration of Billy Diamond, the young grand chief of the Cree. During the negotiations, Billy Diamond, Jim O'Reilly and myself met at my home. At one point during our discussions, Billy dropped a stone into my swimming pool. Concentric circles, one larger than the other, were created around the drop. "You see John," he said, "the centre is the community, but there are rippling effects created around the community." He pointed to the circles. "These are the results of the existence of that community."*

We did not have this problem with the Inuit since there was no precedent for reserves on Inuit land anywhere in Canada. They were given full ownership of the allotted lands. These were the so-called Category 1 lands for both Cree and Inuit.

---

* Unfortunately Billy passed away while I was writing these pages, and my own health prevented me from going to his last rites in Waskaganish. The Great Spirit surely watched over him and inspired him. He deservedly had the respect of everyone.

The government would own the mineral rights of these lands, but minerals could not be extracted without the consent of the communities involved. The Cree and the Inuit would own the soapstone deposits or other materials that they traditionally used. This would protect the production of the much desired and unique Inuit soapstone artworks.

I have already mentioned the importance of hunting and fishing for the Natives. Lands were set aside for their exclusive use – 25,000 square miles (40,000 square kilometres) for the Cree, south of the fifty-fifth parallel and 35,000 square miles (56,000 square kilometres) for the Inuit, north of the fifty-fifth parallel. These were Category 2 lands and their exact location would be determined in the final agreement. Both the Cree and the Inuit would participate in pinpointing the exact location of these lands. The choice would take into account the wildlife productivity and "existing known developments." In other words, the Natives couldn't choose the areas where hydro-electric installations were being built. Severe restrictions were placed on the access of non-Natives to these hunting lands – access could only be granted for scientific or administrative purposes and could not interfere with the exclusive hunting and fishing use given to the Natives.

Category 3 lands referred to the rest of the territory where the Natives would also have unrestricted access to the land, but not exclusive, hunting, and fishing rights. Non-Natives would have restricted rights in these areas. The Natives, however, would have exclusive trapping rights over the entire territory. The purpose of these and other provisions was to preserve the Cree and Inuit ways of life.

A schedule was attached to the agreement providing for the Natives to continue to hunt and fish throughout the territory, even in public parks if they were to be created, and even in areas where there were forestry or mining concessions. Certain categories of fish, animals, and birds were reserved for exclusive harvesting by the Natives. They included fox and coyote, squirrel, polar bear, raccoon and muskrat, whitefish, sturgeon, burbot, and porcupine. Hunting for muskox and other species would be negotiated in the final agreement.

The area of northern Quebec around the project was pristine territory, almost untouched by non-Native human activity. The seemingly barren land, vast and desolate, yes, but alive, seems to go on forever. The hydro project was the first intrusion not only into the lives of the Cree and Inuit, but also upon the land, its waters, vegetation, and animals. Rampant, unchecked development could not be allowed. Measures had to be taken to protect a hardy but nevertheless fragile ecosystem. Although the Cree and Inuit instinctively knew how to preserve their environment, we had to develop ways and means to achieve the same goal.

Those ways and means included changes to the project and remedial work to reduce the impact on the environment, fish, and other animal species. That is why certain species of fish and animals were reserved for the exclusive use of the Natives – to ensure as far as possible that there would be no endangered species in the future. That is why we provided for environmental committees and environmental impact studies – to minimize the impact of the James Bay Project on the environment and to ensure future development in the area would meet strict environmental standards. As stated in the agreement in principle:

> Conservation is the pursuit of the optimum natural productivity
> of all living resources and the protection of the ecological system
> of the territory so as to protect endangered species and ensure
> primarily the continuance of the traditional pursuits of the Native
> people, and secondarily so that non-Natives may satisfy their needs
> for recreational hunting and fishing.

Once these principles had been established, how would they work? What would be the rules of conservation and how would they be applied? First, a hunting, fishing, and trapping regime would be established for the territory. The details would be spelled out in the final agreement. Second, regulations would enforce the principles of conservation. It was therefore agreed to form a coordinating committee that would have the sole power to establish regulations respecting hunting, fishing, and trapping on Category 2 and 3 lands.

One had to consider that the government and Natives might at times have differences of opinion concerning any regulations we established. I wanted to be fair to both parties. The Natives and the government would each name an equal number of representatives to the committee. In addition, there would be a chairman who would hold office for one year, chosen from the Native representatives for the first year, from the government representatives for the second year, and so forth on an alternating basis. In the case of a deadlock in the committee, the chairman would have the deciding vote. Alternating the chairman would create a balance between government and the Natives in the decision-making process.

The agreement in principle was signed on 15 November 1974 by all parties: Cree and Inuit representatives, the government of Quebec, Hydro-Québec, the James Bay Energy Corporation, the James Bay

Development Corporation and the federal government. We were on schedule despite time spent on the conflicts of Bill 22 (Bourassa's language legislation), my vote against the bill in the National Assembly, my suspension from caucus and subsequent reinstatement, and all the myriad details of a newly elected member in a new constituency.

PROCEDURES FOR THE FINAL AGREEMENT

It was time to move on to the final agreement. We had one year to finalize it. If it were not signed by 15 November 1975, everything would be cancelled and our efforts would be in vain. The pressure was on.

The question was how to proceed. The agreement in principle contained many provisions, some more specific than others and some being left for future negotiations. It was necessary to elaborate the details, continue some negotiations, and put the specifics all in final form, spell them out in enforceable legal language. We were not only negotiators. We were legislators.

To put meat on the bones, I needed the participation of all government departments as well as that of Hydro-Québec and the James Bay Development Corporation. I arranged a meeting of the relevant government department heads and explained to them the deadline and the task we had before us. They were aware of my negotiations but not of all the details – in general, they were learning of the commitments we'd negotiated for the first time. I explained the importance of what we were doing and asked for their participation and cooperation.

I had to consider a way to maintain control of the negotiations. I couldn't be at every meeting with all the various departments, corporations, and Native representatives. But nor could I allow crucial details and decisions to be made solely by department heads. I feared that this would restrict the content of the agreement. I wanted the agreement to rise above strictly government-approved provisions. I wanted it to reflect a philosophy and a vision that included the acceptance of a people and their potential for self-development, and which would be an example to the world. This could not come from civil servants alone.

I created seven committees to handle the negotiations, each with a specific responsibility and subject of discussion: lands, hunting and fishing, environment, modifications to the project and remedial work, Native development and economic measures, local government and eligibility, and compensation.

Each committee had representatives from the government department concerned with the items under discussion, the Cree, the Inuit, the James Bay corporations, and Hydro-Québec. I named my personal representative on each committee who would report directly to me. Through my representative I followed the negotiations and gave directions on their content without having to attend all meetings. As the work of the individual committees progressed, we had regular meetings of everyone so that all were informed of progress and slower committees were spurred on.

I chose my personal representatives depending on the subject under discussion. For example, I knew that Hydro-Québec and the corporations had very limited views on the environment, and if left to them, we would not obtain strict rules. I found a member in the environment department who was known for his radical outlook and made him my personal representative on the environmental committee.

I consulted Lucien Chouinard in choosing the leader of the compensation committee. He was the secretary to the executive council, Quebec's highest-ranking public servant (later he was named to the Supreme Court of Canada). I did not want a civil servant as my representative on the compensation committee because I feared that such a person would be parsimonious in granting public funds to the Natives. Chouinard suggested Steve (Severin) Lachapelle from the Quebec City suburb of Ste Foy. He was a practicing lawyer, capable, pleasant, and utterly surprised when I asked him to head the compensation committee. He accepted the offer. We developed a friendship that has lasted through the years.

The contents of the agreement in principle were refined and enlarged. I made several trips to the James Bay region, especially to Fort George, one of the principal communities affected by the project. On my first trip, because of fog, the plane landed at a mining town that produced asbestos, a now mostly banned substance used as insulation and fireproofing. The air seemed so dense with its fibres that when I saw a goose fly by I remarked that it too must be fireproof. We still had to get to Fort George on the shores of James Bay. Local Natives offered to take us across the water in their canoe, but when I saw the size of the white-capped waves, I declined their generous offer.

Denis Chatain, who had been my trusted assistant at Indian Affairs in Ottawa, had followed me to Quebec and continued to be my dedicated right-hand man. He was on that trip with me. The pilot of a helicopter owned by a local company offered to fly us to Fort George. We accepted. The clouds were very low. I was sitting next to the pilot and noticed that he had the kind of road map than motorists could get in any gas station. I asked what he was doing with the map. "Oh I'm following the contour of the shoreline," he said, pointing it out to me. His eyes would dart up and down, from the road map to the window of his helicopter. This did not inspire confidence.

When we finally reached Fort George, the ceiling was so low that when we came out of the clouds, we were very close to the ground. James O'Reilly was there. "John, when I heard the motors of the helicopter, I said to myself, who is crazy enough to fly in this weather?"

On another occasion, midway through some tough negotiations, Chief Robert Kanatewat asked me to go to Fort George to explain the project and the position of the government. It would be a public meeting with a question-and-answer period. I was accompanied by Armand Couture and some other government staff. We were flying in the government plane, a Fokker F27. During the flight, the pilot turned to me and said that he had just received a message. It was a warning that "something bad" would happen to me. He suggested that we turn around and go back. I was surprised. "That can't be," I told him. "Robert Kanatewat invited me." I had confidence in him. After all, he was the chief. "Oh yeah?" replied the pilot. "Kanatewat won't be there. He went fishing." That surprised me. I thought about it. I refused to be intimidated. I made myself believe that nothing would happen. "No," I said, "we're going." The pilot replied, "I have to listen to you because vous êtes le gouvernement. But if I were you, I'd go back."

We reached Fort George in the early evening. It was summer and the sun had not set yet. Robert Kanatewat was not there, and the community hall was not quite filled. Armand Couture and I went onto the stage and faced what was evidently a hostile crowd. Many were heavy set, with scowling faces – not the kind of people we had been meeting until then during the negotiations. Armand and I explained the project, the changes made at the request of Native people, the issues and the benefits so far agreed to, government's flexibility, and the possibility of other concessions. We were often interrupted. The questions were more accusatory than inquisitive. People moved about in the room in a disorderly, aggressive manner.

At about 10 o'clock, I excused myself to go out and see the pilot who was waiting in the airplane. I knew that he had to go to the LG-1 site to pick up other passengers who were going back to Quebec City. I told him that he could leave to get the others, since our meeting with the community was still going on. I didn't know when it would end. He looked me in the eye and said, "I am the captain of my ship. I determine when I leave. I will wait." He knew what was going on in the community hall. He would not leave me there. I went back to the meeting, and after a while the questions and the snarling stopped, and the meeting was over.

The reaction of the Cree was understandable. Walk in their shoes; a project that threatened their existence had been thrust upon them without notice. The land that had sustained them, the land of their ancestors and children, was threatened. Frustration and helplessness can provoke violence.

Couture was shaken. He had seen the animosity and the determination in those faces. On our way out he said to me, "We'll be able to build this project only with the army."

I learned later that there had been a plan to kidnap me. When those who conspired in the kidnapping saw that the plane was not leaving and that the pilot was waiting, they decided to end the meeting. The continued presence of the pilot had foiled their plans. I will always be grateful to him, but I am equally glad that I did not turn back.

That was not all that happened that night. We flew to the other site to pick up the waiting passengers. We were very late, and evidently, by the manner in which they boarded the plane, they had spent their wait drinking. They weren't inebriated but very loosely eloquent, able to express their thoughts without inhibitions. One of them was a judge. "Of course," he declared, "I can be made to wait. I am only a judge. I am not a member of the National Assembly. They don't have to wait!" And he went on and on in this manner. The pilot and I looked at each other and didn't say a word.

Some weeks later, during the negotiations, I received another request to go to Fort George and again talk to the community about the agreement. Once again, I accepted. This time, however, the situation was different. There was a fairly large peaceful crowd in the hall. Members of my staff were with me, and we all sat on the stage facing those who had come to the meeting. Between each government member on the stage sat a member of the Fort George Cree community, all facing the people. It was a show of solidarity, meant to indicate that there would be no trouble. It was the Cree way of giving a message to both the government and their community. I was touched by the gesture, especially since it was in such marked contrast to the intimidation of the previous meeting.

9

Dawn of a New Era

The French have a good word to describe what the James Bay Project had done to Native lives – *bouleversé*, meaning turned upside down, disrupted. It was not only a physical alteration, it affected the mind, spirit, and emotions of the people involved. The changes white society had wrought upon Natives had to be mitigated by our response to their requirements. They were now facing a way of life that was different from what had gone on before. They had to be given the instruments to cope with the new reality.

Changes came not only because of the construction of the project, but also by way of new government structures, new powers given to Natives, a greater participation in the decisions affecting their lives. The white man was no longer the total master.

Long before the James Bay Project, the government had created a new administrative structure for the territory called the Direction Générale du Nouveau Québec – the DGNQ. To Natives it meant "Don't Go Near Quebec," reflecting the perception that their relationship with the Quebec government was not beneficial to them.

But, with the James Bay Project, the whole picture changed. The Natives of the area became decision makers in their own right, recognized as a self-governing people operating within their own culture and language. They were given charge of their local and regional governments but played a meaningful role with non-Natives in the decisions affecting the territory. They were given control of their own social, medical, and hospital services. They became involved in environmental protection and had a say in the future development of the territory.

But perhaps most important of all, they were given control of their own education system. Gone were the days when Native children suffered in residential schools that tried to make white people of them and punished them when they spoke in their own language. Not only would the Cree and Inuit have their own schools with their own school boards, but, as well, Cree children would be taught in the Cree language and Inuit children in Inuktitut.

The James Bay Agreement was the beginning of a new era for the Cree and Inuit of northern Quebec. The final agreement, signed on 15 November 1975, contained thirty-one chapters and 455 pages. It presented an organizational problem in its preparation and timely finalization, resolved by the skills of Denis Chatain. The length of the final agreement was, in part, an indication of the magnitude of the task we had faced. We started with an eleven-point proposal that took four pages. The entire agreement was drafted in precise legal and legislative language.

WHO IS A NATIVE?

First of all, it defined who was eligible to receive the benefits of the agreement. Who was a Cree or an Inuit? The provisions of the Indian Act, first enacted in 1876 with numerous amendments since, were not applied. We were dealing with a different situation at a different time but, more importantly, with a different vision as to the role of Natives and their communities. We had to abandon the overriding powers of government bureaucrats over aboriginal peoples. The Indian Act was unacceptable to the Cree, giving them the impression the government wanted to limit their numbers in Canada. Yes, said the new agreement, they had to be Cree and of Cree ancestry – but their ancestry was not restricted to the paternal line, as provided in the Indian Act. They could be descendants of the male or female line.* The question of eligibility provided a different definition of Cree and Inuit and gave local communities the final say. They knew who they were and didn't need an archaic, restrictive statute from 1876 to tell them.

Inuit communities were given the same rights to recognize Inuit beneficiaries. There was no federal statute defining who was an Inuit. The agreement provided that Inuit communities were those recognized as such by Quebec and by the communities themselves. Adopted children were included as beneficiaries – and the rules of adoption were not limited to the existing laws (federal or provincial) but extended to those who were adopted according to "the customs of the Native people of the territory."

* The Indian Act was amended to reflect this in 1985.

Local enrolment committees were created in each community to supervise the naming of those who were eligible. These committees would be supervised by an enrolment commission composed of four members: a Cree and an Inuit representative, and a government representative each from Quebec and Canada. All the details were spelled out to ensure that no one entitled to the benefits would be left out. Those who claimed to be beneficiaries and had been omitted or were refused could appeal to a Native Appeal Board, consisting of a judge of the provincial court of Quebec. The provisions were meticulous and complete. Legitimate constraints were imposed but Native people were given a role in determining their membership and individuals had recourse if they felt left out.

THE LAND QUESTION: HOW MUCH AND WHERE?

Take courage, boy, the land is all that lasts.
Black Elk Speaks

The James Bay territory is immense – larger than the entire province of Ontario and as large as Texas and California combined – and within the region were competing interests and opinions. On one side were government corporations – Hydro-Québec, the James Bay Energy Corporation, and the James Bay Development Corporation. Their goal was to maintain as large an area as possible for development with as few restrictions as possible, preferably none. They saw their future in that vast plenitude of riches, and they had very able negotiators.

On the other side were Natives. They had been roaming and using the land long before the white man arrived. Even when contact with Europeans was made, few went to this remote territory. The land moulded Native culture and Native character, and it provided their subsistence. They lived on the land but had no concept of its ownership. There was a mystique, a sacredness, to the place, which shaped their lives and sustained their existence. How do you take that away?

I needed allies to help me obtain for Natives the rights over the areas of land that they needed. The final decision would need the consent of the Quebec Department of Lands and Forests. Representatives from the James Bay Development Corporation and I agreed to go and see them.

Sometimes, to achieve honest ends, you create effective strategies. I went to the department one hour before our scheduled meeting with the corporations and met with them alone. I knew that the department preferred green spaces. They maintained a greater authority over undeveloped lands. I explained the need to keep as much green space as possible. Surely 25,000 square miles for the Cree, south of the fifty-fifth parallel, and 35,000 for the Inuit, north of the parallel, were reasonable amounts. They agreed. The corporation representatives came an hour later with their own strategy. They unfurled a map of the territory shown in white, upon which they superimposed the Native areas shown in red. This accentuated the amount of Native land, making it appear enormous, although they were proposing to give much less. But it didn't work. The department members had already made up their minds. The mapmakers couldn't understand why their strategy and arguments had such little impact.

Hunting, fishing and trapping were of vital importance to the James Bay Cree and Inuit, at the centre of their existence. The areas reserved for exclusive Native use were carefully chosen to reflect that by including those where wildlife was most abundant. If the government were to require any part of such lands, it was obliged to replace them with an equivalent and equally productive area.

LOCAL AND REGIONAL GOVERNMENT

Changes began at the local level. The federal Indian Act was changed to give the Cree more power over their reserve lands (Category 1a) and to modify the restrictive definition of "Indian" since it was possible to be a beneficiary under the agreement and not be considered an Indian under the original act. It was necessary, therefore, to provide that those who were recognized as Cree by the local communities would be allowed to remain on the reserve lands even if they did not meet the criteria of "Indian" under the act.

Before the agreement, the James Bay territory had been designated as a municipality. This meant that the James Bay municipality was a governing body, which had authority over all the lands in the territory except reserve lands. The Cree communities were now removed from the jurisdiction and authority of the James Bay municipality. Each community became an individual municipality with more powers than were provided in the Cities and Towns Act, the legislation that defined the powers of municipalities.

Public corporations (which administered the municipalities) were created for each community. To provide cohesion, continuity, and unity, and to avoid duplication and possible conflicts, the members of the band council would also be the members of the councils that administered the corporation and the municipality. In other words, you would have the same administration for Category 1a lands and Category 1b lands.

The public corporations were given extensive powers, including the power to make bylaws for stricter environmental and social protection "by more stringent requirements than those provided by [existing provincial] laws and regulations" and "for the protection and use of natural resources consistent with applicable laws and regulations." The Cities and Towns Act was amended to reflect the new powers given to the Cree.

Another important change was made to Quebec laws. Bill 22 had made French the official language of Quebec and the language of public administration. The agreement still provided that the "language of communication of the public corporation shall be in accordance with the laws of general application in Quebec," but also said that every person could address the corporation in the Cree language and that the corporation had to ensure "that such person can obtain available services from it and can communicate with it in Cree." This effectively recognized Cree as an official language in the Cree communities and could not be changed without the consent of the "interested Native party."

There was more. We had to bring together the administrative structures of each community. We also had to give them a say in the large tracts of land reserved for their use – the lands inspired by Billy Diamond's circles in the water or what we termed Category 2 lands. We couldn't abandon them to the possibly one-sided decisions of the James Bay municipality. "Natives making their own decisions" could not be just a slogan.

The Cree Regional Authority and the James Bay Regional Zone Council were created. The former would coordinate the eight Cree communities that were part of the agreement* and would have jurisdiction over community lands (Category 1). It was made up of the chief councillor, the chief of each community, and another member from each community. The Cree Regional Authority could coordinate and administer all programs on Category 1 lands. The regional authority was the representative of the James Bay Cree when dealing with government. It would also appoint the Cree representatives to the James Bay Regional Zone Council.

* Another community, Oujé–Bougamou, only came later and has its own particular story.

We had to deal with Category 2 lands as well. We couldn't allow the James Bay municipality to be solely responsible for the administration of lands where the Cree and Inuit were given certain exclusive rights. The James Bay Regional Zone Council had authority over the Cree Category 2 lands. It was made up of six persons, three named by the Cree Regional Authority and three named by the James Bay municipality. Although the Zone Council was effectively given control over any measures affecting Category 2 lands, neither it nor the James Bay municipality could make decisions affecting hunting, fishing, and trapping on those lands. Those decisions were governed by a special regime. This was a double protection ensuring participation of Natives in all decisions affecting Category 2 lands.

The agreement protected the Inuit equally and involved them in the government of the region. Since there were no Category 1a lands and no problem of federal jurisdiction in the case of the Inuit, the legal structures for the Inuit were simpler. Each community was incorporated as a municipality, and the Kativik Act was created as part of the agreement. It was effectively municipal act creating local governments for each Inuit community and a regional government for the territory north of the fifty-fifth parallel. A complete description of the powers, rules, organization, and qualifications for municipal office had to be spelled out.

HEALTH AND SOCIAL SERVICES

The full recognition of a people and a break with the approaches of the past required us to cease making decisions for Natives and allow them to make their own choices in all activities. We couldn't pick and choose.

The entire territory was reorganized in terms not only of its administration (local and regional governments) but also in the provision of health, social services, and education. A Cree Regional Board of Health and Social Services was created, with the powers to provide all essential social and medical services to the region. Its members were to be elected by the community and their term of office could only be renewed once – to prevent abuse and allow freedom of action and participation by everyone. The particular difficulties of attracting personnel to this region were recognized. As the agreement in principle stated, "in recruiting and retaining staff ... working conditions and benefits should be sufficiently attractive to accept posts for periods of time ranging from three to five years." Essentially, the Cree Regional Board would assume all existing federal and provincial services with a 1981 deadline by which time they had to be phased into operations.

The Inuit were also given the administration of their health and social services through the creation of the Kativik Health and Social Services Council. Through this council, the regional government was given authority in all Inuit communities and the Category 2 lands. The territory was divided into two areas – the Hudson Bay sector and the Ungava Bay sector. These provided local community service centres that included hospitals, social services, and reception centres. They would extend services to all persons who were normally or temporarily resident in these territories. The establishments in each sector were to be run by a board of directors composed of representatives elected from each municipality for a period of three years.

To encourage public participation in the dispensing of all services, every establishment in each sector was obliged to hold, at least once a year, an information meeting in which the population of that sector would be invited to participate.

The situation with the Inuit was different from the Cree in many respects. For example, many Inuit travelled outside their territory and then returned to their communities. This raised particular problems. A working group would be formed to review the means by which a broad range of services including assistance with transportation, housing, translation, and counselling might be made available to Inuit travelling to centres in the south or returning to their homes in the north. The working group was given a deadline of May 1976 to make their recommendations.

RECOGNITION, RESPECT, AND PARTICIPATION

There were endless meetings, discussions, and proposals. Consciously or not, I was making an attempt to respond to and lift the spirit of a people – telling them we had intruded in their lives, were changing the landscape, but now, together with them, we were prepared to find a way for Natives to be at one with the land. Let us live, work, and travel together in our journey to the future.

James O'Reilly, to his credit, was the person who best understood the Cree and their differences from our society. He, even more than I, grasped the significance of their culture and made proposals to reflect these values in the agreement. He wasn't only thinking as a lawyer. He was thinking as a Native. I accepted his proposals as a humbling discovery, almost in awe, with a greater awareness of who the Cree were and what they needed.

The Cree and the Inuit were to be involved in every aspect of the activities in the territory, governmental or otherwise. We would reach out to them. Therefore, the administration of the territory was totally reorganized with the Cree and the Inuit given a dominant role. They would have control over education, with Cree and Inuit school boards and schools, which would teach in their own language. English or French were secondary choices.

Judges as well as non-Inuit or non-Cree court staff would have to be "cognizant with the usages, customs, and psychology of the Cree and of the Inuit." There were to be programs to train Cree and Inuit to act as stenographers in the courts. Interpreters would be provided in all legal matters and judgments had to be translated into Cree or Inuktitut, without cost to Natives.

Such matters as probation, parole, rehabilitation, and aftercare services would be provided in the Native language, if possible, and had to take into account the culture and way of life of the Cree and Inuit. Precautions would be taken to ensure that the Cree and Inuit did not misunderstand the intervention of the judicial authority.

Judges and courts were relatively new concepts for the Cree and Inuit and alien to their culture. The agreement provided that their role would be explained so there would be no misunderstanding of the intervention of the judicial authority and why it was necessary in the activities of the larger Quebec and Canadian society of which Natives were a part.

The treatment of those who had the misfortune of falling afoul of the laws was important, emphasizing humane intervention and assistance in their rehabilitation. If they broke the laws that we imposed, they were to be detained in institutions in the James Bay territory and not farther south in an environment with which they were unfamiliar. Cree and Inuit units of the Quebec police force would be established, with training programs in English and French and in Cree and Inuktitut where appropriate. These units would have duties in their communities and throughout their respective territories.

I wanted the Cree and Inuit to have the opportunity to participate in the institutions of our society, if they wished. There were also provisions for those who wanted to continue their traditional way of life. I did not want to repeat the errors of the past that I had seen in Ottawa and in the Indian Act where a cleavage was created between Native and white society, under a government control that destroyed the soul of Natives.

A NEW ECONOMY AND NEW BUSINESS OPPORTUNITIES

Billions of dollars were going to be spent in the North on roads, dams, electrical installations, power lines, and a myriad of subcontracts flowing from the investments being made in the region. It was only natural that we give Natives the tools to participate in the economic life of the region and benefit from the challenges of a new situation. A panoply of measures and programs were provided. The framers of the agreement created the James Bay Native Development Corporation, a sort of Cree and government joint venture. Its objectives were to promote and assist the creation and development of businesses. We provided for a Cree Trappers Association under the authority of Quebec, Canada, and the Cree Regional Authority. It would help in providing training programs for trappers. There was a Cree Outfitting and Tourism Association to service an expected upsurge in tourism. We set up a Cree Native Arts and Crafts Association, which would have committees in each community to promote native arts. And we provided for a Cree Central Marketing Service to assist in the marketing of their products.

Canada and Quebec agreed to create joint economic and community development committees to expand government programs for the Cree. Training courses were to be provided so they could qualify for the available jobs.

The language of the Cree was recognized, not only in the school curriculum, but also in the workplace. Quebec and Canada would ensure that unilingual Cree candidates who successfully completed the training courses would have the right to be examined either in the Cree language or with the assistance of a translator. However, if the job application was for the public service, the applicant would have to know either English or French. This made sense because the public service in the region had to deal with non-Natives as well as Natives.

The communities were recognized and strengthened. Canada and Quebec agreed to build community centres in each Cree community and there would be an economic development agent to provide expert business advice. Friendship Centres would be built in non-Native communities to assist Cree who were residing or working there or were in transit. The government also agreed to build roads to join certain Cree communities with the main Fort George–Matagami road.

Similar proposals were made for the Inuit, with certain differences that took into account their own distinctive way of life and thinking.

The regional government was given the responsibility for the adminis-tration of all former federal and provincial Inuit programs. Although there was a hunting and fishing program, the Inuit had specific con-cerns for those pursuing these activities. These included guarantees that people who could not hunt or fish could still get an adequate supply of the produce from these activities. There was also a provision for search and rescue operations in very remote areas.

Hunting, fishing, and trapping were regarded as occupations or industries. Because of the income security they provided, they would be regulated via a labour relations system similar to that provided by unions and management in white society. Standards, qualifications, and conditions had to be set for those involved and were made the respon-sibility of the regional government. The regional government would determine the working conditions, hours, and period of work, with a minimum of forty hours per week. It would establish quotas and train-ing programs. The regional government would create ordinances to de-termine the qualifications of those who hunted, fished, and trapped, would regulate leaves of absence, suspension, and dismissal, and would also determine the number of hunters, fishermen, and trappers to be posted in each community. The selection of those in these occupations would be made by the council of each municipal corporation.

There was also an equivalent to the Cree income security program. Yearly salaries were established for those who exercised these activities – $9,000 per year. Based on statistics taken when the agreement was signed, this meant a total of $477,000 per year payable by Quebec via the regional government. There were additional sums to be paid by Quebec to the regional government: $40,000 to meet the expenses of each Inuk residing in the territory and an additional $51,000 for the administration of the program plus a monthly sum of $4,408.33 to provide for the initial setting up of the program. Everything was calcu-lated based on the existing Inuit population. As a further protection, the agreement provided that these sums would be indexed to the cost of living in Quebec as established by Statistics Canada.

There was more. There would be a joint research program by Que-bec and the Northern Inuit Association to establish the level of equip-ment available to the Inuit necessary to carry out the program. Quebec would supply Inuit communities with enough equipment to ensure they were well equipped to continue hunting, fishing, and trapping. The funding would take into account the conditions particular to the province's far north.

There were also employment and training provisions to allow access to the jobs that would become available in the territory. As with the Cree, programs would ensure that Inuit candidates would be interviewed in their own language or with a translator. The Inuit were also interested in a plan for the training and employment of Inuit staff "within the bureaucracy of the territory," a condition to which Canada and Quebec readily agreed. Specific suggestions were made to ensure that Inuit would obtain both jobs and contracts. Canada and Quebec agreed to hire a qualified Inuit person before hiring a non-Native person for each available job and also agreed to advertise in the communities to give the Inuit a reasonable opportunity to submit competitive bids when the government called for public tenders. The Inuit also demanded the application of "such measures to non-government contracts." There were also obligations imposed on the governments to create programs to promote Inuit arts and crafts. Clearly, they were thorough in their requests.

At some point the Inuit must have been upset with the methods and conclusions of research studies that had been done on their territory because the agreement stipulated that "if Canada and Quebec carry out field studies affecting the cultural and social life of the Native people they will seek their advice as to the best way to carry out such studies." In other words, don't pretend to tell the world about our lives without our own input. This was a very telling condition. Since "Native" includes not only the Inuit, they felt that any distorted interpretation of other Natives, including the Cree, would also reflect on them.

In many respects, the Inuit conditions were more stringent and detailed than those of the Cree. But this is not to say that Natives rejected change. They knew it was coming and accepted it, without abandoning their own identity and culture. And they had leaders who did not fear the future, who had the foresight to see the necessity of adapting and making change work for the benefit of their people. It helped that the people had confidence in their leaders and supported them. About how many societies could that be said?

PARLIAMENTARY HEARINGS

Robert Bourassa was an astute politician. He knew that if the government signed the agreement, the subsequent legislation could be criticized by the opposition in the National Assembly and perhaps by the public. He waited until the last moment to hold a parliamentary hearing to review the terms of the proposed agreement with the intention of getting everyone on side.

He knew it would be difficult for the opposition to oppose the agreement since its signing would allow the construction of a hydro-electric project that would create jobs and furnish provincially produced power at a time when there was a perceived oil crisis. And, perhaps more importantly for the opposition, Quebec would obtain clear title to the entire territory. Not only were Native land rights extinguished, but, as well, federal jurisdiction was severely restricted. Federal authority was anathema to the PQ, and now there was an agreement that excluded Ottawa from many of its former functions in the territory.

The committee hearings began on 6 November 1975, before all of the terms of the agreement had been finalized and five days before it was to be signed. The Cree had set a deadline of midnight, 11 November for its signature. If the agreement was not signed by that time, they had already made arrangements to return to their communities in James Bay. They were adamant.

The committee was headed by Jean Cournoyer, minister of natural resources, the department that oversaw Hydro-Québec and the James Bay Energy Corporation, which was the department most affected by the terms of the agreement. He was personable, placid, a little distrustful, and had a subtle sense of humour. He was accompanied by several other government members. I sat next to him to make my presentation and, together with Cournoyer, answer any questions that would be raised.

Sitting on the other side, representing the official opposition was Jacques-Yvan Morin, the parliamentary leader of the PQ. He was sincere, well intentioned, distinguished, methodical, and persistent.

Often, politics is full of theatrics, and this was one of those times. Apparently Morin had been a professor of law at the Université de Montréal and Cournoyer (as well as others around the table) had been his student. Cournoyer kept referring to Morin as my "esteemed colleague and former professor," and Morin replied, "Yes, my colleague and former student." They kept this up throughout the proceedings. When Cournoyer disagreed with Morin on a point, Lucien Lessard, the other PQ member on the committee, chirped in, "You obviously were not a good student." It was as if we were in the Roman senate, witnessing its theatrics, waving-of-hands, and polite deferences. The only thing missing were the togas.

The hearing had been convened to examine the agreement with Natives even though it had not yet been finalized. This posed a problem.

There was a danger that the questions raised by Morin would be used as a pressure tactic by Natives to demand more. At one point even Cournoyer said to him (rather facetiously, I thought), "Why don't you ask questions on the twenty-eight chapters that have been agreed upon, rather than on the two that are still pending?" We did not want the hearing used as a pressure tactic on the negotiations. At times I warned Morin of this possibility and tried to direct him away from certain subjects that had not yet been agreed on. He understood. Even though he was in the opposition, Morin did not abuse his role. He expressed legitimate concerns, for example about the possible extinction of rights of other Indians in the territory who were not part of the agreement, and he raised the question of dissidents – three Inuit communities were being influenced by an activist working for the provincial government who appeared before the committee and used such terms as "psychological dislocations" and "personality conflicts." These were clearly not Inuit expressions.

I became a little aggressive in my answers, and not as gracious as I could have been, despite the fact that Morin expressed confidence "in the integrity of the member for Mount Royal." I was determined to have a signed agreement that would be acceptable not only to Natives but also to the wider public. I had to manoeuvre between the two sides. In the negotiations I had been speaking to Natives. In the committee I was speaking to the opposition and to the public. So I emphasized those elements that were favourable to Quebec.

Although Quebec would not obtain jurisdiction over Port Burwell (an island off the coast of Hudson Bay now known as Killiniq), the north western boundaries of the province, bordering what were then the Northwest Territories, had been extended to the low water mark, giving Quebec an additional fifty miles (eighty kilometres) along the Hudson Bay coast.

Historically, Quebec never recognized the Labrador border. I was asked pointedly by Morin if the agreement now recognized that contentious border, which Quebec thought favoured Labrador. I pointed out that a map in the agreement indicated that the boundary was not definitive. By accepting this provision and signing the agreement, the federal government would effectively accept Quebec's "nonrecognition" of this disputed boundary. Nothing changed.

We refused the demands of the federal government to create a national park (under federal jurisdiction) at Richmond Gulf. This area would remain under provincial jurisdiction.

The federal government had been operating schools in the territory. Since education would now fall under provincial jurisdiction, all existing schools would be transferred to Quebec, and Ottawa would pay 75 per cent of the budget to operate the schools.

The Canadian constitution gave the federal government jurisdiction over Indians and Indian lands. To curtail, if not eliminate its authority in James Bay, several creative solutions were proposed. First, we limited the powers of the federal government by creating different categories of lands. The federal government would have jurisdiction on Category 1a or "reserve" lands – but even on these lands, the province would have jurisdiction over education, the administration of justice, health services, and natural resources. That didn't leave much.

Second, an additional protection against the possibility of future federal jurisdiction was included in Section 2.10 of the agreement. During the negotiations, the Quebec Department of Justice had raised the fear of a possible federal takeover on the Category 2 and Category 3 lands. Since Natives were given rights over these areas, the department feared that it would be possible for a court to decide these lands be deemed "Indian lands" and therefore come under the federal jurisdiction of the Indian Act. It was a remote possibility, not probable, but unacceptable to Quebec in the political climate of the time.

I could not dismiss this possible interpretation. Courts, at times, can give surprising decisions. Fortunately, I had a legal background. I proposed Section 2.10 say in essence that the federal government would amend the Canadian constitution to render the agreement fully valid if ever a court decided that Canada had jurisdiction over Category 2 or 3 lands.* In the meantime the agreement would continue as originally drafted. Problem solved.

Since Inuit did not come under the Indian Act, the final agreement provided (and Ottawa accepted) that Inuit would come under the jurisdiction of Quebec. One more exclusion of federal power.

Finally, the agreement extinguished all rights that Natives may have had over the territory. Quebec finally obtained full title and authority over all of northern Quebec or *le grand nord*. This was particularly appealing to the opposition.

The reduction of federal power over the territory was presented as a political advantage for Quebec to obtain the approval of the

---

* At the time, it was possible to change the British North America Act (the constitution) by a simple demand from the federal government to the Parliament in London.

separatist opposition, but a further unstated reason was that it made administrative sense. Quebec was already responsible for all of those services to the general population. It stood to reason that they also give these services to Native people. It also happily fed the appetite of civil servants for more control because it gave them more to administer.

These decisions were not made unilaterally. Non-Natives in the territory were consulted. To avoid adverse reactions from them and to promote harmonious relations with Natives, I met with the leaders of the municipalities in the region to explain those terms of the agreement that would most affect them, especially the hunting and fishing provisions. As a result, certain changes were made to the description of the lands affected. Consultation had not been limited to Native groups. All were entitled to be heard.

THE SIGNING

After all the last-minute objections had been met and all who would be affected were satisfied (as much as they could be), the parties involved were summoned to the "bunker," the fortress-like building on Grande Allée in Quebec City housing the premier's offices. There they waited patiently for word that the agreement had been signed. At the eleventh hour of the final day fixed by the Cree, it was. It was literally a last-minute decision. Billy Diamond had already made arrangements for his group to fly back to their James Bay communities. When he was advised that the deal would be signed, he arrived with his people at the premier's office. Charlie Watt and the Inuit leaders were already there.

Leading figures from government and the public corporations were there, including Gérard D. Levesque, the minister of intergovernmental affairs, who would be signing the agreement for the government, and Roland Giroux, the president of Hydro-Québec. Robert Boyd signed for the James Bay Energy Corporation and Charles Boulva for the James Bay Development Corporation. Grand Chief Billy Diamond signed on behalf of his community, Waskaganish, and the chiefs of each Cree community signed on behalf of their communities. Charlie Watt and eleven directors of the Northern Inuit Association, representing the different Inuit communities, all signed.

Smiling faces expressed relief. The arduous negotiations had ended successfully and the James Bay and Northern Quebec Agreement was law.

It was a solemn and for most part, a gratifying occasion. Roland Giroux could stop worrying about obstacles to his financing. Boyd and Boulva were relieved of the task of accepting new terms from the Natives and could concentrate on doing what they had originally been asked to do. Billy Diamond, a defender of Cree rights, no longer needed to create and direct strategies to bring the agreement to a successful end. The Cree chiefs could return to their communities and resume their lives, as could the Inuit. James O'Reilly no longer had to concern himself with legal proceedings against the Quebec government. The Inuit lawyers could feel satisfied that they had represented their clients well. And Robert Bourassa could proceed with his "project of the century." For my part, I could not rejoice or express elation – I was too tired and spent.

THE CELEBRATION

Achieving the James Bay Agreement was akin to building a cathedral, with all the complex elements that includes. A proper foundation, structures, and various elements – some utilitarian, others of beauty but all necessary – must all come together in one pleasing response to the issue at hand. It was mystical and magical.

The magnitude and importance of what had been accomplished, the efforts and sacrifices of so many, the end of a seemingly impossible task called for a celebration. So I invited everyone to my home to honour the event and those who had made it possible.

And they all came. The presidents and senior staff of Hydro-Québec and of the corporations who were responsible for the development of the James Bay Project, the engineers, the lawyers – both on the government and Native sides – the consultants who had so ably assisted the Natives and had developed new concepts and put their talents to the aid of the Cree and Inuit, the civil servants who had so assiduously elaborated and completed what first had been an outline of principles and commitments. Charlie Watt, with his drooping, smiling moustache, was there with Zebedee Nungak and a group of happy Inuit.

A large bus came down the winding driveway of my home and stopped a short distance from my front door. Those who had already arrived looked on with curiosity and surprise. Out of the bus came the Cree and their wives, exuding the spirit of their people in front of a huge Palladian-style white house. They walked in single file or in twos, the women in long dresses, as if showing their deference to our society but undaunted by the unfamiliar surroundings. It was a remarkable sight that has remained embedded in my memory.

Finally, Premier Bourassa arrived. He smiled and chatted with one and all, happy that the obstacles to his dream project had been overcome. There were more than two hundred people, all talking, jostling, munching, drinking, enjoying, and celebrating the end of a negotiating marathon. There was a spirit of camaraderie and gratitude and a sense of history in the making, unstated but present. Then came the highlight of the evening. A Native had brought a violin. He began to play, and the Cree began to dance what seemed to me to be jigs. The women danced, holding up their long dresses not to get entangled in them. We all watched and clapped and hooted, loving it all.

It was a remarkable evening, bringing together people of very different backgrounds: Natives, Québécois, and an Italian-Canadian. We had all worked together. There was a sense of accomplishment and gratitude for what had been achieved.

10

The Elected Representative

Except for the James Bay settlement and the celebration of the summer Olympics in 1976, the three years leading to the fall election in 1976 had been one disaster after another. The language law, Bill 22, had been rejected by both the English-speaking and French-speaking communities. Minority immigrant groups, called allophones in Quebec, were divided and forced to choose between the French and English, with most going to the English side on language and education matters. Labour troubles had been rife, particularly those that disrupted the James Bay Project but also in other sectors such as transportation and public service. Even the Olympics had come at the cost of budget overruns and the taint of corruption, which forced the province to take over the construction of facilities.

As busy as I was during this period, I still had duties as an elected representative of my riding that involved me in other issues, both local and beyond. I felt the need to speak out on all the issues of the day. I saw my role as MNA as an obligation to help constituents and to say what I thought. Was this due to an innate sense of responsibility and a desire to be accepted? Or was it because I was a neophyte in politics and did not see pitfalls and the need for political prudence?

I tried to pacify the English-speaking community about Bill 22, telling Anglos that it was in their interest to speak French in Quebec and to keep social peace, and counselled against contesting the legislation before the courts. In a speech at Sir George Williams University (now part of Concordia University), I made the same point.* Yes, I had voted against the legislation, but now it was time to get on with living and working together in harmony.

* "French needed to operate in province," *Montreal Gazette*, 20 January 1976.

I was invited to speak to Vanier College students on the James Bay Agreement. Striking teachers tried to prevent this event from happening. I was furious and I didn't accept their tactics. They finally agreed to let me speak, provided that I would first meet with them. I did and later declared the meeting "hopeless." I didn't mince words in my reaction to their tactics. I said that they were politically motivated and I wanted politics kept out of the classroom. "Their tactics are not in keeping with the dignity and responsibility of the teaching profession. A very bad example is being given to the children."*

THE AGONIZING CAMPAIGN OF 1976

In 1976, three years into his mandate, Robert Bourassa was pondering whether to call an election, and I was questioning my own place in political life. Before being elected I had not been actively involved in politics. Except for my work on the James Bay Agreement, I felt like an outsider in the National Assembly. Voting against my party on Bill 22, being suspended from caucus, feeling alienated from my colleagues because of their suspicions and my origins, having to be at the beck and call of my constituents (which I took very seriously) – these factors did not encourage me to continue. I asked myself, do I need this?

I called Jean Chrétien and told him my misgivings. He told me that I should not quit – I had an obligation to run. I could not let down the English-speaking community that I had come to represent and which looked to me as their spokesman. He also mentioned that I was the only member from a cultural minority. Appeals to my sense of duty have always influenced me. I agreed to continue. Bourassa was also concerned about my intentions. Knowing I had been disappointed in not being named a minister – the excuse after the previous election being that there were already too many reelected ministers to fit me in – he called to assure me that this time I would be in cabinet "no matter how many ministers are reelected." I thanked him and told him that I had already decided to run again.

The previous three years had been a disaster for the Liberals. They seemed removed from the concerns and feelings of the people. Was their overwhelming majority a boon or a curse? Or had Quebec, with so many different interests and conflicting demands, become ungovernable?

As well as language legislation, which had angered all communities, there were problems with labour unions, especially with workers on

* *Sunday Express*, 2 May 1976.

the James Bay Project who, to pressure the government to meet their demands, had gone on strike, mounted protests, and caused millions of dollars of damage on job sites. Bourassa had taken the unusual and politically fatal step of jailing their leaders.

Then, against the advice of many of his cabinet ministers, the premier called an election for 15 November 1976, with two years left in his mandate, thinking that if he waited the political situation would get worse.

Joyous as my first election campaign was, the atmosphere had completely changed by the fall of 1976. I resumed my visits to the Town of Mount Royal commuter station, but the reception was not the same. Some people walked by with stern unsmiling faces, refusing to speak. The few who greeted me did so without enthusiasm. I persisted, meeting all the morning trains for several days. Nothing changed. The electorate was angry. I was disappointed, worried, and hurt.

The opposition in the riding changed. In addition to the token PQ candidate, Guy Normandeau, I had another, more formidable opponent, Victor Podd, who was running for the Union Nationale. He was a resident of Town of Mount Royal and a member of its municipal council. A well-to-do businessman, he was upset by Bourassa's language law. Since its obliteration in the last election, the UN had risen from the ashes by making an appeal to angry voters from all linguistic communities. Victor was well known, represented a federalist party, and waged a tough campaign. It meant I had to work harder. Fortunately, the local paper, the Town of Mount Royal *Weekly Post*, despite misgivings about the Liberals, said I deserved to be reelected.

The campaign had its lighter moments. During a debate in the working class Côte-des-Neiges district, Podd, who had come from humble beginnings, spoke before a group with similar backgrounds. He told them that he had known hard times and recounted when his father earned only twenty-five cents an hour. "Yes," I told the audience, "and if you vote for Victor and his party gets elected, those times will come back, and you too will be earning twenty-five cents an hour." After the debate, Podd complained to me, "John, that wasn't fair of you to say that." Victor and I remained friends. He later came to Quebec City to see me. Embarrassed, I tried to hide from my colleagues when I disembarked from his Rolls-Royce in front of the National Assembly.

The campaign also had its nasty side. One of my Liberal colleagues, the former football player and now broadcaster George Springate, who was running in Westmount, publicly and tactlessly called Bourassa "the most hated man in Quebec." Indeed, the English-speaking community had rejected Bourassa. On the traditionally Liberal West Island, many voters turned to the Union Nationale. The Italian community, whose children were subjected to the Bill 22 tests if they wanted access to English schools, also rejected the Liberals. The UN and its leader, Rodrigue Biron, channelled the anger of federalists their way. Ironically, Biron later switched to the Parti Québécois.

Bourassa had grossly miscalculated the mood of the electorate. He gambled and he lost. The 102 Liberal members of the National Assembly melted to twenty-six with the Parti Québécois winning seventy-six seats and the Union Nationale eleven, including Bill Shaw on the West Island. I was reelected, but my plurality went from 81 to 51 per cent. Bourassa was defeated in his riding of Mercier, where he lost to the PQ's Gérald Godin. His personal defeat made the rout of his party complete.

There was an air of disbelief in my committee room and tears in many eyes. I had to leave the room momentarily to reflect and collect my thoughts. The unheard of had happened. A government that advocated the separation of Quebec from Canada had been elected. I didn't want to add to the panic and reassured my people that the election of the PQ reflected a split electorate more than it did a desire to separate. And I assured them that we would work tirelessly to keep our country together. We would be a vigilant and prepared opposition.

The election illustrated the law of unintended consequences. The Union Nationale took enough votes away from the Liberals to allow the PQ to win, to the surprise of many, including its leader, René Lévesque. It was a political disaster not only for the Liberals but also for all federalists. Fear and mistrust now stalked the country. The reverberation of this election sent chills across Canada.

We all went home dejected, discouraged, but determined. The next morning I was asked for my reaction. I said that I had slept like a baby – I slept for two hours and then cried for two more.

BILL 101: THE QUEBEC LANDSCAPE IS FOREVER ALTERED

The majority win in the 1976 election had set the table for the Parti Québécois and its agenda. But the Péquistes were about to discover that governing took more savvy than being in opposition. Their big project was language and Camille Laurin was its guiding light. Laurin, a soft-spoken psychiatrist, gave the impression that he was still exercising his profession, especially when he was talking politics. He sometimes used unusual words to impress and befuddle his listeners. Only from the good doctor did I hear the word *superfétatoire*, a seldom-used French expression to describe something as superfluous. With the PQ's language legislation, Laurin put Quebec society on a couch and administered a remedy. Bill 101 was the prescribed therapy.

If Bill 22 had angered the English-speaking community, Bill 101, introduced in March 1977, made it apoplectic. The real exodus of people and head offices from Montreal to Toronto began with this legislation. It was a turning point for Quebec.

I was a member of the parliamentary committee that studied Bill 101. All legislation is analyzed, article by article, in committee before its adoption by the National Assembly. This is standard procedure. There is usually a little banter, a little give-and-take between government and the members of the opposition. This was not the case for Bill 101. The members were often combative and accusatory. We all had a cause – whether it was to protect the French language, promote political independence, safeguard minority rights, or, yes, even to protect the English community. This committee was more like outright war than a skirmish.

I was vociferous in my denunciation of Bill 101 – perhaps too much so. At one point I compared what the PQ was doing to creating a gulag, a place of suffering and deprivation, my point being that anglophones would be deprived of their language. Quebec would become isolated from the rest of Canada, inhabited by people different from those surrounding them. I probably could have said this without calling Quebec a gulag, but perhaps I was influenced by Solzhenitsyn's monumental *The Gulag Archipelago,* which I had been reading. I also felt alienated and was expressing my own feelings of imprisonment in a society where I didn't feel accepted. It was an unfortunate and even dangerous comparison. My colleague Thérèse Lavoie-Roux, the Liberal member for l'Acadie, looked at me with concern but, to maintain the solidarity of the opposition, she said nothing.

Bill 101 did not use a balanced approach – some of its provisions were exaggerated and abusive. These were to be struck down by the Supreme Court of Canada.

THE LANGUAGE OF THE COURTS

Discussions on Bill 101 were not all acrimonious. There were moments of understanding, compassion and elucidation if not illumination. Since the beginning of Confederation, the English and French languages had had equal status before the courts. Bill 101 changed this. It made French the only language that could be used in the courtroom.

Claude Charron, one of the most able and vociferous Péquistes and a junior cabinet minister, explained why he pushed for this change. Apparently his father had taken legal action against a company following an accident. During the court hearing, Charron explained, the company lawyers spoke only English, his father understood nothing, and he lost the case. That, he claimed, was the reason for this clause in the new bill. I sympathized with Charron and told him so. The change he proposed was *pars d'un bon naturel*; in other words, it was well intentioned, and Charron's support was the reaction of a loving son to his father's plight. However, I went on to say that what he had proposed was not the solution. Our legal system had its origins in both the English common law and the French civil code, and the two legal cultures produced something unique in the world. We should continue to benefit from the admixture of two cultures, which influenced and gave so much to each other, broadening our legal system and its approach to problems and life. We would be handicapping young students who had to look at both English and French jurisprudence to grasp a knowledge of our laws.

I proposed an amendment to Article 1 of the bill. "The use of French and English before the tribunal and in the National Assembly shall not be modified by the present law." I pointed out that a contestation of the existing article before the courts would be inevitable since it contradicted a specific provision of the British North America Act, and it would only create dissension and division.* Furthermore, the recognition of both languages in the courts had not affected the growth and strength of the French-speaking population.

But my reasoning came up against a brick wall. There was bitterness and resentment hiding in the PQ government's every gesture. Behind Bill 101 lurked the spectre of independence. Péquistes were convinced

---

* Several years later, the article was indeed declared unconstitutional by the Supreme Court of Canada.

of the rightness of their cause and used every occasion to promote it. Because of their dedication to the cause, sometimes they would even point out that their tactics were meant to advance their aims. On the possibility of legal wrangling over the law at the federal level, Laurin noted that if that occurred, the PQ would be able to tell the populace that Quebec must become politically independent so that they could make their own decisions without the interference of a federal court. Dissension would be used to promote independence.

Obviously, I did not persuade the government. Years of pent-up frustration and, yes, intransigence on the part of the English community had taken their toll. The cup had run over and the Parti Québécois and Bill 101 were the unintended spillover.

THE LANGUAGE OF EDUCATION – IN DEFENSE OF IMMIGRANTS

The objections to Bill 101 were not made out of blind ignorance and knee-jerk opposition. Many valid suggestions were made to take into account language realities and the rights of certain groups. The importance and use of English had nothing to do with the victory on the Plains of Abraham. It was a fact of life that one needed to be able to use this language if he or she lived in North America. English was also becoming the international language of business.

The new law replaced the "tests" of Bill 22 for children of immigrants wishing to attend English schools with a provision obliging them to attend French schools only. I thought that this could apply to new immigrants but not to those who were already here. I believed that everyone should be entitled to learn English. Immigrants had enough handicaps already and would be further encumbered if they did not have the right to learn English. This, of course, was interpreted by the government as a continuation of the integration of immigrants into the English community. The new law would also split up families if younger children could not attend the same schools as their older siblings.

I identified myself as a member of a minority. I pleaded for minorities in a manner that only an immigrant could. I proposed an amendment, not limited to minorities, providing that English had to be taught in French schools. I did not then realize that in the existing political atmosphere that this would not fly. The emphasis was now on the French community as the government sought to make a break with the past. The government claimed that it wanted to break the cycle whereby minorities went to English schools and were assimilated into the English community.

I argued, emotionally, that Italians, and for that matter any other minority, would become neither English nor French if they attended the respective schools of these language groups. "In the same way that everyone wants to keep his identity, and his values, I can assure you that I have kept my values and that I am an allophone. We become integrated into our society, which is composed of both francophones and anglophones, but we are not assimilated," I said in committee.

Was this wishful thinking on my part? Was I trying to convince myself? I was expressing this sentiment in French. Would I have said the same in English to an English audience? Because I insisted that minorities should have the right to learn English, government members interpreted this as my being the defender of the English community. I had failed to break with the past. Once again the minorities were siding with the English!

The commission also had its pedagogical side. In a discussion on French as the official language, I went back into the history of Quebec, pointing out that French was always the official language except for the year 1841 (Jacques-Yvan Morin added "to 1848" – he too knew history), when the Act of Union between Upper and Lower Canada made an attempt to impose English as the official language. It didn't conform to the reality of the times, and so it was a failure. Then I sermonized. "Everything that does not conform to justice and equity, or to reason, will be a failure, whether it is in 1841, 1848, 1974, or 1977." (The last date referred to Bill 101, and 1974 to the adoption of Bill 22, the language legislation of the previous Liberal government.) Strong stuff!

I went into world history and spoke about other countries with minorities. I spoke of the nineteenth century concept of nationalism, since discredited, under which each nation claimed independence. All this was to make the case against separatism.

I referred to Finland where the Swedes formed seven per cent of the population, and yet both Finnish and Swedish were official languages. This was one example among many where a minority had rights. I referred to Article 6 of the constitution of Czechoslovakia, which stated that laws and other governmental declarations were to be in both the Czech and Slovak languages, which had equal status. If there was one country that could consider itself threatened, it was certainly Israel, yet, with 13 per cent of the population being Arab, there were two official languages, Hebrew and Arabic (this was 1977).

After all these examples, I stated that I would still vote in favour of French as the official language. I just wanted to point out what was happening in other parts of the world. When Jacques-Yvan Morin spoke about making French the official language, I retorted that Bill 22 had done the same. "You are plagiarists," I charged.

THE NIAGARA FALLS INCIDENT

Claude Charron had a very negative reaction toward me. Perhaps I was too aggressive in my defence of the English-speaking community and too present in the discussions, offering the government lessons from both Quebec and European history. In the Assembly I intervened often, sometimes out of turn. I kept the Speaker busy. Subtlety was not my forte.

I see now, some thirty years later, that I brought out the worst in Charron. I was unaware of his sensitivity and resentment toward the English community. Many can't rid themselves of certain feelings and memories and get on with life. It can happen to the best of us. During one of my interventions, Charron accused me of having gone to Niagara Falls to speak against the French of Quebec. I vehemently denied it. But he didn't believe me.

Charron's negative feelings toward me seemed to stem from my having rejected French as the official language when I voted against Bill 22. I pointed out that I had voted against that law but was in favour of its Article 1, which made French the official language. "What English subtlety you are showing," he retorted.* You could hear the anger in his voice and feel the resentment he had against the English.

I had been invited to speak in Niagara Falls on the political situation in Quebec. Why Niagara Falls? Hard to say. Perhaps it was because the raging falls symbolized the turmoil in the province. Could we go further and say that after the falls the waters would flow peaceably? I don't remember how a group of businessmen came to choose me. It might have been because I was such a vociferous critic of the new government. Perhaps some of the many who had moved to Ontario after the election of the PQ remembered me. In any event they weren't pleased with what I told them.

The day after Charron's remarks, I told the committee that I would provide the content of my Niagara Falls speech which had been given in English but which I had now translated into French for the benefit of those present. Here are some excerpts from that speech:

---

* "Quelle subtilité anglaise que vous êtes en train de nous manifester."

To understand the nature of the adjustment necessary in Canada to the new social conditions existing in Quebec, let us briefly look at confederation through the eyes of French Canadians. Isolated from the trends of French thought and culture in what they consider to be an English sea, it is understandable that French Canadians feel a certain sense of insecurity.

At the time of confederation, French Canadians outside Quebec were an important part of the population. Since then, millions of immigrants who came to Canada joined the anglophone community, reducing the French Canadian population to a fraction of the whole outside la belle province. Not only did the immigrants add to the anglophone population but a large number of French Canadians were assimilated by them.[*]

It is only lately that this tendency has been slowed due in part to the renaissance of French arts and culture and also to legislation and help from the federal and various provincial governments.

Another concept that French Canadians have of confederation is that the business world, which is mainly anglophone, has dominated, not to say exploited, economically, the French Canadians of Quebec who, after all, were the first to establish themselves in this country and colonize it.

That is why French Canadians outside of Quebec will never accept being considered as just another ethnic group apart from the English.

One can retrace, even before confederation, this unique alliance of the two peoples. The Fathers of Confederation recognized the political association of the two founding people. We know this from a letter of John A. Macdonald to the director of the *Montreal Gazette*. At the time, the anglophone elite of the business world was unhappy with the political alliance between Macdonald and (Georges-Étienne) Cartier. Several months before, this group had burnt down the parliament buildings presided over by Lord Elgin, to protest against the Anglo–French coalition, the reformist government of (Louis Hippolyte) Lafontaine and (Robert) Baldwin.

* What I didn't say to the committee was that at the end of my speech, I was so upset with all those who had left Quebec that I told them, "With the election of the PQ, you left Quebec. Where will you go after Quebec separates and leaves you without your Canada?"

Macdonald wrote to the English of Montreal, "You cannot forget that you were dominant. You are fighting to maintain this supremacy. Treat the French Canadians as a nation and they will react generally as a free people does, with generosity. Treat them as a simple faction, and they will respond likewise.*

English Canadians and French Canadians should remember that confederation would probably never have occurred without the participation and the support of French Canadians.

It is in large part due to French Canadians that confederation was conceived as a system which subordinates the totality of the interests of the nation to the interests of its composing groups. In order for confederation to work, Canada had to become a country where French Canadians keep their nationality. Immigrants, such as myself, can thank the French Canadians for the Canadian mosaic that we speak of rather than a "melting pot."

For the francophones of Canada, confederation is an agreement, a contract, between the two founding peoples, an association, not a fusion. Unfortunately, as Sir John A. Macdonald had predicted, the gulf widened between the idea and the reality.

Mr Speaker, these remarks explain why I am proposing the amendment to Article 69.[†] I don't want to treat Canada as already being divided into two countries – Quebec and the rest of Canada. I believe that in spite of the existing difficulties, the government has not received that mandate to propose legislation presupposing that Quebec is already separated from Canada. That is what Article 69, as drafted, presupposes. It presupposes that in this area there is already a separation between Quebec and the rest of Canada. This is not the government's mandate. I believe that it is more symbolic than the reality and symbolic because there are more Quebecers leaving than anglophones coming to Quebec.

When I ended, the silence was deafening. The Speaker adjourned the proceedings.

---

* In the light of Dr Laurin's language, I told the committee, these words seemed very prophetic.

† Article 69 states that only those children whose parents attended English schools in Quebec would have the right to attend English schools. I was proposing to change "Quebec" to "Canada."

BILL 101: CONCLUSIONS

The Liberals were opposed to Bill 101. However, we realized that the government, having a majority, would proceed with its adoption, so we tried to improve it, to broaden it, and eliminate those clauses that could form the basis of legal contestation and, I thought, adversely affect the social climate.

Fellow MNA Fernand Lalonde, the leader of the Liberal team in the committee, was diligent and firm in his opposition, eloquent and moderate in his remarks. He went beyond the PQ's myopic view of society and was the subject of crass criticism for his trouble. Some Péquistes went so far as to call him a traitor. In fact, he is to be admired for his courage in standing up for his beliefs.

Thérèse Lavoie-Roux was very calm and courteous in her remarks, supportive of her colleagues and firm in her suggestions to change some of the more restrictive aspects of the legislation. Liberals had a very different view of Quebec society – more cosmopolitan, more open, less defensive, less aggressive. This was reflected in the debates. It was probably summed up in Outremont Liberal André Raynauld's approach when he tried to prove that the legislation was not necessary. The former head of the Economic Council of Canada, bureaucrat, economist, federalist, francophone from Quebec who had achieved one of the highest civil service public positions in Canada, presented all the numbers – Quebec's demography and myriad other figures including the increase in the population and the number of French-speaking people as a percentage of the population – to show that a language law was not needed. It was a statistical problem. He meant well but convinced no one. It is curious how our backgrounds dictate our reasoning, despite all the data he had to offer.

My insistence that some of the articles were not legal and would be contested before the courts proved correct. The Supreme Court of Canada struck down the provisions making French the language of the courts as well as those requiring legislation to be tabled only in French. While recognizing the fragility of the French language in Canada, it also declared illegal the prohibition on English signs but suggested a formula making French the preponderant language of signs. This decision was to create problems for a future Bourassa government.

It is sometimes strange how the certitudes that you had at one time in your life can change. Acceptance of certain realities, in this case the passage of Bill 101, can remove anxieties and restore peace of mind.

I now have a different view of Bill 101. Certainly, it contained many provisions that were judged illegal and have now been modified and others that are still overly restrictive, but overall the legislation has benefited the French-speaking people of Quebec. It has enabled them to feel equal in their own province. It has removed many of the anomalies that existed in Quebec society. It has removed some of the sense of grievance, perceived or real, and has improved the social climate.

Generally, the English-speaking community, at least those who stayed in Quebec, have come to accept the legislation as a fact of life. But let's also ask ourselves what would Quebec be like today if the 400,000 who left the province – mostly because of this legislation – had stayed.

ASBESTOS AND THE FIGHT AGAINST NATIONALIZATION

The other dossier that drew my attention concerned Quebec's asbestos industry. In the 1970s, there was not yet the opprobrium attached to this product that exists today. In fact, asbestos had a special place in the economy of Quebec. Indeed, it was so important that there is even a mining town in the Eastern Townships called Asbestos, whose mines contributed to the economic life of the whole region. Adding to industry's mystique, for nationalists especially, was the 1949 asbestos strike, which some said was a spark that later ignited the Quiet Revolution. So, while many western countries eventually prohibited this product, Quebec would not abandon the town of Asbestos. It sought markets elsewhere.

In 1977, the PQ government acquired Asbestos Corporation, the largest asbestos producer in the province, hoping to protect jobs in an industry that was already threatened as evidence about the harmful effects of the fibre mounted. In creating the Société nationale de l'amiante, the Péquistes also saw an opportunity for French-speaking Quebecers to take greater control of the economy in an area traditionally dominated by English-speaking business interests.

I attacked the decision on monetary and health grounds. I demolished the government's contention that it would gain $20 million– the supposed taxes paid by the company on its profits – to invest in promoting the transformation of the raw material in Quebec. In fact, the actual tax dollars paid to Quebec were only $3.8 million. Hiding behind the excuse of "confidential information" Natural Resources Minister Yves Bérubé later admitted that the $20 million figure was perhaps exaggerated and had been used only as an "example."

I pointed out that the primary objectives of the government should be to improve the health and working conditions in the industry. This wouldn't be achieved by acquiring the Asbestos Corporation, which was the most backward of all mining companies in terms of its health and safety records. I argued that there were no market studies to consider the implications of a proposed ban on some uses of asbestos within the European Economic Community, our second largest market, nor had the government considered the implication of increased Soviet asbestos exports to the EEC resulting from growing East–West trade détente.

The government had not made a convincing argument that a state-controlled corporation would be profitable in the future. After questioning several ministers in the National Assembly, I obtained from PQ MNA Pierre de Bellefeuille what a journalist called a "magnificent understatement" when he replied that "perhaps there are flaws in the government plans."*

THE LIBERALS GET A NEW LEADER

The rejection of Robert Bourassa in the 1976 election was so complete that he decided to quit politics temporarily and went to Europe and the US. Gérard D. Levesque became the interim leader during this period of malaise within the party. He was very able but essentially a second-in-command who could bring his demoralized colleagues together. Indeed he was the best person for that role, but we needed a permanent leader.

Raymond Garneau, Bourassa's able minister of finance, was a candidate. However, many of us thought that it was time to make a break with the past. We did not want someone who was associated with the disastrous years of the last Liberal administration. We feared that the public would view this as more of the same.

The person chosen to give the Liberal Party a new image was Claude Ryan, the editor of *Le Devoir*, the small but influential Montreal newspaper that appealed more to Quebec intellectuals than to ordinary citizens. Imagine – we went to recruit as leader the person who had written an editorial during the election supporting the Parti Québécois. Some might consider this self-flagellation. Others would see it as a bold attempt at renewal and an acknowledgement of past mistakes.

* Louis Falardeau in *La Presse*, March 1978.

During the James Bay negotiations Claude had asked to see me. I met him in his office on St Sacrement Street (an appropriate name as we shall soon see) in Old Montreal. He seemed to favour the terms of the agreement. However, the discussion soon turned to Robert Bourassa and his ways of governing. Even then, Claude was critical of the premier. From then on, he seemed to consider that we had more than just a passing relationship.

Ryan's accession to the leadership of the Liberal party followed a tortuous path. He convened a group of us, in whom he presumably had confidence, at his home, with its voluminous library, which I envied, on Laurier Avenue. We met in a small adjoining room. He said he had decided not to run for the leadership and wanted our opinion. Thérèse Lavoie-Roux and Fernand Lalonde were present along with Pierre Fortier, I believe, as well as the person in charge of party financing. They all tried to convince him to accept.

I knew that he was not prone to taking advice if he had already made up his own mind. Moreover, leadership was not usually something one needed to be convinced to take up. It is something that you must want and feel at ease with. Did Napoleon need convincing to become emperor? I told him that it was up to him to decide whether he wanted to become leader or not. I respected his decision.

A day or so later, he wrote an editorial in *Le Devoir* explaining why he would not run for the leadership of the Liberal party.* Some time later, he changed his mind.

It is worth dwelling a few moments on Claude Ryan's leadership campaign. It was innovative, ideologically driven, well organized, conducted with enthusiasm, and successful. It also became, thanks largely to Ryan's supporters, uncharitable, mean spirited, and pitiless toward the other candidate, Raymond Garneau. I regret that I also was harsh and did not show him the generosity and recognition that he deserved.

The campaign was a reflection of Ryan's personality. As a journalist, Ryan was known for his little back notebook, which he carried everywhere. It became his trademark. It was replicated during the campaign as a pocket-sized black memo pad with a red stamp (Liberal red) on the cover of which was written "Leader Claude Ryan" in black and white. It became known as the "Ryan notebook" and was distributed to everyone. When you flipped it open, you saw a signed picture of Ryan, a space to insert your name as the owner of the notebook, and a description of what the notebook was, in French and English. (To his

* *Le Devoir*, 7 November 1977.

credit, Ryan favoured bilingualism.) As you thumbed the notebook's pages you could read words of welcome, which spoke not only of the campaign but also about the issues Ryan considered the challenges we faced: the referendum on Quebec's constitutional future, plans for which the PQ were already discussing; the next general election; and the revision of the Canadian constitution and reestablishment of friendly cooperation among all Quebecers and Canadians.

It contained the program for the leadership convention with precise dates and hours for scheduled events, instructions to the delegates as to what to do and where to go, and a map on how to get to the convention centre in Quebec City. There were extracts of favourable comments on his candidacy by journalists and university professors, biographical notes highlighting his career, a list of the honours he had received, and comments he'd written on federalism and liberty. There was a list of pertinent telephone numbers (e.g. Liberal party and the convention centre but also airlines, telegraph offices, drug stores, medical clinics, and the police departments of both Quebec City and Ste Foy) along with a list of financial contributors to the campaign and some of their comments, pictures of Claude Ryan and his family, the maiden name of his wife, and the names and ages of his five children. The notebook gave biographical data on the candidate, for example, that he was the national secretary of Catholic Action from 1945 to 1962 and that he had undergone postgraduate studies on the church and world history at the Gregorian Pontifical University in Rome. There was even a crossword puzzle with Claude Ryan and his accomplishments as the theme.

The voting procedure for the leadership provided for the election of twenty-four delegates from each riding. The notebook listed twenty-four reasons to vote for Ryan as leader, presumably, one for each delegate – a man who wants a happy Quebec in a united Canada, a great Quebecer known from sea to sea, a great man of politics rather than simply a politician, etc.

There was a "true or false" quiz on every member of the National Assembly and on certain events. John Ciaccia was recognized as a specialist in Indian Affairs; Claude Ryan and Pierre Elliott Trudeau were working comrades at *Le Devoir*.

There was a list of hotels and motels in the Quebec city area where the delegates were lodged. All that information in a little booklet that you could slip into your back pocket. Extraordinary. It was a beautiful document – precise, concise, interesting, and amusing. It reflected the Ryan approach.

OTTAWA VERSUS QUEBEC

Although I was in opposition, I was not always critical of the government. Minister of Communications Louis O'Neill had attended a federal–provincial conference in Charlottetown where discussions had been held on the allocation of powers between the federal and provincial governments. With the election of a PQ government, the division of legislative powers between Ottawa and the provinces had become a heated subject. Redefining these powers and granting more to the provinces might, many federalists hoped, reduce the appeal of political independence in Quebec. I complimented O'Neill for the positions he took in Charlottetown. Then, at a parliamentary committee on communications, I criticized the federal government and made my own suggestions.

The separatists posed a threat, but I believed that we had to do more than merely oppose their objectives. We had to realize that there were reasons why they had adopted their drastic course of action. We had to respond by trying to find responses to the perceived grievances.

To every problem, there is a solution. Sure, there were some intransigents who wanted separatism at all costs, but not all Péquistes were die-hards.

That is why I went to the parliamentary committee on communications.

Communications, which involves the licensing and regulation of television and broadcasting, was and remains a thorny issue. The constitution gives Ottawa exclusive jurisdiction over this area, yet its application affects each province – most significantly Quebec because of the province's language and culture. I maintained that Quebec culture is an asset for Canada and had to be recognized as such not only in Quebec but also throughout the country. The aim of a communications policy should be to assure the specific needs of Quebecers without affecting Canadian unity.

"A central policy on communications cannot function efficiently in situations which are so diverse. For this reason I believe that Quebec must obtain additional powers in this sector ... The needs of Quebecers in the area of communications are different from those of other Canadians."*

As in the case of immigration, I made a plea for shared responsibility in this field, where both levels of government have powers and responsibilities. I made several proposals to achieve this:

* *Le Devoir*, 24 April 1978.

- Give the provinces the necessary powers to formulate and apply policies for all radio, television, cable TV, and pay TV in its territory.
- A province should obtain the powers to issue permits and regulate all other enterprises in the field of telecommunications.
- A charter of rights, which would guarantee the two founding peoples (English and French) the right to receive broadcasts in their language wherever they may be in Canada. The federal government would create a fund to help industries in nonprofitable areas.
- The creation of a federal–provincial commission to coordinate and regulate, where necessary, the policies of both governments.

I commended both Jeanne Sauvé, then a federal minister and later governor general, and Louis O'Neill from Quebec in their attempts to find a solution to a recent decision of the Supreme Court.

Unfortunately, the constitution wasn't changed.

CAMILLE LAURIN AND CULTURE

Meanwhile, the good doctor Laurin's approach to language was replicated in his ideas about cultural development. A white paper on the subject suggested his belief in the all-pervasive role of government in moulding the lives of its citizens. Thérèse Lavoie-Roux and myself were harsh critics. Our major objection was the government's domineering role in matters of culture, "substituting collective choices for individual choices," as Lavoie-Roux explained. "They want to protect the collectivity against the individuals who make it up." We called it "state paternalism."*

Laurin made such controlling and impractical suggestions as the creation of distribution cooperatives for periodicals and newspapers. Claude Ryan, the former editor of *Le Devoir* ridiculed this idea as unworkable.† I said the white paper was not a reflection of what was happening in Quebec, but that it was akin to treating Quebec as an underdeveloped country. I was relieved that Laurin made no efforts to translate his theory on minorities (that they all gravitated to the English-speaking community) into action. "Mercifully, the minorities are spared."

* *Journal de Quebec*, 9 June 1978.
† *Montreal Star*, 9 June 1978.

His was a different way of thinking than I had learned in my schooling. Then again, perhaps I also went a little too far in suggesting, "In a society that is desired in the white paper, we could never produce a Michelangelo or a Leonardo da Vinci. Instead, we would produce a Solzhenitsyn."

OTHER CONCERNS

I involved myself in all the issues of the day. I examined all the government did. I queried all their actions and made my own suggestions on what should be done. I wanted to show that there was an alternative to the present government, a better way to govern.

In 1978, the world reacted in horror to the assassination by the Red Brigades of Aldo Moro, Italy's prime minister. A law professor and a statesman, Moro had held several cabinet posts before becoming head of the Christian Democratic Party and prime minister. He had made significant contributions to both the internal and the international political life of Italy. He was responsible for the creation of the "historic compromise" – the accommodation between the Christian Democratic Party and the Italian Communist Party to work together in government. He was kidnapped by the radical leftist gang the day a government of national unity was to be formed with the inclusion of the Communist Party. At the time, Italy was a society in turmoil. It had known more than twenty years of fascism up to and during the war, and its transition to democracy seemed to be at times threatened by communism. Moro's solution could be seen as a step in the evolution of Italian democracy, although neither the US nor the Soviet Union saw it that way.

Premier Lévesque rose in the National Assembly and eloquently offered his regrets for such a brutal and "contemptible" event. Because I was of Italian descent, I was invited to comment. Speaking extemporaneously, I offered my regrets and added: "It is perhaps an example of what happens when the values of a society are turned upside down. It is perhaps a lesson for us." Journalist Normand Girard of the *Journal de Montréal* commented that these remarks, together with certain others that René Lévesque had previously made, should make us reflect.[*]

I was unaware that the previous year, Lévesque, at a party congress held in Trois-Rivières, had warned his troops that there are limits to

---

[*] "... ont de quoi faire réflechir," 10 May 1978.

the changes a society can absorb. He had continued this message in his inaugural address at the National Assembly. It wasn't the first or only time that Lévesque showed his innate sense of responsibility.

The marking of this event was an occasion for us to ponder and appreciate the values of our society and be vigilant in safeguarding them.

In opposition, I became energy critic for the Liberals. Each year the government decided on the rate increases demanded by Hydro-Québec. At one point, I was heading the parliamentary committee on energy and I questioned the increases authorized by the government. I proposed either the creation of an energy commission that would be responsible for determining such increases or a parliamentary committee, which would have experts available to make a proper judgment on the demands of Hydro-Québec.

(One's perspective often depends on where one is sitting. Later, when I became energy minister, I made the final recommendations on hydro rates and persuaded Premier Bourassa not to create an energy board. By controlling the rates, we would reap the political benefits from fixing reasonable increases.)

I criticized the minister, Guy Joron, for two unusual decisions. He authorized increases for three years, instead of the usual twelve-month period, and he granted Hydro higher increases than they asked for.[*] This was in 1978. The referendum on the political independence of Quebec would be held in 1980. The government did not want to be in a position in which it would be imposing rate increases during a year in which a referendum would be held. Three years would take it past the referendum. Expediency is omnipresent in government decisions. Since he was making a decision that covered increases for three years, he shrewdly covered himself to reduce the possibility of a shortfall in revenues.

On the subject of energy, I also questioned Joron about a study for two new dams that would produce electricity at the Lachine rapids and at the Ste Marie current near Old Montreal. I pointed out that Hydro had already studied the possibility of these projects and found major technical reasons why they should not go ahead at those locations. There was no evidence that this had changed. No matter what the minister proposed, I characterized it as a "referendum balloon," and an incitement to support the government.[†]

---

[*] *Le Soleil*, 8 November 1978.
[†] *Le Devoir*, 4 April 1979.

I didn't leave the minister alone. When the nuclear generating station in Three Mile Island, Pennsylvania, suffered a partial meltdown on 28 March 1979 I rose in the National Assembly to express concern about the Gentilly nuclear plants located near Bécancour, one of which was already in operation (but was soon shut down) and a second that had yet to begin. I remembered the reaction of Robert Bourassa to Jacques Parizeau's initial opposition to the James Bay Project and his proposals for nuclear energy. I asked Joron to create a permanent legislative committee with experts and members of the National Assembly to study nuclear safety. The minister replied that "there is no reason to go off the deep end" but nevertheless assured us that Hydro would launch an information campaign on nuclear safety for the residents near the power stations.* A very minimal gesture.

The federal government announced that it would make available $62 million for urban transportation. This could have helped the operation of commuter trains. In the Assembly, I asked minister of transportation, Guy Tardiff, if he would avail himself of these funds. He replied that the government had other priorities. There was verbal jousting between the minister and Ottawa, but in the end Quebec declined the funds. There was an obvious reason – these funds would help areas such as Town of Mount Royal, which would vote against the government in the referendum. The government did not want to help voters who did not support independence. They had to be punished. So, no funds.

AN INCIDENT IN PENETANGUISHENE

In 1979, in Penetanguishene, on Georgian Bay, the Ontario Ministry of Education refused to build a French school and proposed to send the students to a "mixed" school with other English pupils. Until then, it had been the policy of the government to build schools for the French minority where there was a sizable French-speaking community, many of whom had originally come from Quebec. In this case, the opposition at Queen's Park maintained there were enough students to justify a new school and accused the government of encouraging the assimilation of the French community by sending its children to English schools.

The Ontario government's decision not to build a French school made headlines across the country. Minority rights were more and more important, especially in view of the Parti Québécois's assimilationist policies. There were minorities everywhere in Canada. In my

* *Montreal Gazette*, 11 April 1979.

riding, the minority was English-speaking; in other parts of Quebec there were ethnic minorities. Quebec was a minority within Canada.

I felt compelled to speak out. In a letter to *Le Devoir* which was the object of an editorial in *Le Carillon,* an Ontario newspaper written for the francophone community in that province, I made the comparison with the situation in Quebec and the reaction of minorities there. The malaise, both in Quebec and elsewhere in Canada, resulted from the fear minority groups have of being drowned in a bilingual system that would in the long run be harmful to the cultural interests of francophones.

It would take patience and people of good will who believe in a united Canada to encourage the public to respect minorities wherever they may be," my letter said. "The situation of our francophone compatriots in Ontario or Manitoba is much more difficult in many respects than that of minorities in Quebec.

It is tragic that Quebec, because of its separatist objectives, can no longer play its part in defending minorities. It has abandoned the francophones outside of Quebec. It is absurd to see the government of Quebec interest itself with the francophones internationally (la francophonie) while it has nothing to do with Canada.

As long as the government of Ontario ignores the fact that its French minority has a fundamental right to cultural survival, all of the minorities in this country will have difficulties in being recognized.

We cannot build a country on a democratic basis if equal opportunity is not offered to all, and if fundamental rights are not assured. By adopting policies that deny the cultural identity of minorities, governments are not favouring their integration in our society, nor are they helping them to identify themselves with this country. And that is perhaps the saddest aspect of the Penetanguishene incident.

I urge all Canadians to protest the treatment of francophones outside of Quebec in the same way as they would protest individuals or groups who are persecuted in other countries. Canadians must find the same indignation, which has made them come to the help of those victimized in other countries.

It is clear that we do not physically persecute our victims, but there is moral violence that is just as intolerable.

WE TOO ARE HERE

Claude Ryan was thorough in his approach to politics. He asked me to prepare a policy paper on cultural communities. The document would be presented at a symposium with seminars and workshops. The theme would be, "We too are here."

The Quebec referendum was fast approaching. There were a substantial number of votes in those communities. The PQ government had begun a $2 million "Operation Rapprochement" program. Although it had given up on the English community, which they knew would never support independence, they had higher hopes for the province's ethnic communities. The government knew that they were not unconditional Liberals. In 1976, many minority voters had supported the Union Nationale, which had helped elect the PQ. Ministers were blitzing the immigrant communities. Subsidies were given to their associations. Every day Immigration Minister Jacques Couture would have lunch with some member of a minority community.

The symposium and my eighty-four-page document served as a reawakening and recognition of these groups. They had generally been taken for granted. I did not suggest quotas, but I did ask for a greater role for them in government and in various areas of the private sector. They were inadequately represented in the civil service, in the judiciary, and other public institutions. For example, while forming 12 per cent of Quebec's population, minorities made up only 3 per cent of the civil service. They were almost totally absent from the list of elected representatives.

The document was partly a plea for and to the communities and partly a promotion of Liberal ideas to obtain their support in the referendum. I wrote: "Public representation gives public visibility and public recognition to ethnic groups. It promotes their acceptance within society. It reduces the idea of 'strangeness.' It symbolizes and renders real the notion of equality of opportunity."

I wanted not only the government, but also the public, to be aware of these communities. I wanted acceptance for them and perhaps for me.

In retrospect, the word "ethnic" was itself pejorative, conjuring the idea of difference and unequal status. "Cultural communities" was less offensive but it did not remove a certain climate of mistrust directed towards minorities. The reaction was mutual. Many cultural minorities asked if they were considered full-fledged or second-class citizens. I knew that feeling. Scenes from my childhood came to my mind.

I also expressed concern with the language laws as they affected these communities. I supported the obligation to attend French schools but argued that it should not be enforced retroactively and should not apply to immigrants who were already here when Bill 101 was adopted. It might be divisive if families had children whose older siblings were already in English schools. Imagine if this happened in your family. My plea fell on deaf ears.

I suggested that membership in a profession should not be refused only because a person did not pass a French examination. This was a new rule and couldn't be applied overnight.

In the preparation of my policy paper I consulted many people in minority cultural communities and was ably assisted in the drafting of the document by Rita de Santis, an immigrant who had come to this country when she was nine years old. She became a lawyer and joined one of the most prestigious law firms in Montreal. She was conscientious, indefatigable, and discerning, a devoted volunteer who was to make winning the referendum one of her crusades.

With the referendum pending, I did not miss opportunities to remind minorities that their rights would be better protected in a federal government rather than in an independent Quebec. I tried to allay the fears of the majority that immigrants were taking jobs away from them. Statistics suggested the opposite, that immigrants created jobs that in turn benefitted everyone. Their 12 per cent of the population made up 20 per cent of the gross domestic product.

I insisted on the importance of individual rights versus collective rights, as much an issue for minority communities as for the majority. I also questioned the use of the term "Québécois," saying the PQ had coopted the word, giving it a special meaning that suggested it applied only to francophones born in Quebec. All citizens of Quebec were Québécois, I said.

I urged minorities to integrate themselves into our society by participating in its activities and not limiting themselves to their own communities.

Concerning the economic life of Quebec, members of the province's cultural communities were present not only as entrepreneurs but also as investors. Many of them were employed in lines of work Quebecers no longer wished to do – field work, for example, or, increasingly, owning *dépanneurs* (as corner stores in Quebec are called). I deplored the condition of new immigrant workers who were poorly paid, often receiving only, or less than, the minimum wage.

I disagreed with the existing criteria for the admission of immigrants and urged the government to facilitate the sponsorship of relatives.

Social services were another area of concern. I argued that government should make sure those persons dispensing these services had a knowledge of the language of the people they were serving, so that they could adequately explain the assistance that was available.

I warned against the ethnocentric view of society that would prevail in an independent Quebec, and I maintained that cultural communities preferred a federal system of government where two levels of government would be available to protect their rights. I also suggested that cultural communities could serve as a bridge between the French- and English-speaking populations as a way of promoting mutual acceptance.

Many others helped me in the preparation of the position paper. One, in particular, had his own agenda. In the English version of the document, I suggested that, "the government should give official legal status to the English language. Since a large proportion of the population is English-speaking, such a measure by the government would be more realistic and would contribute greatly to harmonize and stabilize the relationships within our society." This person, who worked on the French version of the document, translated "legal" to "official" language. It was incongruous. I had voted in favour of French as the official language as far back as Bill 22 under Premier Bourassa, and I had not changed my mind.

Was I careless? Was it fatigue? Was it the fast pace of all of my activities, trying to be at too many places and do too many things at the same time? I regretted it as soon as the document became public.

11

The Referendum Divides Quebec

If traumatic experiences are not limited to individuals, then the events of 1980 were a traumatic ordeal for Quebec. The people of Quebec, and all Canadians, were threatened with the possible loss of their country.

Separation involved serious risks to Quebecers's way of life, their comforts, their accustomed loyalties. There are both emotional and material reasons for being attached to your country or wanting to leave it. Canada had an illustrious past. In its early years it had fought off annexation by the United States. It was prosperous. It was respected internationally. Some of its prime ministers had distinguished themselves on the world scene and were well thought of, Lester Pearson, who had won a Nobel Peace Prize, being a prime example. The flamboyant Pierre Elliott Trudeau was another, though he was sometimes viewed more critically from abroad, as the Nixon administration's distaste for him illustrated.

Mostly, Canadians were quietly proud of being Canadian. The separatists didn't see it this way. They felt alienated from Ottawa and rejected by the rest of the country. Years of perceived grievances had left them estranged from the English-speaking community, which they identified with Canada. A lack of understanding of French Canadian aspirations and anxieties in the rest of Canada increased their hostility.

Meanwhile, immigrants were grateful to Canada for having accepted them and improving their quality of life. Some had seen political upheavals in their former countries and didn't want a repetition here. They were probably more concerned and more reactive than native Canadians.

Then there were those in the middle – Quebec nationalists from the French-speaking community – who didn't want to separate but wanted to shake Ottawa and the rest of Canada from its lethargy and indifference. Their attitude was best shown by the slogan adopted by the Union Nationale: "Not necessarily separatism, but separatism if necessary."

There was euphoria among the Péquistes. Their majority in the National Assembly, their nationalization of the Asbestos Corporation – creating a made-in-Quebec product owned by Quebecers – the introduction of stringent language legislation, and the fervour of their supporters all gave a sense that a new era had arrived in Quebec and anything was possible, including the dream of political independence.

However, even most francophone Quebecers were not prepared to support outright independence. It was too drastic. The PQ knew this and that, therefore, they couldn't ask a direct question such as, "Are you in favour of the political independence of Quebec?" This would have been rejected overwhelmingly. Instead, people had to be cajoled into supporting the nationalist cause. So they cunningly drafted a question that they hoped would allay fears. As a matter of fact, the question was noncommittal and would require a second referendum to make a final decision on political independence. You could safely vote "yes" without binding yourself irrevocably to independence. It was a sort of a two-step dance.

The question contained 105 words, all in one convoluted sentence:

> The Government of Quebec has made public its proposal to negotiate a new agreement with the rest of Canada, based on the equality of nations; this agreement would enable Quebec to acquire the exclusive power to make its laws, levy its taxes and establish relations abroad – in other words, sovereignty – and at the same time to maintain with Canada an economic association including a common currency; any change in political status resulting from these negotiations will only be implemented with popular approval through another referendum; on these terms, do you give the Government of Quebec the mandate to negotiate the proposed agreement between Quebec and Canada?

It was not a mandate to "separate." It was a mandate to "negotiate." Who could be against that? The government would negotiate an "economic association" with Canada and have a common currency. No details were given as to what this meant or how it would come about.

The question was vague and crafty, a model of contortion. "Quebec" was mentioned four times, "Canada," three. Very reassuring. Even the word "sovereignty" was misleading. Judicial decisions had already confirmed that Canadian provinces were sovereign in the areas where the constitution gave them exclusive jurisdiction. Perhaps the good Dr Laurin, the healer of stricken minds and troubled societies, had a say in the drafting of this conceivably reassuring but intentionally deceptive question. Without saying so explicitly, it was a path to political independence, the separation of Quebec from Canada.

The referendum and debate surrounding it were tremendously emotional, affecting everyone in Quebec. People had never had to confront such a challenge, to make such a decision, which had so many unknown consequences. And so the referendum campaign – cast as a do-or-die event – became an all-consuming battle for the hearts and minds of Quebecers. It was as if we were fighting the battle of the Plains of Abraham all over again. People reacted as if they were facing the end of their world. Such was especially the view in the English-speaking community and among Quebec's minorities.

I was totally caught up in the fray. I shocked my constituents by telling them that I was not afraid of separatism – I was more afraid of the kind of society promised by the Péquistes with their ideas about "collective rights" as opposed to individual rights, their views of the interventionist role of government, their intransigence, their intolerance. I multiplied their sins. "They don't want to take us out of Canada," I charged in the National Assembly. "They want to take us out of North America." This rallied the federalist forces.

During the campaign, all the issues of the day that a government faced in the Assembly, and on which it is rightfully questioned by the opposition, took on new significance. Even the marking of historical events which would normally be observed and unanimously supported, suddenly took on a new focus. As was customary, the government introduced a resolution on the anniversary of the Armenian genocide. We all denounced the act, expressed our sympathy for the victims, and censured those responsible. But I didn't stop there. "This genocide was perpetrated in the name of blind nationalism against another ethnic group and another nation which had the misfortune of being different. Quebecers, on this occasion, must remind themselves to what extent the exaltation of blind nationalism can lead to."[*]

Fernand Lalonde joined in. "We must remind Quebecers where the white heat of nationalism, as suggested by your Doris Lussier, can

---

[*] "... jusqu'a quel excès l'exaltation aveugle du nationalisme a pu conduire."

lead.* It is something to keep in mind during the current referendum debate."

The PQ members were livid that we should have used the occasion of the observance of the Armenian genocide to castigate the government and warn Quebecers of the dangers of radical nationalism. "It is disgusting," fumed Gérald Godin, the PQ member who had defeated Robert Bourassa in east end Montreal's Mercier riding.

On another occasion, as energy critic, I pointed out that Hydro-Québec furnished only 26 per cent of our energy needs, the rest coming from outside Quebec. Even with the most optimistic predictions for 1990 coming to pass, Hydro would still only furnish 41 per cent of total requirements. Meanwhile, largely because of western petroleum, Canada had 85 per cent self-sufficiency, while the US imported half of its energy. I raised an ominous point about sovereignty-association: "Notice that without Quebec, Canada is self-sufficient. Ask yourself the question and see the considerable advantages that we have in remaining in the Canadian federation."†

When Economic Development Minister Bernard Landry extolled the virtues of Hydro-Québec and claimed that it supplied 50 per cent of our energy needs, I rose in the National Assembly and asked him, "Can Hydro-Québec make your Buick Electra function or do you need petroleum?"‡

Premier Lévesque was interviewed by the French magazine *Le Point* and said that the PQ, "would be best off to forget our plans [for separation] and think of something else if it captured less than 40 per cent of the vote." I responded by stating that Levesque was desperate and "had abandoned all hope of winning the referendum."§

The government enacted special legislation, Bill 92, to regulate the referendum. All those who wished to participate could only do so under the umbrella of either the No Committee (those who opposed the political independence of Quebec) or the Yes Committee, which was for it. The financing was limited and strictly regulated. This favoured the separatists because moneyed interests – the business community – which overwhelmingly opposed independence or people and groups

---

* Doris Lussier was a nationalist firebrand, a diehard *independantise*, and an adviser to the PQ.
† *Montreal Gazette*, 22 March 1980.
‡ *La Presse*, 26 March 1980.
§ *Vancouver Sun*, 14 February 1980.

from other provinces could not organize their own campaigns and flood the province with publicity against separatism.

In the National Assembly debates on Bill 92, I asserted that, "new Canadians who live in Quebec have as much to gain or lose from the results of the referendum as other Quebecers. The Referendum Act prevents the full participation of ethnic minorities, as such, by its ban on organizations representing them." I maintained that these organizations were best qualified to communicate to minority groups the issues involved. I asked for their right to participate in the referendum independently from the national committees set up by the government.

I was also concerned that the civil service, which had been involved in the preparation of a *dossier noir* outlining supposed injustices committed by Ottawa upon Quebec, was being used to promote the aims of the government. I said public servants were at the service of the entire public, not tools for government propaganda. If the expenses of each referendum committee were strictly limited, clearly the potential use of 300,000 civil servants to promote independence gave the Yes side an unfair advantage. I asked for a permanent committee to be set up by the National Assembly to ensure that government publicity would not be prejudicial to the fairness of the contest. Information, yes. Propaganda, no.

I objected to the creation of the Conseil de Référendum, a body that would rule on all disputed matters related to the referendum to the exclusion of the courts. I maintained that this went against the rule of the separation of powers, the basis of our government.

I also tried to look beyond the day of the ballot. The whole process had to be fair and above reproach. Whatever the results, Quebecers would have to live together after the referendum. If uncertainty continued, or if one side believed that the referendum was not a fair reading of the desires of the population, the consequences could be grave for the future economic and social conditions in Quebec.

Claude Ryan was the leader of the No Committee. His past differences with Pierre Trudeau were temporarily set aside and did not prevent Trudeau from assuming a dramatic role in the battle against the break-up of Canada. His rallies ignited crowds and inspired No organizers. As a member of the executive of the No Committee, I was sitting behind Trudeau when he gave one of the electrifying speeches of the campaign. I came out feeling impassioned and encouraged.

We cannot underestimate the role of Pierre Elliott Trudeau in the referendum campaign. Although Claude Ryan was the titular head of the No Committee, Trudeau was the person who galvanized the people. I thought (and still do) that he was the one who made the greatest contribution to the success of the referendum, defeating the *independantistes* and keeping Quebec within Canada. He appealed to the crowds. He inspired them. His rallies attracted thousands who looked up to him and responded to his call. He was the motivator of the No forces. He had the same determination as he had when the FLQ threatened violence in Quebec in the late 1960s. The group had already killed several persons in pursuit of its objective to "liberate" Quebec. Trudeau didn't hesitate to call in the army. When questioned by some doubters as to what he would do, he did not back down: "Just watch me." It was strange, and somewhat scary, to see the Canadian Army patrolling the streets of Montreal.

But the FLQ was no longer a menace. Trudeau had shown who was in charge and had proved that he would take all measures that were necessary to maintain order and the integrity of Canada. Now, in a more peaceful time, he was taking the initiative to defend his vision of Canada. I supported and admired him.

As a committee member, I was active not only in my riding but in other areas as well, especially among minorities. With the emphasis by the Péquistes on French, minority groups felt that the definition of a Québécois did not include them. Certain remarks like those by Premier Lévesque who said Robert Boyd, Hydro-Québec president, was a Québécois in spite of his name, suggested that had his name been from another minority group he would not have been counted among the Québécois. This only added to the feeling of alienation among minority groups.

I spoke at a rally organized by minorities, whose theme was Mon Non est Québécois. It was a play on words because, in French, "non" and "nom" (name) have the same pronunciation. We were affirming that both our "no" and our "name" were Québécois.

Late in the campaign, Premier Lévesque was invited to speak to the members of the Italian community. Perhaps he was tired on this occasion. Perhaps he was irritated by the attitude of an unfriendly audience, Italian Quebecers being among the most pro-Canadian of all the minorities. In any event, he used intemperate language, referring to the audience as "hypocrites," "uninformed," "biased," "child-like" (*enfantins*), "ignorant" and "boneless" (*désossé*), that is, invertebrates or lacking in intelligence. I was incensed and reproached him in *La Presse* for his insulting language and for trying to divide the Italian community.* I criticized him for lashing out at a community that was probably the most francisized minority in Quebec.

The audience wanted to know what sovereignty-association was and the details of the so-called common currency with Canada. I said that Lévesque "skated majestically" over this question. He was vague, and castigated them for the one question asked about language. "If the premier must continue to make speeches, he shouldn't consult the dictionary of insults before preparing them." If he meets citizens who protest noisily during his statements, it is because they object to his constitutional project, not because they have a "visceral" objection to the French language. I ended by acknowledging that the premier had the right to explain and to try and win over the population to his opinion, however, citizens, no matter what their origin, had the right to believe in Canada without being "invertebrates." The referendum debate must rest on the merits of each option, not on divisive tactics. Was that too much to ask?

I considered the referendum issue not only a political question but also an ideological conflict. In my speeches and articles, I analyzed and attacked the PQ government for the philosophy that I believed was behind their policies.

I also wrote articles on "the new society" of the PQ and the choice for Quebecers in the west end paper *The Suburban*. In part they were a response to remarks made in *Ici Quebec*, a newspaper funded by the Ministry of Communications. Its editorial line had racialist and anti-Semitic overtones – it had referred to Israel as "the cancer of humanity." Although Lévesque had dissociated himself from those remarks, I thought they needed to be addressed. "The real confrontation ... is not between Quebec and Canada nor between the French and the English. It is between two radically opposing world views, one being 'liberal' and based on respect for the rights of the individual, the other 'statist' and justified by the rights of the 'collectivity.'" I attacked the views of Dr Laurin and his constant reference to "colonial subjugation." I criticized the PQ's views on their use of state power, advising that there was no need to sacrifice freedom in order to rectify the province's ills.

In retrospect, it surprises me that others were not more forceful in condemning the PQ on their philosophy and tactics.

Voting day, 20 May 1980, was sunny and warm. There was an air of concern and expectancy. There were long lines at polling stations.

* 18 February 1980.

Elderly voters brought their lawn chairs to sit in the sun while waiting to vote. Those who needed transportation to the voting booths called my committee office and volunteers drove them to the polls. There were special vehicles to transport handicapped persons. On one of these, an elderly gentleman was wheeled up and asked if he knew the voting procedure. "I vote Ciaccia," he answered. The volunteers smiled. They explained to him that this was a referendum, not an election, and that he had to answer whether he wished Quebec to separate or remain part of Canada.

During an election I visited all the polling stations, spoke to the persons in charge of the individual polling booths and encouraged my volunteers. The referendum curtailed these practices. I was prevented from continuing my usual routine by a young member of the Parti Québécois. He felt insulted when I told him he was "anti-democratic." Outraged, he complained to a group of voters who were coming out of the polls at Van Horne Elementary School. "Do you know what he said to me? He said I was not democratic." One of the older women looked at me, then looked at him and replied in a thick Jewish accent, "He's r-r-right."

In the end, the No side won by a comfortable margin of 59.56 per cent to 40.44 per cent. Canada, for the moment, was safe, but the debate over independence would continue up to the present and likely for a long time to come.

12

Another Election

Interest in the political future of Quebec was not limited to Canadians. As neighbours, Americans especially were following the province's post-referendum fortunes closely. Premier Lévesque had found it necessary to go to New York in January 1977 and address an influential audience in an attempt to assure them that the democratic process was being followed and good relations with the US would continue.

The Wall Street Journal, the voice of the American business community, gave an analysis of the situation in Quebec, much of which was accurate but reflected a pro-business Republican slant.* The headline on the piece with its one French word was a polite jab at the PQ: "Quebec Election Is Expected in November: Might Well Spell Finis for the Separatists."

It portrayed Claude Ryan as the "wan, serious former editor of the influential newspaper *Le Devoir*. He has run the Liberal Party as he ran his paper – with an iron hand." It then described the "chain-smoking" premier, whose name was a household word, as being more popular. In fact, it unwittingly explained why the Liberal party would be defeated a year later, despite favourable polls. The *Journal* then went on to say: "But personalities aren't the main issues in the race: the interests of business are a stronger consideration." How wrong they were. The mistake was to evaluate a situation through their American eyes rather than the eyes of the Quebec electorate, which was motivated by different considerations. "A Ryan administration is expected to adopt a more pro-business posture than the Parti Québécois. Its philosophy is perhaps best stated by John Ciaccia, assemblyman [even their language bore an American slant] from the district of Mount Royal and

* *The Wall Street Journal,* 10 September 1980.

opposition critic for Energy and Resources. The Liberal Party favours the non-intervention of the government in private industry."

It went great lengths to decry the expropriation of Asbestos Corporation, which had been 55 per cent owned by the American multinational General Dynamics Corporation, quoting my remarks that expropriation was not needed to create more manufacturing of asbestos products in Quebec. "Montreal's English-speaking business leaders, who once dominated Quebec's economy, complain that language and tax measures make it almost impossible to attract promising employees from branch operations outside Quebec to the city for head-office positions. So they have been quietly moving key departments out of the province, usually to Toronto."

This was not an analysis of the issues of separation, but a lament on the exodus of head offices, the increasing use of the French language, the high rate of taxation for those earning over $25,000 a year, all of which made it difficult to attract branch employees to Quebec.

Their reference to the English-speaking community of Montreal having once dominated the economy and who were complaining of the language laws must have been music to separatist ears. It confirmed what they had been saying and provided ammunition for the sovereignty cause.

Reed Scowen, the Liberal Party's spokesman for industry and commerce and finance, was quoted as saying that the Liberals were readying changes in the language and tax laws to meet business objections and to curb the business exodus. This, of course, didn't happen. The language laws were not changed until some twelve years later. And when they were, it provoked another angry reaction from the English community.

THE ELECTION OF 1981

After four years of vigilant opposition during which the PQ's attempt at separation was rejected in a referendum, elections were called for 13 April 1981. The Liberals were ahead in the polls, but, despite the reverses of the referendum, René Lévesque remained popular, more so than his opponent, Claude Ryan.

Ryan was Lévesque's opposite in terms of temperament, outlook, and background. He had been active in Catholic Action, a layman's group that promoted Catholic values, and he had studied in Rome, even spoke some Italian. It must have contributed to his character and way of thinking. Perhaps it is why he tended to be dogmatic and liked to keep stern control over the Liberal party.

He was not helped by the media. Newspaper headlines, like the one announcing his candidacy for the Liberal party – "Claude Ryan says he is guided by the hand of God" – didn't help in a society in which the Catholic Church's influence was waning.* During the campaign, unattractive pictures of him stared out at the readers – gaunt, unsmiling, and severe.

Instead of a triumphant success, the election was for the Liberals a dismal disappointment. Even its conduct was strange. Going door to door to solicit votes is useful in a riding where there is a tight race, but in Mount Royal I found other ways to reach my electors and eventually abandoned this practice. Ryan asked a group of candidates to fly to Val d'Or in the Abitibi–Témiscamingue region, to go door-to-door in the riding of the Liberal candidate. Flying in and out of there, in one day, left very little time for campaigning. Those who opened the door when we called shook their heads. They couldn't understand why someone would travel all the way from Montreal to ring doorbells to solicit votes. The Liberal candidate lost.

With his cerebral approach, Ryan could define Liberal policy, but he never won the affection of the Quebec public. The government had a program for child allowances. During the campaign Ryan announced that, in a Liberal government, child allowances would be paid not from the date of the child's birth but from its conception. Thérèse Lavoie-Roux, the Liberal critic for social affairs, who had not been consulted, was flabbergasted. Perhaps there was a theological reason for Ryan's pronouncement.

He had all the technical abilities that made him a great journalist and editor, but he did not have the talent and people skills to motivate voters. He was an intellectual, not a man of the people. By election day he had won voters over to the adage of American humourist W.C. Fields who said, "I never vote for anyone. I always vote against."

Forty-two Liberal members were elected, more than the previous election, but insufficient to form a government. We were still in opposition. The loss was a bitter one. Ryan was speechless and dejected. The Union Nationale, led by Roch La Salle, a former federal

* *Montreal Matin*, 16 September 1978.

conservative, was wiped out. Its former leader, Rodrigue Biron, had joined the Parti Québécois before the election and became a minister in Lévesque's government.

The political climate was different, and the issues had changed. We were now more involved in day-to-day business, back to the nitty-gritty of politics instead of being entirely focused on saving the country. But there were doubts about our leader, unaccustomed as we were to his style.

HOUSING, A NEW ROLE

Ryan decided what role each of us would have. I would no longer be the energy critic. For reasons unclear to me, he decided that I would be the housing critic. I did not find this very motivating, but I soldiered on.

He had recruited Pierre Fortier, an engineer who had been working in the energy sector, and made him energy critic. In theory, this seemed the right thing to do. Fortier was a decent, capable and sincere person and was knowledgeable in his field. He was a good technocrat. But Ryan forgot about the political and social aspects of the role of an opposition member. One had to go beyond being a technocrat.

At first, I felt limited by the subject of my new duties. It seemed difficult to maintain a big-picture view of government and how it affected Canadians from the perspective of merely promoting better housing – or so I thought.

I pointed out the flaws in the government's housing strategy and its administration of the Quebec Housing Corporation (QHC). The housing minister, Guy Tardif, had announced a plan to subsidize home ownership. I called the plan "wonderful propaganda" and pointed out its flaws. One needed to earn $30,000 a year to qualify – twice the average income of Quebecers at the time. The annual interest rate was 15 per cent when the plan was announced and then jumped to 20 per cent. Tardif said, almost in jest, that, "We're hoping that President Reagan finally decides that interest rates should go down."* Such dependence on America!

I pursued the operations of QHC relentlessly. Just as I had misgivings about the role assigned to me, so Tardif must have wished he had another ministry after I began my assault on the administration of the

* *La Presse*, 7 August 1981.

housing corporation. Tardif admitted that the government had not kept its promise regarding the housing plan – access to property – and blamed the rising interest rates for that fact. But it wasn't the housing plan that grabbed public attention and made headlines.

What changed everything was the corruption inside the housing corporation. A scandal erupted that contained intrigues, accusations and counter-accusations, false bids, benefits to family members, false statements, admissions and denials, dismissals and resignations, political favours, involvement of senior officials, code names and cover-ups, arrests, and convictions – all the elements of pulp fiction or tainted government. And it reached all the way into the premier's office. It began with my questioning of Tardif in a parliamentary committee about discrepancies in the annual report of the QHC. It continued during question period in the Assembly. Helped by information quietly furnished to me by disgruntled employees of the corporation, a sordid picture began to emerge. Essentially, the affair involved illegal acts within the corporation and attempts to obtain pay for political favours in the settlement of certain claims.

In 1978, Luc Cyr, who was active in the PQ, was hired by Jean-Roch Boivin, Lévesque's chief of staff, as director of the QHC division responsible for major repairs in public housing. By the following year, serious doubts had been raised about Cyr's management of the division, but nothing had been done about it. It turned out he had awarded contracts to companies in which he or his family had an interest. The auditor general had criticized the president of the QHC for his failure to report on the operations of the major repairs division and on some $12 million of expenses, pointing out blatant irregularities. For example, in Cyr's office there were letterheads for the companies that dealt with the corporation and which were used by Cyr to make invoices to be paid by the corporation. He also awarded a number of contracts without obtaining the necessary authorization to do so. On one of those contracts, $450,000 of unexplained costs had been added.

There was a dispute between a contractor who claimed $1.3 million and the QHC, which had offered to settle for $60,000. Quite a discrepancy. Tardif had asked Yvan Latouche who was working under contract to the QHC, to prepare a report on this claim. The contents of that report were devastating – the minister obtained more than he'd bargained for. (I had been sent an unsigned copy.) Latouche had invoiced the government $4,600 for preparing the report, and not only did the government refuse to pay that invoice but it also refused to renew his contract. The report was highly embarrassing to the government, revealing:

- The contractor with the claim against the QHC had offered to pay anyone in the government who could get him a settlement of his claim.
- Two individuals used code names. One called Soleil Levant (Rising Sun) was supposedly Lévesque's chief of staff. The other, called Soleil Couchant (Setting Sun), was never identified. Soleil Couchant met the contractor and told him that if he paid $50,000 he would get a "table de négociation," i.e., the government would negotiate the settlement of his claim.
- The settlement of the claim would include an additional $50,000 to be paid to Latouche to keep him quiet ("fermer la gueule de Latouche").

The contractor had met with Boivin and told him that he agreed to pay to the two Suns. A date had even been set for the negotiations – October 1980. Meanwhile, Jean Foisy, a former special counsel to Boivin, now working for Tardif, informed the minister in mid-October 1980 of the existence of the $50,000 demand to establish the *table de negociation*. Tardif was furious and called Boivin, asking him what was going on. Tardif suspended Foisy. In 1981 Lévesque met Foisy, apologized for having had a bad opinion of him and asked him to run as a candidate in the riding of Saint Laurent in northwest Montreal.

During committee hearings, Tardif referred to Latouche as a "master blackmailer" even while, incredibly, he admitted that "an offer would have been made by Boivin" but that no bribes had been paid!

But it must be stated that there was no misconduct on the part of the minister. As a matter of fact, I think that he was as disturbed as I was about the behaviour of the people involved. Some of his answers to my questions almost implicated some of the people involved.

As all of this was coming to light, I repeatedly asked for a public inquiry. During question period in the Assembly, I claimed that the government's refusal to hold one was a cover-up. I reached for all the possible reasons to trigger one, perhaps going a bit too far, even resurrecting the unfortunate accident, five years earlier, in which a car Lévesque had been driving struck and killed Edgar Trottier, a homeless man. I asked Justice Minister Marc-André Bédard to follow the same procedure as had been used then and to deposit the police report and the Department of Justice's analysis on the activities of the QHC. Bédard explained that the premier's accident had been an exceptional case because "when you speak of the PM you aren't speaking of an ordinary citizen but of one who has a very particular responsibility. That is why at the time I adopted that attitude."

Bédard was very precise and shrewd. He affirmed that there was no evidence of fraud at the QHC because no payments had been made. My own legal background made me ask, "but what about other criminal acts such as corruption or attempted corruption?" His reply was that he didn't bring criminal actions on the basis of a newspaper article. I replied that the minister's answer meant that a public admission by a civil servant has no value. To deflect my question, Bédard accused me of demagoguery, applying the adage that the best defence is a good offence.

In the end, he refused to call a public inquiry or furnish a report on the affair.

But the relentless questioning over a period of months had an effect. It was not done just to cause embarrassment or to create a scandal where there was none; there was a basis to the accusations made, and there were consequences. Criminal charges were brought against Luc Cyr, and he was convicted. The image of the government had been severely tarnished. Until then, the PQ had had a reputation for honesty and integrity. During its first mandate, to avoid even the semblance of impropriety it had created restrictive laws on political funding, limiting amounts that an individual could give and forbidding contributions by corporations. With the QHC scandal, this was gone forever. It was, effectively, the beginning of the end of the Lévesque government.

13

A Constitutional Quandary

Prime Minister Trudeau changed the political landscape of Canada. He fought to keep the country intact and to promote the advantages of being Canadian. He played a leading role in the referendum. He also tried to make the rest of Canada aware of how Quebecers felt and why the province should be accommodated. By making both French and English official languages of Canada he was trying to give Quebec a sense of belonging and being respected.

There were times, however, when Trudeau's objectives overlooked the traditional interests of Quebec. One of these concerned the constitution of Canada – then the British North America Act. It was a colonial act, which stipulated that any changes required the consent of the British crown. Trudeau wanted to repatriate the act, make changes, and provide a formula whereby further changes would be made in Canada by Canadians, eliminating the role of the monarchy.

Traditionally, it was accepted that no changes could be made to the constitution without the consent of Quebec, even though the changes would need the final approval of London. Unfortunately, Quebec had a government that still wanted political independence, even though it had lost the referendum, which made it unlikely that it would back any move that might strengthen the Canadian federation. This did not deter Trudeau. He was determined to make the constitution a fully Canadian document, which would confirm Canada's complete independence in the world.

The provincial premiers were invited to Ottawa in November 1981, to discuss the repatriation and other proposed changes to the constitution. Having lost the referendum, René Lévesque could not refuse to participate. He was stuck between a rock and a hard place. But Lévesque was an astute politician. Before going to Ottawa, he presented a motion in the National Assembly reiterating the traditional position and rights of Quebec and asking that no changes be made to the constitution without the consent of Quebec. He wanted the entire National Assembly's support.

Now it was the provincial Liberals who were between a rock and a hard place. Ryan decided to support the motion and ordered all if us to vote in favour. After all, this was the traditional position of Quebec. And thus began another one of my nightmares. Should I support the resolution of a PQ government on the constitution and vote yes, or should I defy my leader and vote no?

I reflected on this. I knew I had a big problem. Two of my fellow Liberal MNAs, Bill Cusano and Cosmo Macioccia, came to see me and asked what they should do. I suggested that they make up their own minds. "Are you crazy?" they shrieked, "The whole Italian community will crucify us if we don't vote like you." Others came to see me – my friend George Holland for one. He knew the quandary I was in. Even a journalist wanted to know what I would do. At one point I broke down into tears in front of them.

I finally made my decision and called Claude Ryan. I told him that I had made a decision. I had called my family, my wife and son, and told them. I would vote no. I could sense Ryan's anger on the line. There were eight other Liberal MNAs who had also decided to vote no. The next day, when the motion was to be debated in the National Assembly, I was told by Ryan's chief of staff that I would not be allowed to speak. "Tell Mr Ryan, that if I can't speak in the National Assembly, I will give a press conference and tell the world what I think," I said.

I was given two minutes to speak. This is what I said:

This motion, which at first glance seems harmless and completely sensible, appears to me after examination to present some very serious problems.

It is not simply about defending the constitutional conventions and rights of the National Assembly, for, on this point, we are all in agreement. If this motion had been presented by a government led by a Jean Lesage, a Daniel Johnson, leader of the Union Nationale, by a Robert Bourassa, or by a government led by Claude Ryan, I would gladly support it.

I agree that the constitutional initiative of the federal government in its present form should not be presented unilaterally. But that is not the only intent of this motion. What is in play is the fundamental and legitimate right of the people of Quebec to take advantage of changes to the Canadian constitution that could benefit them without resort to a government that wishes to separate Quebec from Canada and which has no interest in constitutional changes undertaken within the framework of Canadian federalism. This is the real intent of this motion.

We understand the objectives of the Parti Québécois and we know that it will do all in its power to ignore this aspect of the negotiation. The government that has told us and told us often that it will continue to promote its objective of independence will not negotiate in good faith for the renewal of Canadian federalism. We know also, we who come from minority communities, just as French Canadians themselves do, that the Parti Québécois in no way desires to enshrine a charter of rights that would prevent all governments, be they federal or provincial, from abusing its powers to coerce its citizens.

Yet more importantly is the trap this motion represents, that which gives a green light to the Parti Québécois to advance and promote its separatist agenda in the face of accommodations that might be offered by the federal government. As such, the motion before us permits the Parti Québécois to choose a way in which to amend the constitution that ultimately would permit a province to separate from Canada, and this is not acceptable."[*]

Effectively, Lévesque went to Ottawa while the final changes were made to the plan to amend the constitution, but he was not present at the meeting that concluded the deal, either because of his own refusal or a deliberate attempt to exclude him because of the intransigence that might result from negotiating with a separatist.

The constitution was repatriated and we were all invited to the signing ceremony to be held 17 April 1982, in Ottawa in the presence of Queen Elizabeth. I did not go out of respect for Quebec's position since it was not a signatory to the constitution. My constituents were furious and let me know it. Incidentally, my riding, Mount Royal, was also represented federally by Pierre Trudeau. We represented the same constituents.

[*] *Les Grands Debats Parlementaires*, 1792–1992, 40.

CLAUDE RYAN BIDS ADIEU

Ever since the election loss, Claude Ryan had been having a hard time keeping the confidence of the caucus. Some were still loyal to him, but most were not. And those who were not were vocal. Some even spoke out in public, sometimes viciously. One member, Gilles Rocheleau from the Ottawa region – he later left the provincial party and was elected federally for the Bloc Québécois – openly made unflattering and embarrassing remarks, and, of course, the media never missed an opportunity to report them.

I was chagrined for Ryan. At a public meeting of Liberal supporters where I was called to speak, I criticized those who publicly embarrassed our leader. I asked for restraint and respect. Claude Ryan and his wife were present. They interpreted my statement as a support for his continued leadership. It wasn't. It was a support for human dignity.

The situation got worse. The general council of the Liberal Party, with representatives from every riding across the province, was coming up. At this meeting, it was the practice to vote on the confidence of the party in its leader. Normally, the vote was positive. However, this time the vote was a problem. If the convention voted against the leader, it would be not only a repudiation but a public humiliation as well. The stakes were high.

Claude Ryan tried to stave off his critics while also looking for support. On occasion he was deceived by colleagues who assured him of their support but would tell others that they were against him. This gave him a false sense of security. Some party members asked me to speak to him and let him know the stark reality of the situation – invite him to my house and tell him that he did not have sufficient support to get a vote of confidence at the forthcoming convention.

I was prepared to speak to Claude Ryan but was uncomfortable about inviting him to my house. I happened to live in a house that is not your average dwelling. I was fortunate to have acquired it when practicing law. I didn't have the heart to invite Ryan there to tell him he must resign as leader because I thought it would further humiliate him – here is this person in a palatial home telling him, who lived modestly in a duplex on Laurier Avenue, that he must resign as leader of the party. The lord of the manor dictating to the commoner. Fortunately, by some coincidence, Ryan invited me to his house to talk about his leadership. It was the same home where years before others and I had tried to convince him to run for leader. Life is full of ironies.

I remember going into the room that served as his library, sitting next to him, in one of the most painful meetings that I have ever had with another individual. He told me he was convinced that if I supported him, he could regain the confidence of the party at the convention. He referred to my pivotal role as a spokesman not only of the English community but also as representative of the minorities. He seemed to have an exaggerated view of my power. I think that it was wishful thinking, a refusal to face reality, a grasping at straws. Here I was, in his home, sitting next to him, not only being asked to support him, but being told that I was the only one who could save him. This made my task worse. I took my courage in my hands and told him that I did not have the power he thought I had and that it would be better for him to resign. I lamely suggested that one couldn't predict the future and by leaving now, honourably, there might be an opportunity for him to return.

He looked at me, severely, and dismissively told me, "Alors, il n'y a plus rien à dire." ("So then, there is no more to be said.") Grim.

I did not want to leave it there. I stayed and continued talking to him. He calmed down and a few weeks later, on 10 August 1982, prior to the meeting of the general council, he announced his resignation as head of the Liberal Party of Quebec.

14

The Hearings on the Damage to the James Bay Project

It all started with a newspaper article. In 1983 a great drama was played out in the Assembly, but to set the stage, we have to go back almost a decade.

In 1974, during the Bourassa administration, striking workers at James Bay had gone on a rampage and caused $32 million in damages to the premier's *projet du siècle*. The government took legal action against the striking unions for the damages. After the PQ was elected, the $31-million lawsuit was settled for $200,000. The year was 1979, just prior to the referendum.

On 20 February of that year, Fernand Lalonde, the Liberal member from Marguerite Bourgeoys in Montreal, had asked the premier if the settlement had been reached with the involvement of his office. Lévesque had told the National Assembly that neither he nor his office were involved in the settlement: "pas du tout, ni de près ni de loin" ("not at all, neither from near or from far"). He said the James Bay Energy Corporation – now, under Bill 101, called the Société d'énergie de la Baie James (SEBJ) – and Hydro-Québec had made the decision. "Ça ne nous regarde pas, c'est leur droit." ("It doesn't concern us; it's their right.")

Five years later, on 17 March 1983, *La Presse* made a direct and shocking accusation: Lévesque's statement had misled the National Assembly, and Jean-Roch Boivin, his chief of staff, had negotiated with the lawyers. The article went into the details of discussions in the premier's office that led to the settlement sum of $200,000.*

* Among *La Presse*'s headlines that day were, "The wrecking of James Bay: the out of court settlement," "Lévesque has misled the National Assembly," and "Jean-Roch Boivin negotiated with the lawyers."

Another headline screamed that for a meagre compensation of $200,000, the SEBJ had disbursed $800,000 in legal fees. Details were given to show how the premier had badgered those involved into agreeing on the settlement. Lévesque asked *La Presse* to retract its statements. It refused. He sued for libel and claimed damages of $900,000, which, if awarded, he said he would turn over to charity.

Never doubt the power of the press. All the newspapers pounced on the *La Presse* articles and started their own investigations. Statements were obtained from three prominent persons involved in the lawsuit. Louis Laberge, the head of the Fédération des travailleurs et travailleuses du Quebec (FTQ), the province's largest trade union, admitted that he had asked Boivin to withdraw the lawsuit.[*]

Hydro-Québec President Roland Giroux and Robert Boyd, then its vice-president and later president, both confirmed that the premier had put pressure on them to settle. Boyd had refused, saying that the lawsuit could be won and that Hydro-Québec could not afford to settle a claim that caused damages of $32 million. He maintained that Lévesque gave him an ultimatum; settle or he (the premier) would take the means to settle.[†] Giroux said that the settlement was imposed on Hydro-Québec and that it was done in the premier's office.[‡] These two highly placed officials from the largest corporation in the province obviously did not want to take the blame for the ludicrous settlement.

Lévesque denied the statements of Giroux and of Boyd in the Assembly and mocked our indignation.

The term "Jamesgate" with its comparison to Richard Nixon and Watergate appeared in the media. Fernand Lalonde, the Montreal Liberal member, asked for a parliamentary inquiry to examine what had really happened and threatened to lead all the Liberal members out of the National Assembly if it were not granted. In a show of bravura, Lévesque not only agreed but also suspended the restrictive rule that limited the questioning of a witness to twenty minutes. The time period for questioning became unlimited and could, and did, go on sometimes for days. The parliamentary inquiry, to which I was appointed, was thus instantly transformed into an American-style public Senate hearing. The premier wanted to show he had nothing to hide. (His confidence would come back to haunt him.) He also said that if the

---

[*] *La Presse*, 18 March 1983.
[†] *Le Soleil*, 22 March 1983.
[‡] *Le Soleil*, 18 March 1983.

committee found that he lied, he would quit. It was an easy statement to make since the government had a majority on the committee.

The hearings were a daily drama that continued for two months involving lengthy questioning, emotional outbursts, and accusations, weeping witnesses, stunning surprises. They had the elements of a courtroom drama, with public opinion as the judge and jury.

From the outset, the hearings were more shocking than the newspaper headlines they produced. Claude Laliberté, the director of the SEBJ was more specific about what Lévesque had said at the fateful meeting of 1 February, alleging that the premier had threatened to settle the dispute himself if they couldn't come to an agreement. But he claimed that this had not influenced his decision. This admission only made it worse for Lévesque. For his part, Roland Giroux, Hydro-Québec president, who had indicated that a settlement of $20 million would be acceptable, later testified that he said nothing after this statement by Lévesque.

People were glued to their televisions, following the drama as it unfolded. My half-glasses, over which I would peer to question witnesses, became my trademark. A young man from Alma, in the Lac St Jean region, told a journalist that the television set was always on in the insurance office where he worked so that they could follow what was going on. We were stopped on the streets, congratulated in restaurants, and telephoned with advice from people across Quebec. When my fellow Liberals invited me to speak in their ridings, I would put on my half-glasses, and the crowd would clap and roar. One citizen accosted me and told me to stop; he couldn't go to sleep at night until he had seen the entire proceedings on TV. It became Quebec's new soap opera.

The new rules were a trial lawyer's dream. No time limit, no procedural restrictions, anyone could be treated as a hostile witness. You could speak and question for hours, even days. Witnesses were put through the wringer. The premier did not foresee these consequences when he so magnanimously allowed the suspension of committee rules. His regret probably was the cause of his unusually abusive reactions and name-calling. He accused me of acting like a "small-time crown attorney" using "Lilliputian" tactics.

I had an excellent researcher, Jean Larivière, who not only did his homework on the background and information about each witness but also advised me on how to question them. On one occasion, I wanted to challenge the veracity of statements of a witness, Germain Jutras, a lawyer for Rosaire Beaule, one of the union attorneys. No, said Jean. You have a very expressive face. Just indicate that you don't believe him. This will have a better effect on the journalists. I followed his advice and made a grimace and smiled when the witness testified that Beaule did not speak of the legal proceedings with Jean-Roch Boivin during the time that the settlement was being negotiated. Larivière was right. A journalist reported, "This answer caused deputy Ciaccia to grimace and smile knowingly, suggesting 'I don't believe a word you are saying.'" It was exactly what I had hoped for.

With Lucien Saulnier, a member of the board of SEBJ and a chairman of the executive committee of the city of Montreal under Mayor Jean Drapeau, my questions would often be longer than his answers. He was an experienced politician and a wily one. He used the considerable talents he had acquired in protecting his former superior, Drapeau, to now attempt to shield Lévesque. However, my persistent, admittedly annoying, questioning brought out contradictions in his testimony. He was kept on the stand all the first day of his testimony and asked to come back the next day. One of the important factors was the 1 February meeting in the premier's office during which Lévesque had threatened to force a settlement on those present. Saulnier couldn't deny the meeting in Lévesque's office or what was purportedly said there, since it had been confirmed by another witness. He therefore tried to minimize it or render its effect unimportant by saying that the corporation had already decided on 23 and 30 January to settle the case.

But there were too many unanswered questions that undermined Saulnier's position. He was questioned all day and asked to come back the next day.

He couldn't explain why he would settle a $32 million lawsuit for $200,000. He couldn't explain why the corporation had to consult with the premier on 6 February or why on the same day the board gave a mandate to explore a settlement if the decision to settle had already been made. He did not know that the attorneys for both parties and two members of the board had had contact with the premier's office. He admitted that he did not find this normal. In short, Saulnier did not come out of the inquiry with the same credibility he had when he went into it.

The questioning was so tough that Yves Duhaime, a PQ member on the committee who was ably defending his premier, was furious with me and said my method of questioning was vicious and insulting. He asked that I stop monkeying around (*niaser*) with the witness and accused me of conducting a police-style interrogation where one tries to force the answers wanted. "Your method is an insult to intelligence ... there's always a goddamn limit."* He added that many of his former colleagues from the Quebec Bar were scandalized by what was going on at the committee hearings. To which one journalist added that Duhaime did not specify whether the former colleagues were Péquistes or Liberals.

Hydro-Québec president Roland Giroux, who was ill, came to testify against the advice of his doctor. The meeting of 1 February did not change his mind. Neither Boyd nor Giroux wanted an out-of-court settlement. I knew these people. I had negotiated the James Bay settlement with them.

Rosaire Beaule was a lawyer who represented the AFL-CIO, the American federation that was parent to the Quebec trade unions representing the James Bay workers. He had been a member of the Parti Québécois and had practised law with Jean-Roch Boivin, Levesque's chief of staff. He was appointed legal counsel for the unions on the recommendation of Yves Gauthier a former member of the Parti Québécois and now advisor to Levesque. And, now he was called as a government witness, supporting Levesque's claim that the government had not imposed the settlement. You get the picture.

He was a key player in the legal proceedings against the unions, and he was the witness I kept longest on the stand. He also turned out to be the most hostile of the government witnesses. He had probably thought he would come in, tell his story, and leave. If so, he miscalculated. As with Boyd, the meeting of 1 February did not change his mind – neither wanted an out-of-court settlement.

My questioning of Rosaire Beaule was also a model of confrontation between a witness and questioner. He was determined to protect Lévesque. I was determined to obtain the truth. Although a conflict between us was inevitable, it took on enormous, unforeseeable proportions. Beaule had obvious intent to also protect his former law partner, Jean-Roch Boivin, and Lévesque made him give answers that were not credible. For example, Beaule admitted going to Boivin's office but said that he did not discuss the legal proceedings with him! When I asked him to divulge the legal fees he had received, he refused on the grounds that, "I have the right to my private life." I reminded him that he had

* "Votre façon de procéder est une insulte à l'intelligence ... Il y'a toujours une maudite limite."

been paid with public, not private, funds and that he had to answer. He was finally forced to admit that he had received $300,000 in legal fees in a settlement where the government received only $200,000.

My persistent questioning of this witness rattled him and made him say things that seemed to confirm the accusations we had made against the premier. I asked him for a certain document – a letter he had written on 2 February 1979 to Boivin on behalf of his client, the International Union of Operating Engineers, giving the reasons why he thought his client was not responsible for the damages. He said that he had destroyed it. When? The day before he came to testify. But, he added, the contents had been included in another letter that he had sent. He spoke of a meeting held on 18 January with two lawyers from the AFL-CIO who had come from Washington to meet with Boivin to discuss a possible settlement. He had a "feeling" that this move was studied "with sympathy." When I asked him on what he based his feeling, he couldn't answer. He was trying to prepare the ground for the acceptance of the settlement by the energy corporation without the pressures from the premier.

I linked the offer of settlement by the unions to the fact that the corporation had not yet given its own lawyers the mandate to negotiate. Obviously, someone else – for instance, the premier and his staff – was directing the settlement. Otherwise why would they meet?

Taken aback, Beaule bridled and asked for the protection of the committee chairman, the PQ's Jean-Pierre Jolivet. He complained about the way I was questioning him, that I was violating the elementary principles of justice. The Péquiste committee member Duhaime complained that my questioning implied that the witness had behaved unprofessionally (*actes dérogatoires de sa profession*) during the meetings in the winter of 1978–79, which led to the settlement. I couldn't have phrased it better!

He said that he would present a motion the following Tuesday to put an end to the committee and to liberate Beaule from further questioning.* After two days in the spotlight, either as a diversionary tactic or because he had been cornered, Beaule burst out that he was tired: "I have been hassled by the deputy, Ciaccia. I've had enough. I need a

* This was an idle threat. He would have needed the blessing of the premier who could not allow this – it would have been perceived as a cover-up and would have done more harm to the government.

little rest." Beaule invoked the Charter of Rights, assisted by a lawyer who also made a motion asking that John Ciaccia stop the abusive questioning of her client. Jolivet refused. To his credit, even though Jolivet was a member of the PQ government, he acted objectively as the Chairman of the Commission and applied the rules. And the rules did not give Beaule the right to ask that I stop questioning him. Beaule knew that he couldn't answer. He knew that if he told the truth it would incriminate Lévesque. That's why he objected to my probing and delving into his answers. Duhaime said he would present a motion to put an end to the commission[*]

The hearings resumed the following Tuesday and Beaule was still on the stand. At one point, he defended his position by stating that he would repeat his answer since Ciaccia had probably not understood it the first time "because of the language barrier" – a reference to the fact that I was of Italian origin, a non-francophone. The chairman immediately brought him to order saying that he would not tolerate racist remarks. The next day, Beaule tried to extricate himself by explaining that he had not meant the remark in a racist way. When I had asked him what he meant by saying that he (Beaule) took a remark "with a grain of salt," he assumed my grasp of French was limited. I thanked him for his explanation, but commented that "I take your explanation with a grain of salt," indicating I knew full well what the expression meant.[†]

Denise Roy, a lawyer who represented Beaule at the hearings, complained that Ciaccia had questioned her client's honesty and integrity. She made a motion that I be stopped from questioning her client. Ciaccia was "using a strategy which leads the public to believe that the witness is hiding part of the truth."[‡]

Hallelujah! What a revealing statement! Moreover, I thought, if Beaule really had nothing to hide, why did he need a lawyer to be at his side during the hearings?

Chairman Jolivet refused the motion. Under the rules, I could continue questioning him.

---

[*] Beaule also threatened to sue me for defamation, but it never happened.

[†] "Je vous remercie de vos propos, M. Beaule, mais je les prends avec un grain de sel."

[‡] *Journal des debats*, 29 April 1983.

There were reactions to my bickering with this witness and with Duhaime's threat to put an end to the proceedings. A front-page headline in *La Presse* read "La querelle entre Ciaccia et Beaule envenime les travaux."* Other journalists insisted that the proceedings had to continue.

The reaction to Duhaime's threat was too negative, and he didn't proceed. Had he done so, it would have been an admission of fear of the truth and guilt of the government.

I also questioned Pierre Laferrière, a former member of the Parti Québécois and now a member of the board of SEBJ, who broke down and began to sob after a lengthy interrogation when he was asked to recollect his conversation prior to the settlement at a lunch with Yves Gauthier, an aide to Lévesque. I was somewhat pitiless, telling him not to make us cry. I was surprised when, during my questioning of Yves Gauthier, he too unexpectedly broke down. The proceedings were suspended to allow him to regain his composure.

TRUTH OR CONSEQUENCES

The rules of the National Assembly were severe. If a member accused another of not telling the truth and then did not prove the accusation, he could be ejected from the Assembly. The accusation had to be made in the National Assembly. Statements made to the media would not be enough to invoke these penalties.

In early June, Premier Lévesque appeared before the parliamentary committee for questioning. The verbal jousting between the Liberal questioners and the premier produced some interesting statements. He didn't admit any responsibility in forcing the settlement. He even went so far as to say that he was surprised that they had settled for only $200,000, adding that they should have obtained at least the amount of their legal fees ($800,000).[†]

All but one of the Liberal members questioned Lévesque. Imagine, the premier of Quebec, on the witness stand for hours, answering often probing questions about his own conduct. The following exchange, between Liberal committee member André Bourbeau and the premier gives an idea of the atmosphere and tactics at the hearings. During his session with Lévesque, Bourbeau had asked a question, then hesitated:

---

* "The quarrel between Ciaccia and Beaule poisons the proceedings."
† *Journal des debats*, B4493.

BOURBEAU: Is it then, prime minister, yes or no, your office that considered the decision?

LÉVESQUE: In the end, I don't know that; you are ending your comment with a question?

BOURBEAU: I am still making my comments.

LÉVESQUE: Yes, but are you asking me a question?

BOURBEAU: Not at all. I'm not asking a question.

LÉVESQUE: Ah! Ah! Excuse me. It's because you are looking at me straight in the face and asking: "Is it that the prime minister ——?"

BOURBEAU: Yes, but I'm making remarks and looking at you.

LÉVESQUE: No. All right. Excuse me.

BOURBEAU: You don't have any objection to me looking at you?

LÉVESQUE: You know, I'm not more of a lawyer than you, so the both of us can get mixed up.*

Bourbeau's statements and attitude showed a certain lack of respect for the premier. On the other hand, Lévesque's answer was a subtle and ironic put down of Bourbeau who was a notary. It can be demeaning to tell a notary that he is not a lawyer.

There seemed to be a complete dichotomy between the statements made by other key witnesses and the premier's version, even without considering the contradiction between Lévesque's statements and the version given to the media by other witnesses not allowed by the government to testify. Not allowed to testify because the government didn't want its version of what happened to be contradicted.

I was very deferential in my questioning. At one point during the difficult part of asking Lévesque to recollect what had happen I said, "I am aware that I am questioning the premier."

After having heard the premier's answers, his version and interpretation of the facts, I believed that it was time for me to state what I believed. I summarized what I thought the premier had been trying to do and came to an accusatory conclusion.

Mr President, you have certainly heard the adage that the best defence is a strong offence. That's the course the premier has taken; however in this case the tactic does not change what happened, nor does it change the truth. The facts will not be changed by attacking *La Presse*, the witnesses who were not heard, or the members of this committee. The truth will not be changed by reconstructing an

* *Journal des debats*, B4515.

explanation today to answer for what happened on 20 February. It won't be by the tactics of diversion, by evoking the sad memory of the wrecking of James Bay that will change the truth. And the truth, Mr President, is that there were two parallel operations going on at the same time: that of the SEBJ and of Jean-Roch Boivin who had been given his orders by the premier.

For these reasons well put forward by my colleagues, I am convinced Mr President, that the truth is that the premier misled the Assembly with his answers of 20 February 1979.*

Fernand Lalonde was a shrewd parliamentarian. Rather than openly accuse the premier in the National Assembly of misleading its members, he decided to present a parliamentary motion. All eight Liberals who sat on the committee were party to the motion.

It asked, in effect, for recognition that the premier had mislead the National Assembly. This was unprecedented and, said *La Presse*, "probably unique in British parliamentary history."† All eight Liberal members held a press conference and said that they were ready to put their seats on the line. "Our fate is now in the hands of the government," I said. "It's a risk that we are taking, but I am ready, and my colleagues also, to resign if necessary." I had already gone that far with my speech in the Assembly on 3 June when I clearly stated that the premier had misled it. Curiously, nothing had happened. The government had not made a move against me.

The motion placed the onus on the Speaker, Richard Guay. An acceptance by him to hear the motion implied recognition that Lévesque could have, or had, misled the Assembly. In a well researched statement, Guay started by describing how the recognition of the privileges of the House and its members are rooted in the origins of British parliamentary laws. He quoted authoritative writers: Luther Cushing (1856) and Erskine May, whose work was first published in 1844 and which became the Parliamentary bible. He cited the nineteenth edition, which, incidentally, was published in 1976, the year the PQ was first elected. Then he referred to a noted Quebec authority, Louis-Phillipe Geoffrion, who wrote one of the most exhaustive sets of standing orders in the Commonwealth, and quoted him saying that when a member denies an accusation (in this case of having

* *Journal des debats*, 3 June 1983, B4553.
† 7 June 1983.

misled the Assembly) one must accept his word. "So I take it that under no circumstances can we put in doubt the word of an elected representative."* He made a distinction between "leading in error" and "lying." We were not accusing the premier of lying.

And then the pièce de resistance.

Speaker Guay cited the Profumo affair in Britain. In 1963, John Profumo, the British secretary of state for war, was forced to resign after lying about his affair with Christine Keeler, the reputed mistress of an alleged Soviet spy. After first denying, in the House of Commons, "any impropriety whatsoever" and threatening to issue writs for libel and slander if the accusation were repeated outside the House, he confessed that he had lied to the House and then resigned from cabinet. Curiously, a sexual scandal in Britain served as a reason not to accept a motion of blame against the premier of Quebec. Ah, the anglos can sometimes come to the rescue of beleaguered Québécois.

There were consequences to this very lengthy, sometime amusing, often acrimonious affair. There was obviously no official guilty verdict against the premier, and perhaps that should not have been expected since a majority of the members on the committee were from the government. But the fallout was serious.

Pressure can do strange things to people. Lévesque had always been gentlemanly and respectful of others, although capable of strong emotional reactions, which he expressed in colourful but impeccable language. Now he resorted to name-calling and insults. Speaking on the radio station CJAD, he called the Liberals "bums" and "jerks."† Liberals were "une bande de petits ayatollahs." We were a gang of "bums et de minables" ("shabby and disreputable"). He threatened to muzzle us.

One Sherbrooke newspaper, *La Tribune*, wrote: It is Mr Lévesque himself who has provided a victory, at least temporarily, to the Liberals by his unjustified attacks on *La Presse* and the media in general by way of his threats to muzzle them, and secondly by lowering himself to insults by calling the Liberals a 'stinking band.' "

Everyone was stupefied. This was a Lévesque that they had never seen. The housing scandal had been the beginning of the end of his government. These hearings were the nail in the coffin. What had started

---

* "J'en deduis donc qu'en aucune circonstance on n'a a mettre en doute la parole d'un deputé."
† *Journal de Quebec*, 20 April 1983.

as a breath of fresh political air after the tainted Bourassa years became another example of discreditable behaviour. Ironically, in the next election, the Parti Québécois would be defeated by Bourassa, the man who had so ignominiously lost to the PQ earlier. It was the vengeance of the humiliated.

A RUN AT THE LEADERSHIP

Although Gérard D. Levesque was an effective interim leader, we still had to find a permanent replacement after the resignation of Claude Ryan. A leadership convention was scheduled for the fall of 1983.

René Lévesque was in his second term. Our opposition had been hard hitting and effective and had weakened the government. The Quebec Housing Corporation scandal and the parliamentary committee on the James Bay lawsuit had taken their toll. There was no question that the government was on the ropes. The leadership convention took on a new importance.

There were several hopefuls among the sitting members. One was Daniel Johnson, whose father had been premier for the Union Nationale. Daniel's brother, Pierre-Marc Johnson, would also be premier for a short time with the Parti Québécois after the resignation of Lévesque. A family of premiers, who managed to span the spectrum of Quebec politics by representing all three parties. Pierre Paradis, a very able parliamentarian and lawyer, who had also previously been a member of the Union Nationale before he ran as a Liberal in Brome-Missisquoi in 1980, was another candidate.

And then there was me. When a person is going though emotional stress, he will sometimes make unusual and inexplicable decisions. To try to replace something lost? To soothe wounded feelings? Sometimes the unconsciously chosen cure is worse than the loss. Such was my case.

On a warm summer day in 1983, I invited a friend to my house, a journalist from the *Montreal Gazette*. We sat outside and I spoke to him of my plan to enter the leadership of the Liberal Party. I was more than candid, maybe naively so. I told him I was not convinced I could win. But I would try. In any event I thought that it would be good for the system if a non-francophone were a candidate. We continued to chat.

He reported our conversation, held in my Beaconsfield backyard, writing that there are those who enter leadership races to win and those who want only to prove a point. This was a harmful article for anyone running for the leadership. It certainly put a crimp on possible supporters. A friend and strong supporter of mine, George Holland, after reading the article, said to me, "John, I thought he was your friend!" "So did I," I replied.

But I carried on. My colleague Bill Cusano, who had first been elected in 1981, became my campaign manager. I'm sure that this was done out of devotion and loyalty to a compatriot who was born a few kilometres from Bill's birthplace, Sepino, Campobasso, in Italy.

The contestants were invited to a debate before the youth wing of the party in St Jean on the South Shore. The reactions of the critics to my presentation were respectful if not glowing. I had spoken as a "bon père de famille." The critics favoured the performance of Daniel Johnson. Robert Bourassa seemed to be bored – he was very confident of winning – while Paradis was viewed as somewhat dull.

As the days went on, I became less confident. The *Gazette* article had not helped. The more disturbing aspect of my candidacy was not the fact that I didn't have enough support to win but that the support that I was getting was mainly from minorities. This would defeat the purpose of why I chose to run – to bring communities together, to encourage an open society, where all of its citizens, from whatever linguistic group or origin, would be fully accepted and able to freely and openly contribute their talents. Support coming only from minorities would not only defeat that purpose but also would marginalize them and highlight the differences in our society. I would be hurting the people I was trying to help.

I decided to withdraw and held a press conference to explain my decision. Many were sceptical – a press conference to announce you're not running? I could not however limit the press conference to say only that my candidacy would cause more harm than good to the minorities. I was not a one-issue candidate. I had to show that I was a viable contender and give the elements of my political beliefs, explain what I would do as a leader. I said I believed that the interests of Quebec went beyond its borders. Federalism not only had to be renewed but was also a vehicle to promote the francophone fact in all of Canada, for cultural and economic reasons. Quebec should take a leadership role in making the necessary changes for a new federalism. I also proposed that Quebec should extend its influence throughout North America where all Quebecers, especially the young, could succeed. I was disturbed about Montreal's decline as an international centre and proposed steps to create a climate to attract international investment. I spoke of improving labour relations, increasing productivity, and economic growth.

I deplored the fact that our bureaucracy had become the overseer and not the servant of our society and suggested that the state was not an end in itself but a means to improve the lot of the individual.

Of all the commentaries about my withdrawal, the most positive and gratifying was an article in *La Presse* by Jean-Guy Dubuc, headlined "La qualité du non de M. John Ciaccia" ("The quality of Mr John Ciaccia's no"). "His analysis of the reality of Quebec, of its deficiencies and needs, should inspire many: his perspective is fair and his interpretation couldn't be more comprehensive ... It doesn't require a lot of judgment to appreciate the wisdom and pertinence of this decision."

I was relieved and gratified that my message had been understood and accepted.

The leadership convention was not too far away and Robert Bourassa was clearly in the lead. It would have been easy for me support him. However, I feared that this would make me look like an opportunist, backing the clear winner. I stayed neutral. At the convention, Claude Ryan and I were the only parliamentarians who did not vote for any of the candidates.

DOUBTS AND FEARS

There were times when I questioned myself, my motives, and the direction of my life. It happened when I left my law practice, and then it happened again in 1984, after eight years in opposition. I felt like the Czech dissident writer Vaclav Havel who later became president, when he said, "I knew that between me and those around me there was an invisible wall, and behind that wall ... I felt alone, inferior, lost, ridiculed ... Sometimes I even wonder whether the original reason I began writing, or why I try to do anything at all, was simply this fundamental experience of not belonging."* Similar thoughts were rattling me. What was I was doing – and why? I was overcome by feelings of discouragement and loneliness, of emptiness. In spite of my aggressiveness as a politician, the sense of insecurity that had plagued me earlier in life had returned. I didn't feel accepted. The only times that I had felt confident were my days in Indian Affairs. Those were the thoughts and feelings that went through my mind at 3 a.m. on the night of 30 October 1984.

I turned to my heavily underlined copy of Dag Hammarskjöld's *Markings* for comfort and guidance. To me, he was the paradigm of

* Vaclav Havel, *Disturbing the Peace* (Vintage, 1991), 5.

the dedicated public servant, one who had died in the pursuit of his duties.* Whenever I felt discouraged, weak and uncertain, I would turn to Hammarskjöld. "Thy will be done – to let the inner take precedence over the outer, the soul over the world – wherever this may lead you to." I felt that he was speaking to me, and he made me aware of the importance of inner strength, of our responsibility to others. "Goodness is so simple: always live for others, never to seek one's own advantage."† And further inspiration, from Havel: "It is my responsibility to emphasize, again and again, the moral origin of all politics, to stress the significance of moral values and standards in all spheres."‡

These were words that sustained me as moved into the next chapter of my political life.

OTTAWA OR QUEBEC?

In 1984 Pierre Elliott Trudeau's departure from politics marked the end of an era. He came to his last public meeting in the riding we shared federally and provincially, and we had a reception for him where I was the guest speaker. He was held in awe by all his constituents. I noted at the time that some leaders knew history, but he had made history.

Although we both represented the same electoral turf, my contacts with him had been quite limited. I recalled the cabinet meeting where, as Jean Chrétien's assistant deputy minister, I had presented the new policy for Native affairs and his astute handling of the changes being proposed. During the debates on Bill 22, I had tried to get in touch with him but failed. I understand his avoidance of this issue. It was a matter of provincial jurisdiction, and he shrewdly avoided involvement. I was a distant supporter of Trudeau, but I had my disagreements with him over the constitutional question.

After the meeting, Dahlia Wood, Trudeau's chief organizer, who was named to the Senate, asked me to replace Trudeau and become the new federal Liberal representative for Mount Royal. I politely declined.

* Swedish-born Hammarskjöld, whom John F. Kennedy called "the greatest statesman of his generation," died in 1961 in mysterious circumstances in a plane crash in Africa while on a diplomatic mission. *Markings,* his diary reflections collected into a book, is a testament to faith during a life of spiritual struggle.

† Dag Hammarskjöld, *Markings* (Vintage, 2006), 87.

‡ Vaclav Havel, *Summer Meditations* (Vintage, 1993), 1.

I was more familiar with the provincial issues, having been closely involved in all that had happened since the PQ had come to power. I thought that I could make a more valuable contribution to public life in provincial politics. For me the action was in Quebec where decisions affected the day-to-day life of my constituents. As well, there had to be a counterbalance to the policies and ideology of the PQ.

It is not enough just to be in politics. You must be motivated by and work for the public good. You must look after the welfare of others and not be concerned with popularity at the expense of doing what you believe is right.

I also suspected the federal Liberals would lose the next election, which they did, to Brian Mulroney. I did not relish the idea of continuing to be in opposition. I knew that the Liberals would form the next government in Quebec. So I stayed in provincial politics.

A MESSAGE TO THE ENGLISH-SPEAKING COMMUNITY

It is easy and often politically advantageous to tell your electors what they want to hear. But, there are times when you must go beyond the expected remarks, the safe statements, and say what you believe, even if it goes against the conventional thinking of your constituents. As we were nearing the elections, I was asked to speak to Alliance Quebec, a group formed in 1982 to represent the anglophone viewpoint. After all, I was seen as the Anglo community's spokesman.

"Stop fighting the PQ government on Bill 101, and let us rather open ourselves to the francophone majority of Quebec," I told them in a speech in May 1989. I admitted that certain changes could have been made to the law, favourable to the anglophone community without affecting its intended objective, i.e. to allow the majority of Quebecers to live and work in French.* But what was done was done, and now it was time to move on. We needed a nobler vision of our society, a radical transformation of the relations among the various communities. We needed a more truly open society. We had to identify ourselves clearly, not as a collectivity, but as a part of a population composed of diverse individuals gathered in distinct origins. I was expressing what I felt most, a deep need to overcome what I had not been allowed to express, my own origins. It came out as a plea for a better society.

---

* The courts later struck down parts of the law dealing with bilingual signs and the language of the courts. But unfortunately it wasn't done and we now had to go on.

I spoke of the need to explain the advantages that the presence of the English-speaking community offered Quebec. It was an asset and a resource for our society that contributed to everyone's quality of life. The linguistic and cultural duality of Quebec was (and is) not a handicap but a benefit for all. Knowing both languages would give us a competitive advantage in Canada and other countries.

And when we speak to French-speaking Quebecers in Abitibi, Rimouski, or elsewhere in the province, we must remember the abuses of the past. "Confrontation is a two-way street. And no community has a monopoly on distrust, fear, and lack of communication and understanding. The anglophone community itself must rediscover the enormous benefit for our society of a living and dynamic French-language. Our community must also work to encourage its development and to show that it is ready to accommodate itself to its needs."

FINAL MONTHS IN OPPOSITION

One of Claude Ryan's qualities was his ability to elaborate his policies in a meticulous, complete, and almost scholarly fashion. When he was leader of the party, it was not enough for us to be critical of the government. He insisted that we make specific proposals and expound on our recommendations in a position paper. As a result, I prepared many documents on various subjects – for example, on cultural communities and on energy.

In the final months of the PQ era, I was named transport critic and I prepared a comprehensive transportation policy with the help of Jean Desrosiers, who headed the Liberal party's subcommittee on the subject. It was a substantial document on the subject and the role of government. In the first section, titled "Montreal Back on the Map," I wrote of Montreal being perceived "in North America and in other lands as one of those 'special' cities … with a very particular attraction: the differences of its charm, its flair, and its dynamism." I tried to make the case that Montreal was not a North American city like others – Toronto or Chicago or Cleveland – but that it reached beyond North America to Europe, where historically its roots were. French and English, two important international languages, made Montreal the largest bilingual city in the world – though this was not seen as an advantage by many French-speaking Quebecers. It was almost a nostalgic hope to bring back what had changed.

As a politician, you can't solve all the problems, but you must give people hope. Such was the case with proposals I had made on other subjects and now again with the transportation white paper. I saw transportation as an important tool in planning economic development, pivotal in various sectors of the Quebec economy: pulp and paper, mining, manufacturing, agriculture, and tourism. Transportation also had an effect on regional economies. For example, the construction of roads and airports made possible the completion of the James Bay hydroelectric project. I stressed the importance of the transportation equipment industry for the economy. At the time, 20 per cent of its products manufactured in Quebec were destined for other parts of Canada and 50 per cent for foreign markets. Those substantial figures necessitated policies that would grow this sector and its ancillary activities such as engineering and aeronautics.

I emphasized the importance of research and development, its impact, and the need for government support. I made proposals on how to improve the system, how to make it respond to the needs of the users, and how to encourage growth in the industry. I indicated that five of Canada's fourteen national ports were located in Quebec. The Port of Montreal was booming.

However, I also identified certain anomalies resulting from the policies and objectives of the PQ. It had reduced funding for research and development, and, as a consequence, many companies had been forced to close. I also asked how many manufacturers like Pratt & Whitney had chosen to create subsidiaries outside of Quebec so as "to have access to a larger labour pool." Not wanting to offend the government and possibly lose out on future tax breaks and subsidies, they used this euphemistic language to express fear of PQ policies. There was no doubt that the objectives and policies of the PQ worried many who, rather than expand in Quebec, made alternative plans outside the province.

Regarding public transit, I found it unacceptable that in Montreal passenger fares were not sufficient to cover more that 40 per cent of public transit costs, whereas in Toronto they met 70 per cent of those costs. Moreover, the government, which had proposed a plan to use highway tolls to finance public transit, reversed itself and decided to remove them altogether.

That last criticism was unfair on my part. I was the one who had made a motion in the National Assembly to remove all tolls for the Laurentian highway. The motion was debated and both the Liberal party and the government agreed to it. Abolition of these tolls saved users some $50 million dollars annually.

Essentially, my recommendations suggested that we encourage research and development, reduce energy consumption, stimulate urban transit, implement certain corrective measures for the taxi industry, upgrade and improve the quality of the road system, improve road safety, revise the provisions of the "régime d'assurance automobile," maintain a Quebec trucking industry, ensure the complementarity with other provinces of intercity buses and passenger train service, exploit our maritime advantages, expand air service and favour improved access to the regions, and, finally, secure our foreign markets. Suggestions were made on how to accomplish our goals in each of these areas.

Following the tabling of the transportation paper, there was speculation in the press that I would be tapped as the minister for this portfolio in the next Liberal government.*

During this period, I also expressed my opposition to the PQ's so-called Prôjet Archipel, which proposed the building of six dams on the rivers surrounding Montreal and Laval, supposedly to prevent flooding. This would not only have ruined the Lachine Rapids but would have cost a billion dollars in return for a meagre 485 megawatts of surplus electricity, power not needed in Quebec but for export to the US. It was a ridiculous project and during the election campaign I promised a Liberal government would scrap it.

While involved with such larger issues, I still managed to be concerned with the mundane problems of my riding. There had been an infestation of cockroaches in the Côte-des-Neiges area. I called for all three governments – Ottawa, Quebec, and Montreal – to attack the vermin plague. From the sublime to the ridiculous.

LÉVESQUE'S FAREWELL:
THE END OF A POLITICAL PHENOMENON

He had made his mark as a Lesage Liberal; he had achieved the nationalization of Hydro-Québec, had stood up for the role and rights of French-speaking Quebecers, and had brought the province to the edge of political independence. René Lévesque played a unique role in changing Quebec society. Now, after losing the referendum and in the midst of a worsening economy, he was being rejected by the party that he had founded, by the people that he had brought to power. The ingratitude of the shortsighted. Quebec was fortunate to have a man like

* *Montreal Gazette*, 3 December 1985.

Lévesque as leader during uncertain and turbulent times. You could disagree with his beliefs, but you had to respect his way of operating.

He had been humble, magnanimous, and still hopeful after losing the referendum. He believed in the democratic process and in peaceful change. Disappointment had not altered his beliefs. But his star began to wane during the James Bay hearings, when, under the pressure of his opponents, and even of his supposed associates, he lost his composure.

When Ottawa convened a federal–provincial conference on Native issues, Lévesque asked me, a member of the opposition, to attend the conference and represent his government, an implicit acknowledgment that I was more qualified than the members of his own government to deal with the Native portfolio. He made a choice unencumbered by partisanship. To my knowledge, he is the only premier in the history of Quebec to have appointed a member of the opposition to be the sole representative of the government in a federal–provincial conference. That I was a federalist, opposed to the government's separatist aims, makes it even more remarkable.

But Lévesque was not radical enough for the nationalist and leftist extremes in his party. Six prominent members of his cabinet and caucus resigned after he declared that the next election should not be fought on the political independence of Quebec. The PQ lost four by-elections provoked by these resignations. The split in the party led to Lévesque's resignation on 20 June 1985. The PQ went into the next election unmindful of Lévesque's counsel, and it would cost them dearly.

15

Back in Power

"And the Liberal party's time has come." Those were my words on the eve of the elections of 1985 after nine long years in opposition. "People want a change of government," I told the voters. "They believe in federalism and they know the PQ hasn't abandoned the idea of independence."

It was an effective line. Following the 12 December vote that year, Bourassa and the Liberals won in a landslide, electing ninety-nine members. The PQ under Pierre-Marc Johnson, who had replaced Lévesque, obtained twenty-three seats. The only sour note in the triumph was the personal defeat of Robert Bourassa in the riding of Mercier. After the Liberals assumed power, Bourassa was elected in a by-election in St Laurent.

The premier had succeeded in attracting a very able and eminent group to run for office. They had to go through the tedious and sometimes arduous electoral process – nomination as the candidate, meeting the electors, soliciting votes, and waiting for the results on election day. If you were the senior vice-president of a bank or a CEO, it took a certain amount of commitment and motivation to exchange a high-ranking position for the nitty-gritty of the electoral process. Among the talent who formed the government were:

- Pierre Macdonald had been the senior vice-president of the Bank of Montreal. He was made minister in charge of foreign trade.
- Paul Gobeil was executive vice-president, finance and administration, of Provigo and had become president of Loeb Corporation, a retail food chain. He was named head of the treasury board.

- Gil Rémillard was a Quebec City lawyer and Université Laval professor who had served as an advisor to Prime Minister Brian Mulroney. He became minister of intergovernmental affairs.
- André Vallerand had been vice-president of the Montreal Chamber of Commerce. He was named minister responsible for small and medium-sized businesses.
- Herbert Marx was a professor of constitutional law at the Université de Montréal. He was named minister of justice.
- Pierre Fortier had been president of Canatom Limited, a large nuclear consulting firm. He was named minister of privatisation.
- Claude Ryan, the former party leader, was named minister of education.
- Daniel Johnson, the brother of the PQ leader Pierre-Marc Johnson and son of former UN premier Daniel Johnson Sr, had a doctorate in law and an MBA from Harvard University. He was named minister of industry and commerce.

To the surprise of many, not only was I named minister of energy and resources, but I had two "junior" ministers reporting to me: Robert Côté, minister of forestry, and Raymond Savoie, minister of mines. Côté was a knowledgeable forestry engineer. My responsibility over forestry proved crucial later in a decision concerning a paper mill project in Matane.* Raymond Savoie was also given the responsibility for Native affairs. This indirectly and shrewdly made sure that I was still involved in this delicate area and would oversee its activities. (The Oka crisis would one day make me rue this decision.)

I was overjoyed and almost lyrical in my hopes for Montreal, trying to reverse the effects that the Parti Québécois, a party that favoured the francophone regions over the multilingual metropolis, had had on its growth and dynamism.

I was considered an anglophone representative in the new government. After my nomination as energy minister, the *Gazette* reported that the English-speaking community had excellent representation in cabinet – I was one of four English ministers, the others being Herb Marx, Richard French, and Clifford Lincoln. But as future comments and positions on issues would show, I was not an unconditional defender of the anglophone cause. When interviewed after my

---

* The *Gazette* didn't fail to point out that I had been an outspoken critic of Bourassa's controversial language legislation, Bill 22, 15 December 1985.

nomination, I said that I understood some of the frustrations of the French-speaking majority. In an interview, referring to my growing up in an Italian immigrant family, being in a French neighbourhood and then attending an English school, I admitted that, "As a little kid I always felt like No. 3."*

GOVERNING: A PLETHORA OF PROBLEMS

After the election, I hit the ground running as Bourassa named me energy minister on 5 December. Despite the nationalism that was in the air, he did not hesitate to name me to head a department that was responsible for Hydro-Québec.

The energy appointment came soon after Gulf Oil announced it would close its refinery in east end of Montreal on 31 December. I wanted to prevent the shutdown, and there wasn't much time. I didn't accept that this was strictly business. It could have serious consequences for Quebec. The loss of refining capacity would affect the price of gasoline. Workers would lose their jobs. The petrochemical industry would be seriously affected.

I tried everything to get the refinery to stay open. Gulf had sold the plant and other retail locations to Ultramar, with the obligation to close the refinery. Because Ultramar at that time was not a Canadian company but a subsidiary of its British parent, the consent of the federal government was required. I sent a telegram – emails were still almost a decade away – to Pat Carney the federal minister of energy asking for a delay in its decision so that I could explore other possibilities. No answer. I tried to get the Quebec company, Gaz Métropolitain, involved, and participated in negotiations with a consortium led by Salomon Brothers, a New York investment firm, to purchase the refinery. I went to Toronto to meet the Ultramar executives to try and persuade them to keep the refinery open. The best that I could obtain from them was a slight delay in the closing and an agreement to expand their refinery in St Romuald near Quebec City to take up the slack both in refining capacity and the number of jobs lost. All but one hundred of the lost jobs would be saved. Through all of this there was a threat from Shell Oil that it would close its refinery in Montreal if Gulf stayed open.

The refineries issue became a political hot potato for the Conservative government of Brian Mulroney in Ottawa. Michel Côté, the

* The *Globe and Mail*, 27 December 1985.

federal minister of consumer and corporate affairs, released a report stating that Quebec was paying $300 to $500 million more per year for gasoline because of the shortage in refining capacity.[*] When asked how Pat Carney, the federal minister of energy, could deny this, Côté's answer put in question Carney's knowledge of the boundaries of Quebec. The reactions of federal ministers were an indication of the turmoil and doubts caused by Gulf's decision.

When the federal government allowed the sale to Ultramar, Suzanne Blais-Grenier, the minister of state for transport, resigned. She said publicly that Quebecers did not have enough influence over major economic decisions made by Ottawa because ministers were advised by an English-speaking bureaucracy that was insensitive to Quebec's needs.[†] Ouf!

It was not a pleasant spectacle of the federal government at work.

As it became evident that the Gulf refinery would close, I tried to save its petrochemical installations. I was so persistent in my calls to the Canadian president in Toronto, that, to get rid of me, he agreed to transfer certain facilities to the Quebec government for $1. They were worth some $20 million, but he probably figured that, hey, if they closed, what could be done with them. I was taking them off his hands, nothing would happen, and he would be rid of my constant harassment.

But I had other plans in mind. I met with Bernard Lamarre, the president of Groupe Lavalin, the large Quebec engineering firm (it had not yet merged with SNC). He came over to my home with his brother Jacques, and we discussed their taking over and operating the installations that I had obtained for $1 to produce a substance called "phenol," an important industrial material produced from oil. The government would transfer the plant to Lavalin for $1. It was a great deal for them. They agreed to reopen the facility as a phenol plant.

When the Toronto director of Gulf found out that Lavalin would reopen the plant, he called me. He was fuming. He was sputtering on the phone. I hadn't told him that I had a possible buyer who would reopen the plant. I had misled him. He insinuated that if he had known he would not have given the government a $20 million plant for a buck. He said he had the impression that when he transferred the plant to the government, as a gesture, it would remain idle. I listened to him calmly but did not budge. I never heard from him again.

---

[*] *Montreal Gazette*, 31 December 1985.
[†] The *Globe and Mail*, 8 January 1986.

Of course, the press releases by Ultramar on the $1 transfer did not reflect this conversation. I remember the press conference with Bernard Lamarre to announce the new project. Lavalin had formed a subsidiary Phenolmont to operate the plant. A group of journalists asked me what the product, phenol, was used for. With remarkable candour, I answered, "I don't know. All I know is that it needs this plant to produce it." One of the journalists, shaking her head, and also speaking for the others, gently answered: "Mr Ciaccia, we will not report that."

While I was trying to help maintain the petrochemical industry, Ultramar was working to dismantle it. It began demolishing all of the installations at the Gulf refinery. I blew a fuse. How could they deliberately destroy plant and equipment which I qualified as "the patrimony of Quebec" that could still be used and hopefully revive a troubled industry? It's one thing not to reopen a refinery, but to tear it down? I had initially spoken to L.D. Woodruffe, a director of Ultramar in its England head office who had not mentioned the destruction of the refinery after I had asked him what would happen to the plant and its equipment. He had left me with the impression it would remain idle. He had undertaken to maintain the equipment. However, Ultramar was now destroying it to assure there would be no future competition in refining capacity. This time a new federal energy minister, Marcel Masse, who was from Quebec, supported me. I called Jean Gaulin director of Ultramar's Quebec operation. I did everything I could to stop further destruction. But to no avail.

A newspaper called it Ultramar's scorched earth policy. An editorial in *La Presse* by Jacques Bouchard reminded Ultramar that in any society a company should not only have money making as an objective; it also has responsibilities and moral obligations.* If the business world had always heeded this advice we might not have had Karl Marx and *Das Kapital*.

I decided to enact a law to deal with the possible abuses by petroleum companies (called an Act Respecting Petroleum Products and Equipment RSQ chapter P-30.01, and later renamed the Petroleum Products Act). Unfortunately, it could not be applied retroactively to the Gulf–Ultramar sale. I considered petrochemicals an important sector in Quebec, not only for the direct jobs that it created but also for

* "Une compagnie ne doit pas seulement avoir comme objectif de faire de l'argent: elle a aussi des résponsablities et des obligations morales dans une société." *La Presse*, 25 August 1986.

its spinoffs. I dealt directly with the companies involved – for example, Polysar – I met with Pat Carney and obtained federal financial help for Petromont, a plant in eastend Montreal. I remember the meeting being short and tense. She gave me the impression of being ill at ease and wished to keep her distance from Quebec.

CONVERSION OF A PIPELINE FROM SARNIA TO MONTREAL

My involvement with the petrochemical industry began with the installations I had obtained from Gulf Oil on the closing of its refinery in Montreal and my negotiations with Lavalin to open a phenol plant there. I tried to do more. The phenol plant was only the tip of the iceberg, and it showed a possible solution to a larger problem that existed. Refinery closings indicated a need to create the conditions to maintain and increase investments, also that the industry needed a secure supply of competitively priced feedstock. The Soligaz project would meet that need.

The industry needed liquefied natural gas (LNG). It cost $4 a barrel to bring it to Quebec by train but less than $1 if carried through a pipeline. This could be done by converting the Sarnia–Montreal pipeline, owned by Interprovincial Pipeline (today Enbridge, Inc.), a company based in Edmonton created by Imperial Oil, to allow it to carry liquefied natural gas. At the Montreal end, it would require a plant to reconvert the liquid gas so it could be used to create the various products needed by the petrochemical industry. Such a plant essentially produces the required chemical products – ammonia and methanol, for example – that are used in various other products. The Quebec company, Soligaz, would build and operate such a plant to feed the other petrochemical plants. This could be the basis of a healthy industry, stem the loss of companies, and hopefully encourage new investments.

I pressed for the conversion of the pipeline but getting a decision to achieve this was a complicated process. There were conflicting interests – different regions of the country with a stake, powerful corporations with varying interests that wielded much influence, all levels of government. In addition, the consent of the National Energy Board was required. Quite an array. I did not let this deter me. The greater the difficulties, the greater the effort.

The negotiations for the Soligaz project were long and arduous, and I was directly involved in all of them. Usually the investments of this sort are considerable, but the advantages are so great it is worthwhile to invest government money.

I thought it important enough for me to go to Alberta along with the promoter of the Soligaz project, André Lapalme, chairman of the Soligaz board and CEO of the petrochemical company Pétromont. We would meet with government officials and with executives from the Alberta Natural Gas company, who would be partners in the project with the provincial agency La Société québécoise d'initiatives pétro-lières (SOQUIP), Gaz Métro, and SNC, the engineering firm that later merged with Lavalin.

The Alberta government obviously was interested in delivering more of its natural gas to eastern Canada. The *Calgary Herald* reported that, "Quebec has offered Alberta a boom in propane sales and help to prop up natural gas prices in exchange for support for a pipeline project designed to boost Montreal industrial growth."*

I needed the support of the federal government. In addition to it being an interprovincial pipeline, the consent of the National Energy Board would be required. I worked with Marcel Masse, the federal minister of energy. He was very cooperative. However, at one point he said to me that he could not get his civil service to agree to the project, and he could not make a decision without their approval. Ultimately, Masse had the power to make the decision but was reluctant to do so without his ministry's backing. This illustrates the power that civil servants wield. But rather than back down, he did a very unusual thing. He called me and asked me to come to Ottawa to convince his senior officials to approve the project.

I met with the senior officials of his department. I drew on my experiences as ADM in Ottawa with Indian Affairs where I often had to overcome the decisions of the civil service to make the changes that I wanted. I was glad when after some discussions they agreed that it was a good project and would support it. Mission accomplished.

Interprovincial Pipeline objected to the conversion, saying that the project could not be realized for technical reasons dealing with safety. "When we can send a man to the moon, technically nonfeasible doesn't exist," I shot back.† Interprovincial proposed that the Soligaz group build its own pipeline. "There is no question that we're going to build another pipeline when there is one that is hardly used," I retorted.

I accused Imperial Oil of a conflict of interest when it objected to the payment of the cost of conversion by Interprovincial. I pointed out that Imperial (and Gulf Oil) owned 20 per cent of Interprovincial Pipeline

* 5 May 1988.
† *La Presse*, 12 August 1987.

and also had interests in the Sarnia petrochemical industry. Therefore they had no interest in doing anything that would promote the petrochemical industry in Montreal. The president of Imperial Oil denied my claims. I also pointed out that an expanded Montreal petrochemical complex would not compete with plants in Alberta or Ontario. I tried to calm their fears by pointing out that their markets were concentrated closer to their operations while the Quebec output would be exported to the northeastern United States.

To increase the possibility of investments, I even went to Italy with Ghislain Dufour, the president of the Conseil du Patronat, where we met with his counterpart, the President of Confindustria. My main objective, however was to meet officials of ENI and ENEL, Italian energy corporations which operated worldwide. I thought that there were opportunities for investments by both sides. I figured my Italian background could help.

ENEL signed an agreement with Hydro-Québec to study underwater transmission lines. ENI was interested in a plant in Montreal to produce MTBE, an octane increasing gasoline additive. Later, a representative from the company met me in Montreal to discuss this project.*

Meanwhile, I was anxiously awaiting the decision of the National Energy Board.

The Montreal–Sarnia pipeline conversion would cost $200 million. I wanted the owner, Interprovincial Pipeline, to pay since they would be receiving the revenues from its transformed use. Finally, the board acted. It allowed the transformation of the pipeline, but refused to impose its costs on the owners. The users, Soligaz, would have to pay.

I still heaved a sigh of relief. We had the decision to convert. The project would go ahead! I would find another way to pay for it. I asked Ottawa to contribute $150 million, the cost of the conversion and part of the total project. It refused. I had overcome too many obstacles to let the project die because of inadequate funding. Premier Bourassa agreed to provide the $150 million. Soligaz would invest the other $50 million.

In September 1989, we announced the project. Premier Bourassa was present, as well as Finance Minister Gérard D. Levesque and Minister of Industry and Commerce Daniel Johnson. The project would assure the development of the petrochemical industry in Montreal and

---

* This product was later proved to be toxic to the environment and its use discontinued. It was one of the few times that failure to attract an investment proved to be beneficial.

benefit from provisions of the free trade agreement with the US, signed a year earlier.

The project had all that was necessary to go ahead – construction of a Toronto bypass, conversion of the pipeline, developers who were ready to invest and proceed, subsidies from the government, approval of the NEB, approval of three governments – federal, Alberta, and Quebec – and yet it did not go ahead. Another election and my transfer to Ministry of International Affairs derailed it. The PQ brought the issue up in question period, but to no avail. To be realized, the project needed a driving force, the same persistence and tenacity that had got it approved. This was missing and it died. Pity!

PORT CARTIER

Port Cartier, a town in northern Quebec near Sept-Îles, had a paper mill that had been shut down for many years. I was determined to reopen it. When I was in opposition, I remember going there with other MNAs and Claude Duhaime, the PQ minister. We were sitting in the closed mill, a large, dark building with huge idle, dust-covered machinery rising above and behind us as the sun streamed in from large windows on its upper side. It was a phantasmagoric, unreal scene. As we sat on the equipment eating sandwiches for lunch, Duhaime smiled and said that it reminded him of a set from the film of the neo-realist director Roberto Rossellini.

I don't remember why, but there were two projects that I was determined to complete: the reopening the existing mill at Port Cartier and the building of a new one at Matane in the Gaspé. Perhaps Port Cartier because I had been there with a PQ minister and his government had been unsuccessful in restarting it, and perhaps Matane because for the past twenty years every government had promised, and failed, to build a paper mill there. Port Cartier involved an investment of $50 million, and Matane, originally some $450 million, then scaled down to $250 million.

After I had successfully concluded an agreement with the company Cascades and the Lemaire brothers for the reopening of the Port Cartier mill, I was at the Queen Elizabeth Hotel having dinner. From across the room came Brian Mulroney with four husky bodyguards. At the time his electoral riding was in northern Quebec and included Port Cartier. He congratulated me for reopening the plant. Robert Bourassa was also there. He smiled at me and said, "John, t'es super." I glowed.

HYDRO-QUÉBEC

As energy minister I was the government overseer for Hydro-Québec, a role I summed up in a remark to the Quebec City newspaper, *Le Soleil*: "Hydro-Québec has a responsibility as a business, while I have a responsibility to the people of Quebec."

Hydro-Québec was an immense enterprise with a monopoly in the province, except for a few small municipal companies that distributed but still bought their power from Hydro. However, there was a role for the minister of energy and I took it seriously. I believed that Hydro-Québec needed guidance in its directions and overseeing in its operations. Without interfering in its day-to-day activities, I saw myself as the final decision-maker in major matters – exports, investments, and services to consumers.

Each year Hydro would present its development plan to government. Questions would be asked, reasons for proposals outlined, and approval given by cabinet on the recommendation of the minister of energy. Only then could the plan be implemented. An example of how this worked: during the presentation of the 1986 three-year plan, in a parliamentary committee, I was concerned with the trends and market prices of other fuels that could have an effect on electricity sales. If natural gas or petroleum products were cheaper it would dissuade certain customers from using electricity, especially businesses and, potentially, those with new plants. This, and the exchange rate of the Canadian dollar, which would affect exports and debt payments, would seriously impact the profits of Hydro. To cushion such a loss, I wrote to President Guy Coulombe and asked that Hydro reduce its operating expenses to counter the effects on its profits. He proposed to reduce Hydro's expenses by $42 million. He based this on the assumption that the price of oil would stay at $13 a barrel and the exchange rate for the Canadian dollar would be 71.5 cents US. How times have changed! However, his proposed reduction included the calculated risk of postponing repairs to the distribution system that, he considered, would not affect services to the clients. I told him that this worried me. The development plan also included a duel-energy program whereby Hydro would help subsidize the installation of equipment that could use both electricity and oil or natural gas – the intention being to utilize electricity and switch to the alternative fuel during peak hours. It seemed like a good program to increase the sale of electricity.

Some time later my son Mark, who was administering my properties, told me he had just signed with a private contractor to install a duel-energy system for one of the buildings. Hydro would furnish a subsidy of $50,000 to pay a part of the cost of the new system. I told him that I couldn't accept that because as the minister of energy I felt that it would be a conflict of interest. Mark was astonished. "But this is a public program that is available to everybody. There's no conflict. Do you think it's a conflict of interest for you to go and buy liquor at a liquor store owned by the government? It's the same thing." He had made a good comparison – buying a government product that is available to everybody. I told him that I would check with the premier. When I asked Bourassa, he brought in a legal advisor who examined the facts and told me that it was perfectly permissible and legal. I could go ahead. But I decided not to. When I told this to my son, he asked why. "Because I don't want to wake up one morning and see a headline in the newspaper saying, "Minister of energy accepts $50,000 subsidy from Hydro-Québec." Even if it weren't an accusation of wrongdoing, it would create the impression of not being above suspicion. Mark cancelled the contract and we lost the deposit of $7,500.

At one point I was meeting regularly with Hydro president, Guy Coulombe, and his staff to review various issues and problems. We kept minutes of the meetings and followed up on proposed actions. I signed an agreement with Ottawa to promote energy saving and instituted an energy saving plan called "Forum-énergie-centre-ville," hoping to reduce energy consumption by some 20 to 30 per cent for Montreal building owners. Nouveler was created as a subsidiary of Hydro-Québec to promote energy efficiency.

I opened an office in Milan to promote Quebec's forestry industry. I went to the official opening with Guylaine Saucier, president of l'Association des manufacturiers du bois de sciage du Québec (AMBSQ) and other Québec industrialists from this sector. I also dealt with the export of electricity to the US, and I involved myself with two major projects that I considered important for regional development and the creation of jobs. I wanted to get things done.

EXPORTING JAMES BAY POWER

The development of the James Bay Project was Robert Bourassa's grand vision. My agreement with the Cree and the Inuit had cleared the way for it to proceed. Now as the energy minister I wanted to make sure that Native agreements were respected and that all aspects of the project moved forward. Since there would be an excess of capacity, both in the short term before demand went up and during nonpeak periods (usually the time of day outside meal times), exporting the power seemed a profitable idea.

Although the James Bay Agreement was quite a complete document, and sensitive to Native needs, there were still certain aspects of the project that weren't covered, including unforeseen changes in its development. I signed three additional agreements with the Cree at Chisasibi for $110 million. This allowed the government and Hydro to build five power stations on the La Grande Complex, which would provide an additional 300 megawatts of power. Ted Moses, one of the community leaders, said this would give a solid thrust to Cree self-government and to the Natives' objective of economic self-sufficiency.[*] It was important to maintain the goodwill of Native people. Meanwhile, Hydro was pleased that these agreements would allow the completion of Phase Two of the La Grande Complex.

So, I was very active in promoting exports of electric power. I participated on a committee created by the premier and formed another internal government committee to help achieve our objectives.

Premier Bourassa had a remarkable ability to make friends with prominent people in other countries who occupied influential posts dealing with important public issues. One such was James Schlesinger a former secretary of defence under Presidents Richard Nixon and Gerald Ford and the first secretary of energy, a post created by President Jimmy Carter. Bourassa succeeded in recruiting him to head an advisory committee for Hydro-Québec on American energy needs and our relations with the US to help fill those needs.

Bourassa saw the importance of having a committee that had a deep knowledge of the American political milieu and would be helpful in advising Hydro on its dealings with American clients. Guy Coulombe announced the formation of this fourteen-member advisory committee in February 1986. I remember attending a meeting presided over by Schlesinger at the St James Club in Montreal. He was jovial, with a pleasant smile, and amusing yet serious in discussions. His presence as our advisor added to our credibility when we were dealing with the various American authorities and state governments.

This committee was important in bringing together decision-makers in both countries. However, I believed that we needed more. We had to do some internal organization and promotion, and all those in government who were affected should be involved to facilitate exports. I advised the premier's office that I would form a Hydro-Québec–government

[*] *La Tribune* (Sherbrooke), 7 November 1986.

coordinating committee, which I would head, with representatives from the environment department (Clifford Lincoln), intergovernmental and international affairs (Gilles Rémilliard), and from Hydro. Rémi Bujold, from the premier's executive committee, would attend all meetings. Hydro would be represented by President Coulombe and its vice-president for external markets, Jacques Guevremont. The agenda of this committee covered many topics and indicated the allotted time for each item to be discussed.

For example, the meeting of 7 November 1986, provided for a discussion of the objectives of the coordinating committee and its method of functioning. We then went on to the plan of action for the governments and the input expected from each one concerned with exports. We examined all the areas that had to be covered in analyzing the markets and their impact on the various elements and sectors affected (equipment, financing, rates, and technical studies, including an analysis of profitability are some examples) so that a plan could be prepared to meet all of the requirements and the profitability necessary for exporting electricity. We also provided for the distribution of all such information to all government departments involved.

We talked about the various contracts under review, especially with New York and New England. We discussed Hydro-Québec's acquisition of the Cedar Rapids Transmission line, in New York State, which would help in the delivery of our exports. We also discussed the contracts in New England – with Central Maine Power. We were concerned with a report to the New England governors by their power planning committee. We had obtained a preliminary copy of the report that outlined some reservations on imports. The decision was made that I would visit the governors of the six New England States, or their representatives, as well as the New England Power Pool (NEPOOL), which acts on all matters affecting the New England region's wholesale electric power arrangements, and I would give a speech in Boston. I would be accompanied by a representative of Hydro-Québec.

In Boston, I remember seeing my name on a bulletin board in the lobby of the hotel where I was to give my speech: "John Ciaccia – Veritas" (Truth). I flattered myself by thinking that these people seemed to know me, and I was pleased with their acknowledgment of my qualities. I was soon brought back to earth when I realized that "Veritas" was the name of the room where I was scheduled to give my talk.

I was mandated to attend the National Energy Board session in Ottawa, which would examine our contracts with NEPOOL. At the time, the federal government maintained jurisdiction on exports to the US, including power contracts. I objected to Ottawa claiming jurisdiction and to a federal report that recommended it should intervene in our power exports. This was a matter of provincial jurisdiction. I found the report inconsistent. Their suggestion was to reduce federal regulations for gas and oil exports and yet increase them for electricity. It wasn't until September 1988 that Ottawa accepted our arguments and Energy Minister Marcel Masse announced that Quebec could export its electric power without federal intervention.

NEW YORK AND GOVERNOR MARIO CUOMO

New York State was an obvious possible client for our exports. Its population was greater than that of Quebec, and New Yorkers paid 17 cents a kilowatt-hour, more than three times Quebecers' rate. We couldn't have asked for a better market. This opportunity brought me into contact with New York Governor Mario Cuomo. Although we had not met before, we immediately felt at ease with each other, in part, no doubt, because of our shared Italian background. In 1986 he came to Quebec with the head of the New York State Energy Office for the signing of an electricity export agreement and to discuss a collaboration agreement on energy economy and various subjects dealing with electric power, including New York's energy needs and the potential for exports.

It was not Cuomo's first visit to Quebec City. That had occurred in 1983 when he met Premier Lévesque to discuss buying Quebec power. Although the James Bay Project was begun by Bourassa, Lévesque took great pride in its tremendous potential. Bourassa and I had been invited and attended the official opening of LG-1 soon after the PQ was elected. The reporting of the Quebec City event by the *New York Times* could not avoid reflecting and commenting on the political situation with a slant similar to that offered by *The Wall Street Journal* in 1980.

> At the news conference, held mostly in English with some French, Governor Cuomo ... asked John Dyson head of the New York Power Authority how much additional power the state could reasonably ... acquire. Mr Dyson said 2,000 megawatts. Mr Lévesque, who had made power exports a key factor in his economic planning* since he first nationalized Quebec's electric

* This was news to many in Quebec.

companies nearly two decades ago, beamed. Mr Lévesque's pro-separatist government has been eager to expand its ties to New York, both for economic reasons and as a counterweight to relations with Canada's national government.*

While looking to the future, I thought it would also be a good idea to do a little housecleaning in Hydro legislation. I enacted Bill 11, which repealed the Rural Electrification Act and the Office de l'Electrification rurale.

In 1945, 80 per cent of Quebec farms had no electricity. The Rural Electrification Act created seventy electricity cooperatives that allowed people to have access to a long-desired essential service. In 1963, with the nationalization of electricity, Hydro took over from the existing distributors, except for a few, such as municipalities and the Co-operative de Saint-Jean-Baptiste-de-Rouville. Since the law was no longer necessary, and the office was not operating, I abolished the law.

One day, Richard M. Flynn, the head of the New York Power Authority, called me saying that he was getting nowhere in making an import deal with Guy Coulombe. It wasn't clear whether Coulombe was playing hard to get or just not showing enough interest. Flynn seemed anxious to conclude an agreement. I asked him to fly to Montreal and meet me in my office. I reviewed with him the proposed terms of the contract and the issues that were holding up its finalization. Then I told him to call Coulombe and suggested an approach that he could use with him. He did so, presenting the conditions of the purchase. When certain difficulties would arise, Flynn would put the line on hold, I would suggest his replies and proposals, which he gave to Coulombe. This went on for some time until they finally agreed on terms.

That is how the largest contract in the history of Hydro-Québec – worth $15 billion – was negotiated.

We went to New York to sign it. Governor Cuomo invited me to visit his offices on the eightieth floor of the World Trade Center. There was friendly banter – the governor pointed out the view from his office and told me that he told his friends and relatives from Italy that all this was his. They interpreted this as meaning that he owned it. But he was only saying that he had authority over it – a play on words. He smiled mischievously as he explained this to me.

* 18 December 1983.

BLACKOUTS

One evening in mid-November 1988, I was having dinner in a restaurant while on my way to Quebec City. Hydro president Guy Coulombe was at another table. When I finished, I waved to him, got in my car with my driver, and continued my journey. We hadn't gone a block when all the lights went out – street lights, buildings, everything. It was the beginning of the worst blackout Hydro ever experienced, covering the entire province. I thought of the timing, the energy minister and the head of Hydro having been in the same room just a few minutes before.

I continued to Quebec City where the emergency lighting system of the hotel enabled me to make my way to my room.

There had been too many blackouts affecting too many people – two other big ones, in April 1987 and August 1988, as well as the one on 15 November. I was fed up. Something had to be done. I tried to get Hydro to present a plan of action as to the causes and remedies, but at a subsequent meeting with them, I wasn't satisfied with their answers and proposals. Consequently, I named a working group of experts in early December 1988 – Nicole Côté, a consultant, Francisco Galiana from McGill Universtiy, Théodore Wildi from Université Laval in Quebec City, and Yves Gervais from l'École Polytechnique in Montreal. Their job was to examine the causes of the blackouts and come up with ways to avoid them in the future.

Claude Boivin from Hydro was upset with my course of action. He feared the group would embarrass the corporation, which had more than 1,100 engineers who supposedly knew what they were doing. "Candidly, I am surprised that three university professors would reveal something we don't know," he told *Le Soleil.** He felt it was not necessary to have a commission of inquiry on the three blackouts that Hydro had in April 1987, and on 25 August and 15 November 1988. "But I realize that I am both judge and jury," he said.

My differences with Hydro were out in the open.

The corporation came up with its own plan to remedy the situation. It planned to spend some $850 million dollars to improve the system. Part of the work involved shortening the length of the transport lines, supposedly to make them more efficient. However, one of the members of my committee pointed out that this would not solve the problem of blackouts but would make the situation worse. "The reliability of the

* 12 December 1988.

system could be seriously affected to the detriment of the customers," said Theodore Wildi, speaking on behalf of the committee.* Putting Hydro's recommendations into effect would mean setting aside fifteen years worth of data accumulated by Hydro, including thousands of simulation tests, which would have to be done over. It would require an adaptation period of several years.

I immediately suspended the proposed works.

I was surprised that Hydro, with all of its expertise, had not realized this. However, there was an explanation – though not a justification. Hydro had suggested these changes to satisfy the demands of its export markets. Those clients demanded certain standards to conform to the problems of their own systems. Effectively, Hydro's proposed changes were intended to meet the demands of the American purchasers of electricity but would not necessarily reduce the blackouts in Quebec. However, the last blackout had been serious enough that Hydro was forced to cut off its exports to its American clients on 15 November.[†] (Under the terms of its contracts, Hydro was allowed to stop exports to fill domestic needs.) But the dependability of our system worried our American clients and I tried to reassure them.

Meanwhile, my group of experts discovered many deficiencies in the system and made twenty-two recommendations to remedy them. One of the proposals involved the regular visual inspection of overhead hydro lines. This may seem banal, and Hydro did do some inspection but not regularly on a province-wide basis, but when you consider that it had 85,000 kilometres of lines, you begin to realize the amplitude of this recommendation.

Wildi also said that one of the reasons for the blackouts was the lack of maintenance over many years. I think this was the product of the previous government's policies. That government had had less revenue because of reduced investments and an economic condition caused in part by its political program of independence – the exodus of hundreds of thousands of people hadn't helped the public purse – so they'd cut costs and maintenance in an effort to increase Hydro revenues.

I said, "We will accept (the committee's) standards if they answer Quebec's needs and if they are necessary for the reliability of our system." I immediately suspended Hydro's proposed action plan and

---

* *Le Devoir*, 5 May 1989.

† I found the date ironic – the blackout occurred on the anniversary of the first election of a PQ government in 1976.

enforced the committee's recommendations. (Hydro had just got a new president, Richard Drouin, and obviously he had not been responsible for this problem.) He accepted the new recommendations.

In the end, Hydro agreed to implement twenty of of the committee's recommendations (the other two dealt mostly with labour relations). They required investments of $600 million. I assured consumers this would not result in an increase to their electricity rates. The money would come from the reduced dividends payable by Hydro-Québec. The required improvements were made to the system, and Hydro returned to its customary efficiency in its services to the consumers.

OMBUDSMAN

Because of the particular difficulties that Hydro had gone through, especially with the blackouts, the corporation's 2.6 million customers had many complaints. Hydro was a monopoly. It had a captive market. What could aggrieved consumers do? They couldn't go to court. A remedy was necessary. I decided to enact a law providing for an ombudsman to handle their grievances.

The purpose was to ensure that customers would be treated more equitably in cases of billing disputes, services, interruption or delays in the reconnection of services, and in the event of blackouts. The ombudsman would intervene only if the parties did not come to an agreement within thirty days. He would have adequate personnel and a budget of one million dollars. In the event of a prolonged interruption of service, the ombudsman had the authority to award damages because of lost service.

Any consumer or group dissatisfied with the results of their claims could ask the ombudsman to intervene. He would examine the problem and suggest an appropriate solution. He would also have the power of inquiry. The distributor (Hydro or one of the dozen or so private furnishers) would inform the parties of the measures it would take to remedy the problem or would give the reasons why it could not. The ombudsman would make a report to the minister twice a year and would table, annually, in the National Assembly, a report of his activities and the application of the law.

To assure the impartiality of the ombudsman and avoid a possible conflict of interest, I provided that he would not answer to the minister of energy but rather to the minister responsible for consumer protection, the minister of justice. I named a lawyer, William (Buddy) Schwartz, as the first ombudsman. I had known him when I practised law with the firm of Chait, Salomon, Gelber, Ciaccia, Reis, and Bronstein.

HYDRO RATES

At the time, the minister of energy and resources, with the approval of cabinet, made the final decision on the electricity rates demanded by Hydro-Québec. At one time, Bourassa suggested that I create an energy board to deal with rate increases, and I myself had promoted the idea as energy critic in opposition. That was then. This was now.

I pointed out to the premier that it was a great advantage for the government, and not an independent board, to set rates as we would have better control of the outcome, and we could reap the political benefit of controlling and fixing reasonable rates. We would be the protectors of the public interest by curbing Hydro's appetite for greater profits. Guy Coulombe was disappointed that the rates that I approved did not get him the return a privately held company might have. I accepted the reasoning that maximized returns were fine for commercial rates, but I believed that as the shareholders of Hydro, the public was entitled to certain benefits, too, advantageous rates being one of them.

I adopted what I thought was a fair increase – the cost of living. For example, in 1989 Hydro asked for a rate increase of 5.7 per cent. I pointed out that this was 29 per cent above the rate of inflation, I therefore granted an increase of 4.5 per cent. I suggested that the company increase productivity rather than penalize the consumer.[*]

I applied the inflation rule even in extraordinary circumstances as, for example, when the blackouts occurred. The cost of repairs to the system would be some $600 million dollars, but I decided that Hydro would cut its dividends to the government and use the money to finance the repairs.

I wanted to help the consumer within what I thought were reasonable limits. For example, the rate for the first 900 kilowatts of usage was lower than the normal rate. To get more revenue, Hydro tried to decrease this to 750 kilowatts. This would have provided government an additional $12 million, but it would have been on the backs of those who consumed the least electricity. I refused.

This system worked well at the time. There was, in my view, a proper balance between the needs of Hydro and the savings to the consumer.

[*] *Le Soleil*, 8 March 1989.

However, it was also possible to abuse the system for political purposes as happened in 1978. That was when then PQ energy minister Guy Joron increased rates for a three-year period (rather than annually as he'd previously agreed) in order to avoid alienating voters with a Hydro rate increase during the referendum year.

Was it too much to think that the memory of this event inspired the PQ to create an energy board the next time they were in office?

A MEETING WITH LOUIS LABERGE

Guy Coulombe, then president of Hydro, wanted to eliminate subcontracting and give all the necessary work to its employees. Since this would eliminate competitive bidding, it could only increase Hydro's costs. I disagreed with the decision. But how could I acceptably overrule this internal hydro decision? I had to find the right reasons and the proper method.

I asked Bourassa to hold a parliamentary inquiry to hear representatives from Hydro and from private industry present their positions. The inquiry members, including representatives from the opposition could question them. We would discuss the pros and cons of subcontracting. The press would be there and report the results to the public. I was convinced that when the facts were presented it would be evident that subcontracting would allow the work to be done at the best possible price – that's why you have competitive bidding. Hydro would have to give cogent reasons why it wanted to change its practices and eliminate subcontracting. It would then make it easier for me to overrule Hydro if it became necessary.

Bourassa was concerned about the reaction of the labour unions and especially of Louis Laberge, the president of the FTQ, the largest union in Quebec. The Hydro workers were members of the FTQ. Bourassa didn't want to antagonize them or Laberge, who he had imprisoned in 1972 after the James Bay riots. Holding a public hearing, which could affect the rights of Hydro-Québec employees might do just that. I understood Bourassa's concerns.

However, I still wanted my parliamentary commission. So I decided to meet with Laberge. I called him and he readily suggested that we meet for lunch. We got together at an Italian restaurant on Sherbrooke Street, east of Pie IX Boulevard. He told me that he loved Italian food. It was a very pleasant lunch. We connected and felt at ease with each other. He was very jovial and friendly. After we had ordered and were enjoying our food, I broached the subject of subcontracting at Hydro. I told him that I was aware that the Hydro workers were members of his union, but, I also pointed out, the subcontractors also had workers who were likewise members of his union. I suggested that a parliamentary committee would not be detrimental to the union members, and that Coulombe's decision to eliminate subcontracting would hurt non-Hydro workers who were also members of the FTQ.

I didn't have to do much convincing. There was no argument. As a matter of fact, there wasn't even any discussion. He just listened and said, with a smile, that I could go ahead with my parliamentary inquiry. He seemed pleased to let me know. I went back to my office and called the premier. There would be a parliamentary inquiry.

Various representatives from the private and public sector were heard, including Hydro-Québec. The private sector representatives were especially keen to present their case. It became clear that public tenders, by providing for competitive bids, kept costs down. Hydro had to abandon its initial position to perform every function itself. There would be public tenders.

PROTECTING THE ENVIRONMENT

Being in charge of an essentially economic area of government didn't mean that I would not be interested in the environment and the cost of protecting it. In 1986 I was faced with an unusual situation that was solved in an unexpected way. Hydro-Québec was building a transmission line from Radisson, in the James Bay region, to Massachusetts – a distance of some 1,100 kilometres. It would service Quebec and the northeastern United States. The line would cross the St Lawrence River at Lotbinière-des Cantons, in the Appalachian region situated between Quebec City and Montreal.

Towers 140 metres in height would be built to carry the line over the river. Artificial islands would have to be built to accommodate three of the towers. You can imagine the impact on one of the most picturesque areas of Quebec. You can also imagine the reaction of the people in the area.

A group aptly calling itself Contestension threatened legal proceedings to prevent the crossing at that scenic location. They contested the right of Hydro to expropriate the land for its towers and invoked the Canadian constitution. When I was informed and given the name of the lawyer representing them, Guy Bertrand, I smiled. He had been a stalwart separatist. I found it amusing and ironic that he, of all people, would be invoking (and recognizing) the Canadian constitution. Politics and law make strange bedfellows. When he met me, he too smiled.

The people affected would be entitled to damages, either for any part of their land that would be expropriated or for the inconvenience caused by the construction. My immediate reaction was to ask Hydro if it had considered an underwater crossing at that area. For some unexplained reason, Hydro told me that it had not developed the technology. However, I found out from Roger Warren (a partner of the engineering firm Rousseau Sauvé Warren), that an underwater line could be built. There were specific proposals on how it should be done – by boring, rather than using dynamite, to protect the environment and by covering the interior of the underground structure with concrete. When I discovered that a study existed on the feasibility of an underwater line, I felt that I had been misled by Hydro. I could not ignore this. Was it a genuine error? Had someone forgotten? Was it a deliberate deception?

I called Hydro executives to my Montreal office. Yes, I said, there was a study validating the feasibility of an underwater line. It did not become clear whether this information was deliberately withheld, and I didn't press the issue, but I had made my point. The technology was available and Hydro officials knew it. I told Guy Coulombe to dig in order to cross the St Lawrence River. Since he could no longer claim that Hydro didn't have the technology, he found another excuse. "We can't proceed with the underwater passage. We would not be able to deliver the electricity to the US on time. We would be in default under our contracts with the Americans," Coulombe told me.

"Oh yeah?" I said. "Well, here's what you're going to do. You're going to build the overhead cables to meet your obligations to the Americans, and you're going to start building the underwater crossing. When you've finished the underwater crossing so that it can deliver the power to the Americans, you will then dismantle the overhead cables."

I left him sputtering.

A few minutes later, I got a call from Mario Bertrand, the premier's chief of staff. "What did you do to Coulombe?" he asked. "There's a blinding snowstorm, and he just called me saying he's driving right away from Montreal to meet the premier."

I was told that my decision would cost close to $100 million. I didn't bat an eyelash. The whole project, from Radisson to Ayer, Massachusetts, would cost more than $1 billion. I said that in any project, environmental protection could take up to 10 per cent of the overall cost. We were within the norms. Indeed, subsequent figures seemed to indicate that the cost of the changes was much less.

Of course, there were others involved in this process. Clifford Lincoln, the minister of the environment, voiced his objections to the original Hydro aerial crossing and worked with the residents of the area. There were other incidents, a little more amusing. When the project was first announced in the area and the residents vehemently objected, I went to see Micheline Beauchemin, a textile artist who had her studio in Grondines. She would be affected by the Hydro construction and entitled to damages. I was very impressed with her and her work – so much so that I got carried away and agreed that she would be paid damages of $1 million.

Premier Bourassa was a very respectful and deft person. He knew that the sum I had agreed to give Beauchemin was highly inflated, but he didn't want to overrule my decision. My experience with him was that he would never directly contradict you. If he did not agree with your decision or recommendation, he found other ways to let you know. So, others close to the premier questioned my decision until I finally realized that he thought that it was excessive. In the end, the amount obtained by the artist was nowhere near the sum I had agreed to.

All decisions affecting the environment must be approved by the BAPE (Bureau d'audiences publiques sur l'environnment). My reaction to Coulombe, telling him to build an underwater line and then demolish the aerial one, had to follow the environmental procedures, the decisions of the BAPE, and of cabinet. I had to formalize the decision – it was not just my saying so on the telephone. On 9 January 1987 I gave the president of Hydro a text which essentially provided for the following:

- Hydro would accelerate its studies to establish the technical feasibility of an underground passage at Grondines parallel to the overhead line.
- Following these studies, Hydro-Québec would undertake to construct a parallel line under the aerial line. At the same time, a notice of project would be deposited with the minister of the environment and an environmental study affecting the project and the modification must be made.
- Following this study, the cabinet must formally authorize its construction.

- Following the construction of the underwater line, and if the operation of the cables is viable and efficient, Hydro-Québec will then dismantle the aerial line.

This text was also submitted to BAPE on the same day – it had started hearings on the project in May of 1986 and was now holding a hearing in the auditorium of the Gabrielle-Roy Library in Quebec City. It held the hearing at 7:30 p.m. after having received my note to the president of Hydro-Québec. The decision of the board, made that same evening, repeated the instructions that I had given to the president of Hydro. The president of the board, after questioning various witnesses including representatives of Hydro, authorized the construction of an underwater line.

That is how state-of-the-art technology was employed to build the 4,000-metre-long tunnel under the St Lawrence River at Grondines-Lotbinière. The towers went up and then were removed in 1992, as were some of the artificial islands. The scenic beauty of the river was restored and maintained.

BATTLING THE OIL COMPANIES

I had many skirmishes with the oil companies, starting with my attempts to keep the Gulf refinery open. There were many issues, from refinery closings to gas prices, to mergers with possible effects on competition and pricing, to pipelines affecting supplies, and jobs. I felt impelled to act to protect the public. I didn't always succeed, but I tried. At least the public was made aware of the problems.

I was looking for a reasonable response from the oil companies. After all, they knew they were taking advantage of their ability to set prices.

An example: Gérard D. Lévesque, who was finance minister, fulfilled a Bourassa election promise to reduce the gasoline tax in the outlying northern regions of Quebec. However, this reduction was slowly being eroded. Prices crept up and the savings, instead of going into the pockets of the consumers, were being absorbed by the oil companies. What else is new?

Everyone looked to me the Minister of Energy. What would I do about it? I tried to persuade the heads of the companies to respect the tax reduction and got nowhere. I even threatened to create an energy board on gasoline prices with powers to allow it to intervene "with firmness." There was such a board in Nova Scotia. The oil companies ignored my threats.

A parliamentary committee was held in September 1987 at which the oil companies presented their positions and were questioned on their proposals. Esso, Ultramar, and Shell Oil, and even Petro-Canada, had the nerve to suggest that if we wanted to help the residents in these regions we should reduce the cost of their licences instead of cutting gasoline taxes. Imperial Oil's spokesman told us this measure was already in existence in northern Ontario and was easier to administer. They had no shame!

I was amused by the reaction of Vincent Della Noce, a federal Conservative member of parliament, who said indignantly that according to him the oil companies "take their pumps for revolvers and the government has to abide."* But not this time.

Competent civil servants are worth their weight in gold. One such was my deputy minister, François Dicaire, who informed me that a law adopted in the early 1970s, during an oil crisis, allowed the minister to fix the price of gasoline. However, that law had never been promulgated. It was not in effect.

Premier Bourassa was in Nova Scotia, attending a conference with the eastern Canadian premiers and the northeastern United States governors. I flew to Halifax to explain the situation and get his approval to take the necessary steps to promulgate the law. On 16 June 1987, I fixed the maximum price of gasoline that oil companies could charge in the outlying regions of Quebec. The decree would last for a period of three months with stiff penalties for noncompliance.†

I had become a one-man energy board.

After three months I renewed the decree to the end of September 1987. However, I was realistic enough to realize I could not fix the maximum price forever. During that time, all gasoline prices went up by two cents per litre to take into account the increase in the price of crude oil. This increase could not take place in the outlying regions because of my decree.

But I didn't just let the decree lapse.

I created an office to inspect gasoline prices – le Bureau d'inspection

---

* *La Presse,* 14 May 1987.

† The highest prices were on the lower North Shore – 54.3 cents per litre for regular and 56.2 for super leaded. Wouldn't we love to have these prices today!

des prix de l'essence (BIPE). It had the power to inspect gasoline prices and to inquire about their evolution and to publish the information in a monthly bulletin available to the public. The bureau would inform the public on refinery margins, wholesale prices, the cost of transportation, margins for the retailers, and posted prices on a comparative basis between the outlying regions and the urban areas. In other words, there would be a breakdown of the cost of the items that made up the final gas price. I believed that this would exert a downward pressure on prices. If, for example, it became evident that a retailer was taking a higher profit, the consumer could go to another station. The other information would certainly have an effect on the oil companies.

I claimed at the time that we were the first in North America to give such powers of inquiry, inspection, and provision of information in matters of gasoline prices to a board.* When it was created, the board operated under the powers of the ministry of energy; however, it would take legislation to give the board its proper powers. At the next session of the National Assembly, in November 1987, I presented Bill 93, an act respecting the use of petroleum products, amending and elaborating on the original act. The Act provided for the control by government of the sales price of petroleum products. This could even include the cost of an oil change, although that was not the intention.

The Act, since amended by subsequent governments to remove some powers, also allowed the government to monitor the price of gasoline and its components. The government had the right to obtain from oil companies and retailers the cost of all items that went into calculating of the price charged to the consumer. This information would be published in the monthly bulletin of the inspection bureau. Permits for the operation of gas stations were to be obtained from the minister of energy. They would be issued on a yearly basis and renewable on the payment of the required fees. There were substantial penalties for those who failed to comply with the conditions of the legislation.

This legislation saved the consumers several million dollars in the summer of 1986. I showed concern for the consumers and expressed this publically. I thought it my duty to protect and help consumers.

Before the Act was passed, however, most oil companies, except Imperial Oil, had increased their prices. I publicly accused Ultramar of taking advantage of Quebecers by hiking their prices. I said I was surprised because I had spoken to its president, Jean Gaulin, who had told

* *La Tribune* (Sherbrooke), 25 September 1987.

me earlier that his company would not be the first to increase prices in Quebec, and I found it peculiar that Ultramar had not increased its prices in Ontario where they had a smaller share of the market. "It would certainly appear that perhaps Quebec consumers are being taken advantage of," I told reporters.[*]

Another occasion when I took on the oil companies was when Imperial Oil announced that it had purchased the assets of Texaco. I was concerned about the effects of such a merger on market competition. Imperial had 11.5 per cent of the Quebec market. If it were allowed to keep all of Texaco's stations, that share of the market would rise to 24 per cent. This would give Imperial a dominant position, especially in some regions of the province where there would be almost no competition. The consumer would suffer. I wanted Imperial to cede to private retailers 225 of the 563 stations it was acquiring from Texaco. After I was unsuccessful in getting any commitments from Imperial to reduce or avoid this possibility, I asked the competition bureau in Ottawa to intervene. The competition bureau stepped in, forcing Imperial to sell many of the stations it had acquired from Texaco, not only in Quebec but in other parts of Canada as well.

Years later, after my retirement, I met someone at a Liberal fundraiser for Jean Chrétien in Shawinigan who came up to me and said, "Mr Ciaccia, you saved my life."

"How did I do that?" I asked, surprised.

"Many years ago, you opposed the sale of Texaco stations to Imperial Oil. I was able to keep my gas station and continue earning my living because of that. I want to thank you."

That felt good. All the time, effort, and hard work in politics were sometimes rewarded.

AN ENERGY POLICY

I believed that the energy sector was a key area in our activities and our economy. It affected many aspects of our lives and of our economy. It needed direction, organization, and rules. The government needed a plan to give direction in this sector. Providing one became my task. I called it "Energy: the Driving Force of Economic Development." The policy's objectives included:

[*] *Montreal Gazette*, 6 November 1986.

- Using energy to stimulate economic development and to support regional development, for example, by using Quebec's low electricity rates to attract industries.
- Maximizing the industrial benefits of energy-related activities. For example, what additional actions can be promoted when a project is in construction? What can be done to increase the benefits after a project is completed?
- Developing and maximizing the use of our hydroelectric resources by government. I pointed out that Quebec was the fourth largest world producer of electricity after the United States, the USSR, and Brazil. Quebec produced 8 per cent of the total world production of hydroelectricity, 28 per cent of North American production, and 54 per cent of Canadian production.
- The government would aim to assure a secure of supply of energy. This included not only maximizing our hydro potential but making sure that we had access to all sources of supply, Canadian and international, at competitive rates. I stressed the resources available from Canada to make a point with sovereignists who were still pursuing their political objectives.
- We would favour open competition within the energy industry to benefit the Quebec consumer. The consumer should have access to all forms of energy – oil, natural gas, or electricity. Although we promoted the use of electricity, we would make sure that other energy sources were available to the consumer to maintain competition.
- The policy would be applied to respect the environment. The best example was the government decision to oblige Hydro-Québec to build an underwater line across the St Lawrence river at Lotbinière-Des Cantons.
- Finally, the policy provided that the government would favour the growth of the petrochemical industry by assuring it access to all possible sources of supply. Support for the Soligaz project was a prime example.

There were other elements as well. Because of the size of Hydro-Québec, it was not suited to develop small projects. I took the initiative to allow the private sector to build projects involving small dams producing 300 megawatts or less. They could generate investments from the private sector of some $150 million. These would have important economic consequences for small businesses and for the regions involved.

A PAPER MILL AT MATANE

I wanted to bring investment to Quebec. In my view, this represented a significant contribution to the province's prosperity, and it was my role as minister to help it happen. That's why I had worked on the Port Cartier reopening. I approached these projects with determination and passion. I felt impelled to make them work.

There had always been an interest in building a paper mill at Matane.

For close to twenty years, various governments had made promises to bring about such a project. In 1980 Pierre de Bané, the federal minister from that area, got into the act. He changed the location of the proposed mill to Matapedia, a nearby town. The strangest thing is that Yves Bérubé, the Quebec minister who represented Matane, agreed with him. The result was that the mill was not built in Matane, but wasn't built in Matapedia either. It had become another talking point, another empty promise from both levels of government. I was determined to change that.

I began negotiations with Norske Skog Saugbrugs, a firm from Norway. It proposed to build a plant to manufacture supercalendered magazine paper. The investment would be $327 million. Obviously, government subsidies would be sought. I went to Ottawa and obtained an agreement to participate from Sinclair Stevens, the minister of regional industrial expansion. When I sent him the document containing our agreement, he refused to sign it. I even added a provision that the majority shareholder of the Matane project should be Canadian to allow Stevens to furnish federal funds.

I had accepted the Tory government's withdrawal from Port Cartier for political reasons. Mulroney didn't want to appear as investing in his own riding, thus opening the door to accusations of buying his electors. This I understood. But I didn't understand Stevens's about-face on the Matane file, and I expressed my disappointment publically. (In fact, he was giving in to pressure from other paper mill companies that didn't want more competition.)

In desperation, I denounced Stevens for refusing to respect his commitment and warned him that his actions threatened the project. Other countries were anxious to obtain this investment. "I tried everything, even speaking to Stevens who is in Arizona," I told the press. "If Stevens doesn't want to help the people in this region, let him say so."

When Saugbrugs saw the reticence of the federal government, it backed away from the project. We had lost an investment that could have provided 3,000 jobs during its construction and 800 direct and indirect jobs in a needy region. I deplored this missed opportunity. But I didn't give up.

Pierre Péladeau, the owner of Quebecor, was interested in acquiring Donohue Forest Products, of which Rexfor, a Quebec government corporation, was the principle shareholder. Péladeau's partner in this venture was Robert Maxwell, the Czech-born, London-based media baron. I told Bourassa the government could sell Donohue with the condition that the purchasers agree to build a mill at Matane.

Maxwell invited me to meet him at the Ritz-Carlton hotel in Montreal. He was a burly person, with a British accent, jovial, and friendly – what I would call captivating. We had a pleasant talk about conditions in Quebec. He even accompanied me out to the lobby where he bought a copy of *The Economist* from the newsstand on the ground floor of the hotel. He left me with a confident feeling about his intentions to invest in Quebec.

The premier had scheduled a cabinet meeting in Lac Beauport, near Quebec City. When the sale of Donohue came up on the agenda, I suggested that a condition of the sale be the construction of the mill at Matane. Finance Minister Gérard D. Levesque looked at me questioningly. The premier said nothing. The decision was made to sell Donohue, but there was no mention of the Matane mill. I closed the files that were before me, put them in my briefcase, looked at Bourassa, and walked out of the meeting. My colleagues looked at me in shock. You don't stomp out of a cabinet meeting in session. They all thought that I would resign.

I left Lac Beauport. I left Quebec City. I left Quebec. I went to Florida on a holiday to calm down and think.

I didn't resign. Instead, when I came back, I met with Péladeau, and we made the deal to build the Matane mill.

At the press conference announcing the construction of the project, a journalist asked Péladeau how he would cover the $250 million investment. Péladeau, never shy, said, "C'est pas de tes maudites affaires. Est-ce que je te demande combien t'as payé pour ta cravate?" ("None of your goddamn business. Do I ask you how you paid for your tie?") To lighten the atmosphere, I looked at the dumbfounded journalist and chipped in, "I wish I could answer the press like that."

At the time, Matane had an annual shrimp festival with a parade and a patron. That year, I was the patron, and I still have the ceremonial shovel given to dignitaries at the ground-breaking ceremony. Later, the mill experienced certain difficulties and was taken over by Tembec, a Canadian forest products company.

A GENEROUS GESTURE

There was an old law, passed in 1884, which gave the government ownership of all lakefront property for a distance of "three chains" (about sixty metres) along all the province's nonnavigable lakes and rivers. A decision by the Supreme Court in March 1987 had confirmed the validity of the law. Most of the 100,000 landowners affected didn't even know that such a law existed. They believed they had become owners of the waterfront when they had bought their property.

Public servants wanted the government to profit from this decision and sell the land to those who occupied it. The government lawyer who argued and won the case called the property owners in question "squatters." In a similar situation in Ontario, the government's decision was that the land could be sold by the municipalities to the adjoining owners at full market value. My reaction was that these people had already paid for the land once when they thought that they had bought it.

I decided to amend the law and give the land back to the owners free of charge. It seemed the fair thing to do. Presenting this law in the National Assembly also allowed me to make another point – one that was directed as a message to all of Canada.

At the time the bill was being drafted, a language issue was stirring things up in Alberta. Léo Piquette, a member of the Legislative Assembly, attempted to address the house in French. He was ruled out of order and prevented from doing so. He had to speak in English.

I had always spoken French in the Quebec National Assembly. However, this time, in my presentation of the amendment to the law of 1884, I made some of my remarks in English. At first the other members were surprised, especially those from the PQ. Then they understood, and some of them smiled. I was deliberately speaking English to make the point that in Quebec we could speak both languages. We did not prevent a legislator from speaking English instead of French. I was giving a message of tolerance.[*]

---

[*] Later, I told reporters that what happened in the Legislative Assembly in Alberta was "not the kind of incident that promotes harmony in Canada." *Montreal Gazette*, 16 April 1987.

16

Another Language Crisis

Bill 101, the language law, provided that all public signs had to be in the French language only. Anglophones obviously objected to this as it effectively erased them from the face of Quebec. A group from the community took the case to court, claiming that such a prohibition was against the Canadian Charter of Rights and should be declared illegal. The case went all the way to the Supreme Court of Canada. The court decided that, yes, this section of Bill 101 went against the Charter of Rights and thus was illegal. The decision allowed for bilingual signs but stipulated that the French language must be predominant, an indirect judicial admission of the special status of French in Quebec.

Many opposed the Supreme Court decision. Some 60,000 demonstrators took to the streets to protest any changes to the language law. Bourassa was placed in a difficult position. On one side was the Supreme Court decision, and on the other were the demonstrators and possible social unrest.

The PQ must have known that some of the provisions of its language bill could be interpreted as a violation of the Charter of Rights. To override such a contestation, they inserted the "notwithstanding" clause, a provision in the bill that could be invoked to override the charter. This clause would have a maximum time limit of five years.

The discussions in cabinet were long and arduous. My position was to respect the court decision. Bourassa wanted to use the notwithstanding clause, and he was supported by Claude Ryan. The final cabinet decision was a uniquely Bourassa approach – an attempt to placate both sides. But, when you try to please everyone, you end up pleasing no one.

Respecting the court's decision would mean riots on Quebec's streets. Bourassa didn't want this. No political leader does. But he knew he couldn't just invoke the notwithstanding clause – he didn't want to totally abandon the English community– so he made a compromise. He would use the notwithstanding clause but allow for the use of bilingual signs inside an establishment. On the outside, however, all signs had to be in French only. This would still require an amendment to the holy of holies, Bill 101. The result was a howl of indignation from the English community. They took it as an unacceptable affront to their rights. They couldn't accept the problems that Bourassa faced. For them it had to be all or nothing.

The elected representatives of the English community were put under tremendous pressure. Richard French, Herbert Marx, and Clifford Lincoln resigned. I decided to remain. It wasn't easy to vote for a law that, in the words of Hubert Bauch of the *Montreal Gazette*, "confines English signs to places where the sun doesn't shine." I thought that it was time to change tactics in the language disputes. We had to live together. It should be done in harmony not in acrimony. In the past we had always loudly opposed language laws, looking at them as a question of us or them. These past tactics hadn't worked. The language laws had passed, and our reactions perpetuated a conflict between communities. Maybe it was time for a new approach – an approach based on understanding the problems and fears of the other community. Why not try? Both francophones and anglophones had legitimate concerns.

In this case, Bourassa had taken a risk – the risk of amending the "untouchable" law, Bill 101. Why not accept his act as an interim gesture? "We've used the same tactics every time up to now and they haven't worked. So let's not repeat the mistakes of history. Let's make new history. There's a difference between appeasement and dialogue. Why not change our approach?"* Patience. Generosity. Understanding. Moderation. I told the community that this new amendment could last for a maximum of five years, the duration of the notwithstanding clause's effect. The next step would be a full recognition of English signs everywhere.

But anger doesn't listen to reason. I was pilloried by some. I spoke to a meeting of Alliance Quebec, the organization that represented the English community, and tried to explain this new position. I was yelled at and insulted. The moderator, Peter Blaike, an eminent lawyer, did his best to keep order, but it was an evening I would prefer to forget.

Clifford and I made our speeches in the National Assembly. His was one of resignation ("rights are rights and will always be rights") and mine explaining why I was staying. Cliff and I were very close. After

* *Montreal Gazette*, 12 February 1989.

our speeches – one had followed the other – we put our arms around each other, an affectionate parting of the ways.

From that point, the English media no longer considered me an anglophone or a representative of that community. I became an "allophone," a representative of a minority immigrant community. All of a sudden, I had an Italian name. The past fifteen years had meant nothing. Now there's loyalty. It doesn't take much to change people's thinking. Perhaps my few words in Italian, during my speech, may have had something to do with it. Such are the vicissitudes of politics.

I was affected by what had happened, feeling disillusioned and abandoned. I considered retiring from politics prior to the 1989 election, but, because of my vote on the language law, I had to stay. Otherwise my retirement might have been interpreted as an admission that I had made the wrong decision and couldn't face my electorate. The Equality Party, created that year in protest over Bill 178, ran a candidate against me in Mount Royal. Although I garnered fewer votes than in previous elections, I still won comfortably, beating both the PQ and Equality Party candidates. So did my party, handily coming out ahead of the PQ by ninety-nine seats to twenty-nine. The Equality Party won four seats. It would be the high-water mark of their electoral success.

After the elections, and before the expiry of the notwithstanding clause, Bill 178 was amended and signs, both inside and out, were allowed in both the French and English languages. I don't want to crow "I told you so," but I told you so.

A FINAL LANGUAGE LAW – REALISTIC AND ACCEPTABLE

In 1993, the time had come to make another decision: Renew the notwithstanding clause or change the law. The government decided, in accordance with the Supreme Court decision, to change the law to allow other languages on outside signs, but with French predominating. It meant that other cultural communities would also have the right to have signs in their languages.

The PQ was against the revision, of course, wanting no concessions for anyone. *Pur et dur* – pure and firm.

This was the fourth language debate of my political career and the only one in which the decision being taken was one that I wholeheartedly accepted and supported. For the first time, I was elated in making a speech on language in the National Assembly. On 8 June 1993, I stood up and said, "During the debate on Bill 178, I tried to promote understanding and avoid confrontation even though the law was not accepted by the English-speaking community. But in my mind, it was part of the evolution of our society which eventually and inevitably had to go beyond the law of that time."

I told the Assembly that the situation in Quebec was incomparable to anywhere else in the world. Here, a vibrant English-speaking community and many diverse language communities all work in a French milieu to contribute to the cultural and economic development of Quebec. Our society is unique and our laws have to reflect that uniqueness. The new language law was doing just that. It would further the interests of Quebec by allowing the full participation and contribution of all to its development.

By then I had been appointed minister of international affairs in the new government, and I noted how the language issue was affecting the perception of Quebec in other parts of the world. Most countries don't usually interfere in the internal affairs of others. In my experience there were only two areas where this was not observed – the question of language and Quebec separation.

I was constantly being asked about our language laws, whether it was in America, Europe, Asia, and the Middle East; maybe not in Sana'a, Yemen, but certainly in Riyadh, Saudi Arabia. The world was aware and took an interest in what we were doing and questioned it. Of course I had to defend the government's decisions, but these weren't always understood. It affected our image and raised questions about our credibility. Businessmen who accompanied me also had to overcome this burden. And, the language issue was not just an economic question. It was perceived as a matter of human rights. The obligation to use French on signs was not the main problem. What people in other countries couldn't understand was the prohibition of the use of English or any other language. I tried to explain that we were an open, tolerant society, but that is not the image that we gave to the world. People questioned what they saw and reacted to it.

How do you tell your biggest commercial partner, and your neighbour, the Americans with whom we have not only commercial exchanges but also institutional relations, that you won't allow outdoor signs in their language? It's not easy explaining that. I had to do it before the editorial boards of newspapers in Los Angeles, Chicago, Detroit, Boston, and New York. It wasn't easy.

I thought that Claude Néron, a Chicoutimi newspaper columnist, expressed the essence of the attitude and approach that should guide

Quebec when he wrote: "Quebec must show its maturity and learn to consider English, not as an enemy, but as an ally essential to its success and fulfillment of its potential."* This is just as true now as it was then.

The law was adopted and for some time we had language peace.

* "Le Quebec doit faire prévue de maturité et apprendre à considerer l'anglais, non pas comme un ennemi, mais comme un allie essential à la réussité et a son épanouissement," 14 December 1992.

17

Minister of International Affairs

A few weeks before the 1989 election, on a sunny Saturday afternoon, I was on my terrace with two friends, David and Diana Nicholson. The phone rang. It was Premier Bourassa. He told me that he wished to change my portfolio in an upcoming cabinet shuffle. He assured me that he was doing this, not because I wasn't doing a good job as minister of energy, but because he wanted to offer this portfolio to Paul Gobeille to entice him to run in the next election. Apparently Paul had indicated that he wouldn't run again. Bourassa told me that he would appoint me minister of international affairs.

I was surprised. "Isn't that a department with a lot of bullshit?" I jokingly asked. The department, created by Daniel Johnson's Union Nationale government in 1967, did not have the scope and importance that it later acquired. "Don't worry," Bourassa replied, "I'll give you an assistant minister in charge of the bullshit."

And so I became minister of international affairs, with a delegated junior minister, Guy Rivard, responsible for the francophonie, which was, in fact, an important sphere for Quebec – so it wasn't BS. I quickly became aware that events occurring in other lands could affect all of us.

TOUT LE MONDE EST UN PAYS

I became minister of international affairs at a time when the world was rapidly changing, and we in Quebec had to adapt or fall behind. The Berlin wall fell in 1989, and I was there, in January 1990, as it was being demolished. I crawled through an opening, meeting Russian soldiers on the other side who just looked at me and let me go by. I scooped up a piece of the broken wall and kept it as a memento. I went to Checkpoint Charlie, the American gate to East Berlin. It was deserted and empty. The streets seemed abandoned, forlorn, almost lifeless. There was sadness and misery in the air. When East Berliners crossed to the western side, you could immediately recognize them, poorly dressed, driving beat-up Russian Ladas, sad looking – they were the victims of history.

There were other events that had a profound impact: the creation of the European Common Market followed by the European Union, the freeing of eastern Europe from the grip of the Soviets and the subsequent collapse of the Soviet Union bringing the Cold War to an end. Nelson Mandela was released from prison. In Beijing a popular uprising in Tiananmen Square was crushed by tanks. In Canada, the North American Free Trade Agreement with the US and Mexico was concluded. It changed not only the way North Americans perceived each other but how we did business.

I made a presentation to cabinet about the importance of these changes. I was convinced that we could no longer have a viable domestic policy without a coherent international policy. I reviewed the various trade missions I had made and the various agreements that I signed with other countries.

I believed in a holistic approach to international relations and understood the importance of the international domain not only for economic reasons but also for cultural ones. To act strictly for economic reasons didn't necessarily give one an advantage over competitors. What made the difference was the cultural component. By showing who we were, we added something other countries did not include in their economic missions. Most of my economic trade missions to other countries always included representatives from the cultural sector.

And so I set out to develop a new international affairs policy to reflect this concern – a global approach to a global domain.

Essentially, the objective of the policy was to use international affairs as an instrument for promoting Quebec's economic, social, and cultural development. To achieve this we would set priorities for international activities and promote partnerships as a course of action. The policy would support an integrated approach, that is, making sure that the economic, cultural, social, and political factors were considered and included when conducting international affairs. Whether through joint ventures, exchanges of technologies, or investments, Quebec businesses were encouraged to be more present in other countries. We also welcomed and sought investments from other countries. It was an age of interdependence.

I gave a talk in Montreal during the Quebec–Italy week, an annual event that highlighted rapport between the Italian community and Quebec. This was part of my efforts to involve the cultural community in international affairs.

"My interest in economic development is always accompanied with my concern for cultural development. The dynamism of a society is not compartmentalized. The cultural domain is an important field both for our specificity as well as for its economic spinoffs," I said.[*]

Man does not live by bread alone. Our international policy had a role to play in maintaining our Quebec personality. For example, our links with the francophonie represented an important way to preserve our francophone identity. Our English-speaking and other cultural communities, which had become integrated into Quebec society without abandoning their languages or identities, were all important to the province – all of Quebec benefited from this diversity. To reflect that, I involved the cultural communities in my policies because I believed they could contribute to and participate in our international activities, especially with their countries of origin.

As minister of international affairs, I didn't have a shortage of issues to deal with. Add to that the local concerns of my constituents, constitutional questions, and my legislative functions such as being on hand for question period in the National Assembly and for legislative committee meetings. I travelled extensively in other parts of the world and to various regions of Quebec to promote an interest in international trade – over the course of my time as minister, I made more than fifty missions in forty-one countries. I was a "busy fellow" as I once had been described in the *Weekly Post*, a Town of Mount Royal paper,[†] and that was *before* I went to international affairs!

I needed the authorization of the premier's office to travel to another country. I was never refused, except once. I had been to France on several occasions and on this particular occasion I would have once again met the minister of French foreign affairs Roland Dumas. But the premier asked me not to go. I was not told why, and I did not ask but found [find] it curious that the only request to which he said "no" was a mission to France.

Shortly before I was made minister of international affairs, the Mulroney government's Free Trade Agreement with the United States was

* *Le Devoir,* 14 November 1990.
† *Weekly Post,* 3 July 1986.

signed (2 January 1988). Talks for the North American Free Trade agreement with Mexico had not yet begun. Canada was also preparing to negotiate the World Trade Organization Agreement. These were major events that would affect the conduct of our economies of Canada and Quebec and all of their citizens.

THE FREE TRADE AGREEMENT WITH THE US

Trade is the motor of our economy. As minister of international affairs, I believed it was my responsibility to make sure we did all we could to promote access to world markets, and especially the American market, while protecting some of our more vulnerable sectors, agriculture, for example.

Obviously, our relations with the US were of paramount importance. I had paid particular attention to our American neighbours when I was minister of energy, going to Washington to meet members of their Department of Energy and negotiated Quebec's largest electricity export contract with New York Governor Mario Cuomo. I had also met James Schlesinger, the former US secretary of energy and with Paul Volcker, the former chairman of the Federal Reserve Board.

I continued to do so as minister of international affairs. Once, in Rimouski, I met with the business community and urged them to take advantage of the American market. One businessman sheepishly said during the question period that followed, "I'm afraid to sell in Montreal, so how can I do it in the United States?" I encouraged him to stop being afraid and start acting in his own best interest.

Free trade agreements were something new. We didn't know exactly what to expect. Each province had its particular industries that they wanted to protect and not leave to the complete mercy of the marketplace. For Quebec we were concerned primarily with agriculture and with textiles. We knew that we could provide protection for some in agriculture and interim measures for others in textiles where there were 91,300 jobs in Quebec. In 1989, Montreal was the Canadian centre for women's apparel design – but with globalization that was going to change.

There were also other areas where decisions could not be left entirely to market forces, including communications, language, and cultural matters.

Then there was the whole question of provincial jurisdiction. One could understand the concerns of Quebec with regard to a Free Trade

Agreement that gave Ottawa the power to make commitments that would bind the provinces. That was one reason I wanted the province to be involved in the administration of the FTA as well as hold a seat on the panel created to resolve disputes between Canada and the US.

The federal government was aware of our concerns. It did not involve the provinces directly in the administration and decisions of the FTA – I now realize this would have been too clumsy, anyway – but did sign an agreement with the provinces creating a commission on cooperation, implementation, and development of the agreement (the CFTA). This meant that Ottawa and the provinces would work together on any dispute submitted to the settlement panel created under the FTA. The panel would have representatives from both the Canadian and American governments. To safeguard provincial interests, the federal government agreed that if the matter referred to the panel was one of provincial jurisdiction, the provinces, or the affected province, had to agree on the Canadian submission to the panel. In such a case, the affected province would be invited to participate in the dispute settlement process as members of the Canadian delegation.

The federal–provincial meetings of the CFTA were numerous and productive. The commission ensured that Quebec had full participation in the administration of relevant problems and in the dispute settlement mechanism of the agreement. The commission also initiated various meetings with provincial ministers to discuss potential problems and concerns. For example, I wanted to establish a common position among the provinces for the application of the FTA. I invited all of the provincial external trade ministers to a meeting in Ottawa on 9 May 1990 to discuss the issue. After we had agreed on our approach, we met with the federal trade minister, John Crosbie, at the first meeting of the CFTA. It was agreed that the application of the FTA would respect the distribution of powers under the Canadian constitution.

Ottawa suggested that the provinces use a "Team Canada" approach to international relations and activities. For example, Ottawa might represent a province overseas in its bid to obtain foreign investments. This, obviously, would reduce the need for a province to have its own representatives in other countries. At the time, Quebec had twenty-six such representatives around the world. I thought this was really an attempt by the federal government to control the international activities of the provinces. I also thought that this could lead to a conflict of interest because the same negotiator – the federal government – would represent all provinces. This approach would take away the neutrality of the Canadian commercial representative. Would he favour a more populous province – Ontario for example? How would a decision be made as to which province would be promoted for a particular investment? I politely refused to participate.

I prepared a free trade action plan that would enhance the performance of all Quebec delegations then attempting to penetrate the American market. It began by identifying the major products that we should be concentrating on in each of the markets where we had delegations: Boston, New York, Atlanta, Chicago, and Los Angeles. (In New York, for example, I identified clothing, furniture, and agro-alimentary products, construction materials, software, and aeronautics as most important. I did the same for the other delegations.)

The success of the FTA is seen in Quebec's trade balance with the US. In 1988, prior the signing of the FTA, Quebec had a positive trade balance of $7.1 billion. Six years after the agreement was signed, in 1994, that trade balance had increased to $17 billion.

THE NORTH AMERICAN FREE TRADE AGREEMENT

After the FTA, a continental free trade agreement that would include Mexico was on the table. I wrote to John Crosbie in September 1990, suggesting that Canada should be a party to the negotiations, which were to result in the North American Free Trade Agreement (NAFTA). I also pointed out that the application of any agreement would have to respect the division of power in our constitution, that is, the provincial legislative powers. Ottawa could not make commitments in those areas without provincial consent. That included, social policy, communications, language, and culture – everything that contributed to the specificity of Quebec society. I also maintained the right of Quebec to approve the agreement or not, depending on the evaluation we would make regarding our fundamental interests.

Our objectives were to maintain the advantages that we had under the FTA, to benefit from the potential of the Mexican market, and to develop comparative advantages for Quebec to attract foreign investments. In other words, access to the Mexican market could be an additional advantage that we could offer a potential investor.

After the failure of the Meech Lake Accord, Quebec, as a mark of protest, decided to restrain, as much as possible, its participation in federal–provincial conferences. However, Premier Bourassa was smart enough not to cut off his nose to spite his face. When such conferences dealt with international trade, I would attend and Bourassa would explain in press releases that our presence was essential to protect "les interets superieur du Québec."

Bill Clinton had just been elected president. Because of protectionist tendencies among Democrats in the US, trade negotiations with Mexico became uncertain. I went to Washington to speak to various groups, suggesting that America should sign the free trade agreement with Mexico. The US had been in the middle of discussions with Mexico when the American elections took place. I remember the surprise of many American representatives that a provincial minister would go to Washington to talk about signing and participating in international agreements. Americans were concerned about some of the problems that such an agreement would have or would create, even though President Bush had initiated negotiations with Mexico. I told them that building an economy that involved 360 million people worth $6 trillion US would only increase everyone's potential for prosperity. Moreover, economic reforms in Mexico would produce stronger growth in that country and, therefore, even greater wealth opportunities for all.

Quebec's participation in NAFTA had five objectives:

- To maintain the advantages that we already have with the FTA
- To preserve Quebec's position in the American market
- To profit from the potential offered by the Mexican market
- To develop comparative advantages for Quebec designed to attract international and foreign investments
- To compete with Mexican products on the Canadian and Quebec markets

The final agreement basically met Quebec's major concerns. The province's agricultural industry continued to be protected, supply management programs were maintained, and we obtained certain delays to allow the textile industry to adjust to the new conditions.

Signed on 17 December 1992, the North American Free Trade Agreement created the largest trading bloc in the world. Meanwhile, we were also negotiating the world trade agreement. These were busy and consequential times.

INTERNATIONAL TRADE

Rules to facilitate international trade were not new. The General Agreement on Tariffs and Trade (GATT) had existed since the end of the Second World War. There had been many different stages to the expansion of these agreements. (Negotiations were called "rounds." For example, when I was minister of international affairs, the GATT negotiations were known as the "Uruguay Round.") When these were concluded in 1994, GATT became the World Trade Organization (WTO).

Since Quebec was directly affected by the GATT decisions, I worked closely with John Crosbie, then Michael Wilson who replaced Crosbie as trade minister, and finally with the Chrétien government, elected in 1993.

After one of my meetings with Crosbie, we stood together with others to have a relaxing drink. Crosbie had an empty glass in his hand and a waiter asked him how much scotch and water he wanted. "Just two fingers," said Crosbie. "Yes, two fingers," I said. Then I held up my hand and indicated the two fingers. "Two fingers of water" showing my index and the next finger together, "and two fingers of scotch" showing my index and little finger, with a wide space in between. Crosbie laughed.

There were key issues for Quebec in the GATT negotiations. These rules affected our trade with individual countries, including those that came with NAFTA. We wanted easy access to other markets, which meant reducing trade barriers. At the same time, governments faced pressure to protect some industries, which meant that certain barriers would remain. In a sense, we wanted to have our cake and eat it too, a tricky proposition. I did not want to rely strictly on Ottawa to finalize the negotiations. I wanted to be involved because of the particular interests of Quebec. We could not protect all of our industries. It was inevitable that some, like the textile industry, would be affected. All we could hope for was to give the industries time to adjust by providing delays in the reduction of import duties.

I wrote to Crosbie on 25 October 1990, setting out Quebec's position with respect to the Uruguay round of negotiations. In agriculture we wanted to maintain our system of supply management, which controlled the amount of product reaching the market and provided stable revenues for farmers and processors. We supported the Canadian position to eliminate all subsidies with respect to the export of agricultural products. This created a distorted and destructive market, which could destroy local producers and local markets. We also asked that all cultural services be exempt from the negotiations.

I realized that the textile industry was in a particularly fragile situation. Wages in many other countries were very low. So, as with NAFTA, the best we could do was propose certain protective measures intended to give the industry time to adjust to the new situation. Unfortunately, these only postponed the inevitable decline of this industry in Quebec.

The GATT proposals that came out of the Uruguay round were included in a report by Arthur Dunkel, its general administrator. It contained two provisions I found unacceptable: the prohibition of supply management programs in the agricultural sector and the elimination of subsidies by non-national governments. In other words, Ottawa could grant a subsidy, but a province could not. This would reduce, if not eliminate, Quebec's ability to attract foreign investment.

Curiously, Alberta disagreed with us on the agricultural provision and was ready to accept the Dunkel report. At a federal–provincial conference on 12 February 1992, I argued my position and received the support of all the other provinces. Federal Trade Minister Michael Wilson said that Canada had not changed its position. In other words, my position was maintained.

The second proposal – subsidies by provinces – was more difficult. Although Canada supported allowing provincial governments to grant them, this stance continued to be refused by GATT. The *Globe and Mail* noted, "'This is a key element in attracting industry,' the Quebec minister says."*

We overcame an American proposal on electricity that would have obliged Hydro-Québec to have the same rules for internal markets as for exports. This would have prevented Hydro from granting preferential rates to local industries, a tactic often used to attract investment. The American proposal questioned Hydro's monopoly on electricity production on sites that provided more than twenty-five megawatts, by applying the principle of national treatment to investors who would want to acquire and manage electricity production installations. In Quebec the private sector cannot suddenly decide it has a right to produce and sell electricity as if it were on the open market. We did allow the construction of small generating sites by the private sector – I myself had initiated many such projects – but this was strictly under government control. The American proposal tried to apply to the electrical sector the same rules that applied to petroleum. They wanted free competition in this field, giving the private sector the right to bid and construct electricity producing projects, ignoring Hydro's monopoly position.

I stated that Quebec demanded the maintenance of state monopolies in the production of electricity in accordance with an article in the free

* 13 February 1992.

trade agreement with the US that allowed for that. We weren't there to renegotiate the FTA.

There was a close collaboration between myself and Michael Wilson to make sure that Quebec's position would be respected in both the agreement with Mexico and the GATT negotiations. When I thought the GATT talks were stalled, Wilson seemed less worried. I guess that for the whole country there was not as much at stake as there was for Quebec. I was outspoken and blunt, and a newspaper headline from the time reflected this, "The GATT negotiations: failure could hurt the Quebec economy."* I was quite direct in expressing my concerns. The deadlines for finalizing had been postponed several times, and I was losing confidence that they would ever be finalized.

I was also growing impatient. There was another issue I found totally unacceptable – the question of subsidies. Subsides were still prohibited for non-national (provincial) governments. The federal government was getting nowhere on this issue, so I decided to do something about it. I decided to go to Geneva and meet the international GATT negotiators to express my concerns. The fact that I was not a national representative did not bother me. I wanted to see those negotiators face-to-face. I wanted to renegotiate that clause myself. I persuaded the federal government to allow me to go.

On 9 November 1993, I flew to Geneva.

I obviously needed the cooperation of the federal government to meet with the GATT negotiators. The intervention of a provincial representative was quite unprecedented. I was accompanied by the federal ambassador, Gerald Shannon, who arranged and attended my meetings but did not intervene in discussions.

There were two areas that created problems for Quebec – subsidies and agriculture. As outlined above, we wanted as a province to be able to award subsidies and to continue our supply management programs. On the first day I met with all of the members of the Canadian mission. They briefed me on the status of the negotiations and on the various representatives who were conducting the talks.

The federal government and Ambassador Shannon spared no effort in organizing my meetings and making sure that I was well briefed and met all of the key people involved in the GATT discussions, including M.P. Sutherland, who had replaced Arthur Dunkel and Anwarul

---

* *Journal de Quebec*, 18 July 1991.

Hoda, the assistant director general. I felt at ease in the discussions, so much so, that others confided their own concerns to me. The chief negotiator from Japan, a Mr Akawo, for example, complained to me that the others did not understand that rice was a cultural item for Japan and should not be the subject of stringent international restrictions especially in terms of subsidies to Japanese farmers.

I was quite firm in my talks with each negotiator, especially the ones from the European Community. I told them that Canada had a constitution that allowed the provinces to grant subsidies to businesses. It was not the role or right of GATT to amend our constitution. Not only were the negotiators not respecting our constitution, they were encouraging those who wanted to break up our country. GATT was feeding nationalist arguments that Quebec would have more power if it became independent. My point appeared to be quite effective. A representative from France, after my outburst, smiled and said, "You know Mr Minister, that condition was really aimed at Bavaria." Apparently the Bavarian state government was quite aggressive in taking business away from France. I was told that GATT would remove that restriction, which it did. Of course, Ottawa took credit in the Canadian press, but I guess that is part of the game of politics. The bottom line: Quebec maintained its supply management system in agriculture.

MISSIONS TO OTHER COUNTRIES: FRANCE

Quebec had a special relationship with France. The province even owned a building in Paris that it had acquired in 1964 for $1.4 million and which was in 1992 worth $42 million. I had a very productive and revealing meeting with Roland Dumas, the minister of Foreign Affairs of France. I told him I was glad that France was my first official visit to another country as Quebec's minister of International Affairs. I felt obliged to explain that my previous trip to Bavaria (prior to my voyage to France) was strictly to accompany a firm that had asked me to be there to finalize a contract. It was almost an apology. Such was the view of France in Quebec at the time.

We discussed the activities and objectives of France in foreign affairs and the participation of Quebec in activities of mutual interest – how we could help each other and benefit our respective economies. I spoke of the possibilities for France and Quebec in the context of both the European Union and the North American Free Trade Agreement. They opened up possibilities for both of us – we could enter the European market via France and they could take advantage of the Free Trade Agreement via Quebec. I gave as an example the joint venture of the French company Bouygues with the Quebec company Pomerleau for a multimillion dollar contract in James Bay.

He asked me about Quebec's reaction to the Free Trade Agreement. I said that Quebec supported the agreement even though Ontario was against it (because Ontario already had a form of free trade via their automobile pact). I was very positive in explaining NAFTA's advantages for Quebec.

The discussions went further than the economic sector. I referred to the twinning of a French city with one in Quebec (Dordogne and Jacques Cartier) and the possible visit of the French premier to Quebec. Dumas thought that it was good idea and he would be pleased to ask the premier to make such a visit. He then spoke of the Francophonie – the support and promotion of the French language in countries that have a significant number of French-speaking people or where there is an affiliation with the French culture. He was interested in the promotion of French in Eastern Europe, especially in Poland, Rumania, and Bulgaria where there were a significant number of French-speaking people. He asked if we could work together, France and Quebec, to put French back on the scene in these regions. I answered that Quebec was interested in all actions that would help reinforce its own identity. Working with francophone countries could help strengthen our identity. He was clearly interested in increasing the role of France and its influence in the world.

At the air show Le Bourget, near Paris, contracts for $397 million dollars were signed for Quebec enterprises. That represented 70 per cent of all Canadian contracts with France. The sale to France of the Bombardier plane built at Canadair originated with this salon. On that same trip I had met with Prime Minister Edith Cresson who was the first (and so far the only) woman to hold that office. Unfortunately she resigned after barely one year in office.

There were visits in alternative years both from the French prime minister to Quebec and the Quebec premier to France. There was a big fuss in 1992 when French Prime Minister Pierre Bergevoy wrote to Bourassa and declined an invitation. I explained to a critical press that over a long telephone conversation with Alain Juppé (who later became prime minister) I was told that Bergevoy's absence was just a question of postponement – not a refusal.

CHINA

There was great scope for business with China, but the fallout from the Tiananmen Square prodemocracy demonstrations in 1989 initially dampened our enthusiasm for closer ties with the Asian giant. We gradually resumed contacts with various Chinese agencies and representatives to promote projects that would be mutually beneficial. We reasoned that economic development projects would contribute to the improvement of conditions for the Chinese people. We instituted scholarship programs and other projects that could contribute both to our own interests and those of the Chinese.

We also thought that scholarships to Quebec would be instructive for young people. These would help to expand their knowledge of a different world and way of life and the possibilities of freedom. Rather than concentrating only on business relationships, we believed that a broader approach would be more helpful. Human rights would be a delicate question, but I believed that we had to distinguish between the leaders and their acts and those of the Chinese people. Moreover, mentalities do not change from one day to the next. I thought the process of promoting change in China would be a long one.

Quebec delegations and I made many trips and held meetings with Chinese representatives in various regions. The country was changing. The influence of Mao was waning, but China remained a communist regime. There was still a picture of Mao Zedong prominently displayed at the entrance to the Forbidden City. A representative from Foreign Affairs, Sui Hui, accompanied me through an itinerary that began in Beijing and continued to Shanghai. When we reached Wuhan, she showed me the spot where Mao had swum across the Yangtse River. She wore the "uniform" of Mao's time – a red beret and green jacket. She dressed like this until we reached Shanghai where she surprised me one morning by appearing in a casual dress. The politics in Shanghai were different, it was more "Americanized," and Mao's influence less. This could be seen in the restaurants and nightclubs where a combo was playing American jazz that had been banned during the Mao years. Sui felt that she would have been out of place in a Mao costume in Shanghai. It seemed that even in dictatorships public sentiment was still a force to be reckoned with.

Conditions in China in the early 1990s were difficult. I remember a January meeting in Beijing where we all wore overcoats while sitting around a desk because there was no heat in the building. But such negotiations could be productive for the Quebec business representatives who were with me. In one instance I was in the province of Hunan with Quebec companies seeking a contract to furnish electrical equipment. The Quebec company was borrowing money from the federal government. The interest that it was paying on the loan was the difference with the lowest bid. If the federal loan were interest free, the Quebec company would have the lowest bid and would get the contract. The Quebec businessmen who accompanied me were surprised when I persuaded the Hunan officials to suspend their decision on the contract. I wanted time to persuade Ottawa to give an interest free loan. I figured that the amount in taxes that would be paid by the company from its profits and from the wages paid to its employees who would be building the equipment if it obtained the contract would more than compensate for the lost interest.

I came back to Canada and tried to meet the Conservative federal minister who could make such a decision. It was during an election, and he did not even bother to meet me. The contract was lost.

Many contracts were signed with Quebec companies and their associates. In Chengdu, the engineering firm Dessau International and Hydro-Qubec International (along with BC Hydro International) signed an agreement with the Commission of Industrial Electricity of Sichuan for a 500 kilometre transmission line. An agreement was also signed to provide a hydroelectric plant in Hubei. I met with the China National Post and Telecommunication Appliances Corporation in Beijing and signed a contract with Ingénierie Electro-optique from Quebec City. We also signed contracts in Shanghai, for example with the company M3i from Longueuil.

I enjoyed meeting with officials in the various regions that I went to, sharing the powerful Chinese liquor, Moutai. Some of those officials later came to Quebec, and one day at a luncheon, we almost got into a drinking contest – my host would lift his glass of Moutai and gulp it down in one shot. I had no choice but to do the same. I did this a few times with my smiling host. Fortunately, we were advised that our next meeting was awaiting us. This saved me. I couldn't have taken more Moutai and stayed sober.

My second visit to China in 1992 covered telecommunications and energy. I met with the minister of Posts and Telecommunications, the vice-minister of Exterior Commerce, and the vice-minister of Hydraulic Resources. Representatives from eight companies accompanied me on that mission, and many of them signed agreements for their particular products or services. At Wuhan, SR Telecom signed an agreement with Posts and Telecommunications in the province of Hubei for the sale of its products to facilitate rural telephones. With financing from Ottawa, it could provide thirty such systems. I set up most of the meetings with the Chinese officials and was present during the discussions between the Quebec and Chinese representatives.

VIETNAM

Despite an American embargo, I went to Vietnam. On my first trip I met with various government representatives and identified areas that could be interesting for Quebec firms: banking (this piqued my curiosity since Vietnam had a communist regime), manufacturing, agroalimentary, and energy.

Many of the government people I met said they wanted a market economy in spite of the country being officially a communist state. They were also hoping that their withdrawal from fighting in Cambodia would help lift the embargo. They would welcome foreign investments. I believed that Quebec had to position itself strategically to serve a population of 68 million people. Because of its ties to its former colonial master, France, whom the Vietnamese threw out in the 1950s, it was a full partner in the Sommet des pays francophones.

The Vietnamese were proud to show me Dien Bien Phu the site of the decisive battle that resulted in the defeat of the French. They had accomplished the almost impossible task of dragging heavy cannon up the side of a mountain to rain it down on the French army below. They also showed me wreckage of American airplanes that they had downed in their successful fight with the Americans. In Hanoi, on 16 January 1992, I signed an agreement with the socialist Vietnamese government for economic and technological cooperation as well as collaboration in the banking sector.

Before that trip, I had met with members of Quebec's Vietnamese community. They were concerned with human rights in their homeland. In Vietnam I spoke with the Foreign Affairs Minister M. Nguyen Manh Cam on the question of human rights and the case of a Dr Que, an activist who had been imprisoned by the government. The minister took note of my concerns, but it was just lip service. As had happened with others who spoke up for the doctor, my message fell on deaf ears.

Because of the American trade embargo, cities such as Vancouver and Montreal served as a bridge for many private transactions with

Vietnam. A financial infrastructure to facilitate the transfer of funds sent to Vietnam by the community in Canada was deemed appropriate. These transfers were estimated to be between $200 million and $300 million dollars annually. If channelled properly, the funds could be used by the Vietnamese government to purchase Quebec products.

There were banking needs. However, I didn't think it would be appropriate to bring a large Canadian bank to Vietnam. I thought that a cooperative financial group such as Caisse Desjardins would be ideal. It could not only serve as a conduit for the transfer of funds but might be a model for the same type of institution in Vietnam. Desjardins had already contacted the government in Hanoi. I went to Viet Nam with Desjardins and twenty-one other Quebec companies. My visit was sponsored by the Popular Committee of Ho Chi Minh City, Vietnam's capital city, and banking agreements were signed with the Vietnamese government.

Vietnam was a good example of the cooperation between industry and government and the identification and use of markets for Quebec products and services we strove for. And, for the Vietnamese it was an opportunity to get around the American embargo and penetrate the North American market.

CZECHOSLOVAKIA

At the end of 1989, after massive demonstrations, Vaclav Havel was elected interim president of Czechoslovakia. It was an historic occasion as he presided over the first democratic government the country had seen in more than fifty years.

I decided to go to Prague.

I went in May 1990 and I met Havel. He was a pleasant down-to-earth person. Although a bit withdrawn, he still made you feel at ease. When I saw him I was reminded of the London financiers who had arrogantly told Premier Bourassa, during one of our visits to their city, that they wouldn't let a poet become head of a European country. Well here I was in Prague with the poet who was the new president.

In Wenceslas Square, I stood between him and Alexander Dubcek, the person who had started the "Velvet Revolution," which transformed his country. The occasion marked what Czechoslovakia had overcome. Rows of Nazi Flags with their black swastikas on display were a reminder of what they had been through and had survived. It was a very moving moment for me and I felt privileged to share in their celebration triumph over the unspeakable. Havel had just published *Disturbing the Peace*. When I read it later in Montreal, I understood better why I connected with him. "I knew that between me and those around me there was an invisible wall, and because of that wall I ... felt alone, inferior, lost, ridiculed" (5). Today I believe this childhood experience influenced my entire future life including my writing." (6). So, we are not alone.

The message that I brought to the Czech people was that Quebec supported them and wanted to be a part of their new economic reality, which included more trade. I met with government officials and was offered a location in Prague that I agreed to rent as a centre de commerce et de la culture du Quebec. It soon reached its objective of becoming self-financing, and in fact, during its first five months of operation, made a profit of $50,000 from leases to Quebec businesses.

I went to Bratislava. I noticed a different atmosphere and different reaction from the people there. At one point, they started discussing some legal problems, and I was surprised to see that their point of contention was similar to a part of the Quebec civil code. I was taken to a hotel for lunch. Although it had only twelve rooms, I noticed very lavish common areas that seemed to take more space than the rooms. I asked how this hotel could afford this. I was smilingly told that this used to be the secretariat of the Communist Party.

I went back to Prague in 1992. By then the country was in the process of splitting into the Czech and Slovak republics, both of which were recognized by the United Nations. Havel resigned prior to the breakup. He knew what was coming and did not want to preside over the end of Czechoslovakia. I was concerned as to what the country's dissolution would mean to Quebec. Separatists would point to the peaceful breakup of the country as an example that might be followed in Quebec. However, I needn't have worried. The history of Slovakia and the Czech Republic were totally different. There could be no comparison with the situation in Quebec. Havel came back and was elected president of the Czech Republic.

Czechoslovakia was a good example of what could be achieved by a provincial overseas mission, promoting our business interests and making Quebec better known through cultural and other activities. The world order was changing in many ways, politically and economically. New countries were emerging, out of the breakup of the Soviet Union and asserting themselves on the world stage. Dictatorships were being replaced by democracies. We had a responsibility to support these changes and countries. Our successes in Czechoslovakia were just a few examples of how we could take advantage of those changes while helping emerging countries and those with shifting governments.

THE SYMBOL OF POLAND

The ascent of Lech Walesa as the first postwar democratically elected president of Poland deserved to be noted and applauded. Poland had had a turbulent history. In the 1990s, with the collapse of the Soviet Union, Eastern Europe was entering a new era and needed the support of the West.

On 15 December 1990, I presented a motion in the National Assembly to congratulate Walesa and give him our best wishes for success. He represented a symbol of hope for people oppressed by totalitarian regimes and a sign that justice might be achieved in those countries. Quebec, I said, could have a role to play in this process. I urged our business community to establish relations in Eastern Europe. The speed with which it might be done would support the interests of the region and the world. I related how I had met Walesa in 1989 when he told me that the reconstruction of Poland could not be achieved through pious wishes or charity. He was realistic. Poland would establish serious economic connections with its commercial partners.

I went to Poland with twenty-one members of our business community, representing various sectors of the economy including pulp and paper, industry, energy, telecommunications, transport, and agro-alimentary businesses. We were able to support the businessmen who were with us, give them access to higher levels of government, and help them to proceed with their projects. In the context of the dramatic changes in Eastern Europe, it was more than a commercial voyage – in supporting a new democracy it felt like there was a nobler motive that made our efforts more rewarding.

EGYPT AND QATAR

In January 1993, I went to Egypt and Qatar with eighteen representatives of Quebec business firms. The Canada–Arab Business Council and the Council of Egyptian Businessmen were to sign an agreement considered important in the promotion of business between the two countries.

In Egypt, I met with the Energy and Industry Minister Abdula Ben Hamad; Finance, Economy, and Commerce Minister Mohammed Bin Khalifa Al Thani; and Communications and Transport Minister Salah Hama Al Mana. We had fruitful meetings that resulted in agreements between Quebec and Egypt and contracts for B.G. Checo, engineering firm Robco Inc., Imex Foods Inc., Hydro-Québec International, and Rousseau Sauvé Warren, also an engineering firm. I struck up a friendship with Roger Warren, which continued long after our trip to Egypt.

Egypt is the land of an ancient civilization – captivating, strange, and mysterious – different from any other. I felt it in the atmosphere and in my surroundings. I saw glimpses of it in the Cairo museum with its carved tombs in bright blue, gold, and green – one with the mask of Tutankhamen at the top, slightly open and empty. I went to the pyramids at Giza where I mounted a camel and rode by the pyramids. Yes, I was in Egypt with a number of businessmen, promoting their services and products, hoping for profitable agreements, but there was more to the world than our own interests and our own history. It would be a different world if we could put everything in perspective. It might make us more complete and change our outlook on the world.

I had been invited to Qatar by Sheik Mohammed bin Khalifa Al Thani. I met him as well as the ministers of finance and of energy and industry. We signed an agreement for economic cooperation that covered many sectors: transport, communications and professional services, and electric energy and its distribution to distant areas by means of a technology developed in Quebec.

I was invited to the sheik's home. He had young children, and I remember seeing all sorts of playthings for his children, seesaws, ladders, slides. It was like a miniature park. I was impressed that he would do this for his children. I thought that when I got back home I would do the same for my grandchildren.

IRAN AND YEMEN

I went to Tehran with a group of business people and met several government officials. I remember seeing the former American embassy, abandoned and surrounded by barbed wire. Across the street were stores selling documents supposedly taken from the embassy and containing articles allegedly written by Americans and critical of Iran.

We went to the public market, called a suq, where people, dressed in their Arab garments, sometimes long and flowing, mingled with merchants. They were ordinary people doing their shopping but for me it was quite a spectacle.

The business people who were with me were able to conclude several agreements with the Iranians. SNC-Lavalin, Hydro-Québec International, and Rousseau Warren were involved in a hydro project. A friend of Roger Warren, Lambert Toupin, was also with me, representing the Canada-Arab Council. He was from a well-known Montreal law firm, Martineau Walker.

Construction Polypus International was involved in a project to build a thousand homes and Multimedia signed an agreement with the group Rayan Afzar Ing. to provide "enseignement à distance," a system of learning from home by sending assignments in the mail.

Construction Polypus also came with me to Yemen where they also dealt with a housing project of 900 units at Sana'a and Aden.

ISRAEL

In 1992, Montreal's Jewish community sponsored a conference on Israel called Issues and Prospects. I was invited as a guest speaker to one of the workshops, provocatively called "Israël-Québec – État des relations ou relations d'État." In other words the community wanted to know if we were attaching enough importance to Israel by recognizing relations at a high government level or just observing the events that occurred there.

My trip to Israel was doubly meaningful for me. First of all, I was going to the land where Christianity began. Secondly, from my days at Steinberg's and subsequently in the law practice of Sam Chait's office, I was close to the Jewish community.

I met with the consul of Israel in Montreal and identified particular areas of interest for both countries: medical instruments, aeronautics, telecommunications, and agricultural technology. These were areas that were well developed in Israel and important for us. It was not difficult to interest the business community. Israel was our most important client the Middle East. Our trade relations annually sent $63 million worth of Quebec products to Israel, representing 44 per cent of all Canadian exports to Israel.

There was a plethora of business opportunities to be had in Israel. There were technological transfers for companies such as I.A.F Biovac, Haemacure Corp., Ibes Technologies, BioCapital and Lab-Elite Ltée. There were research possibilities for the Sheldon Biotechnology

Centre at McGill University, the Cancer Institute of Montreal, and the University of Tel Aviv. It was almost a unique situation with great opportunities for all.

What I found most significant were the research institutes in Israel. Not only would they research a particular subject but they would then continue their research until they actually produced a final product. Very innovative and practical.

Because there were elections happening in Israel while I was there, I wasn't able to meet with government leaders. But, I met with the vice-premier and minister of Industry, M. Nissim. (I later met Prime Minister Yitzhak Rabin when he came to Montreal.) Our hosts were very gracious, and two young men took us to various sites that were especially meaningful. We went to the synagogue of Capernaum, a town much cited in the Gospels. We entered the Church of the Holy Sepulchre with the site of the crucifixion of Jesus. We went to the Mount of Olives and the Sea of Galilee where Jesus gave the Sermon on the Mount. We stopped and one of the young men read to us the sermon. It was a very moving and touching moment. We were there, where it all began.

SYRIA AND LEBANON

Between 1975 and 1990, the civil war in Lebanon had caused massive damages, and it would require $13 billion to restore the country. The large Lebanese community in Quebec was asking us to strengthen our links with their homeland and participate in its rebuilding. There would be opportunities for Quebec entrepreneurs. In 1994, I led a delegation to Lebanon of fifteen representatives from the Quebec business community.

I hadn't realized the full impact of the war, especially in Beirut, until that visit. Nothing could have prepared me for what I saw. First of all, five members of the armed forces, dressed in army fatigues and fully armed, with rifles, met and escorted me throughout my stay in Lebanon. The devastation to what had been one of the most beautiful cites in the world was unimaginable. The centre square was a mass of rubble. The buildings had not been levelled but what was left of them made the scene much worse. They stood, damaged, empty, windowless, broken, like ghosts, no longer alive, gazing at their own destruction.

Those who accompanied me saw the devastation but also the commercial potential of rebuilding. One was Hervé Pomerleau, who looked at the heavily damaged Sheraton Hotel and could see it being repaired. He later opened an office in Beirut, but soon abandoned it. The time was not right for a North American business model, so he left.

Elsewhere in Lebanon the countryside was lush and peaceful. The armed guards accompanying me tried to be jovial, but I couldn't get the image of Beirut out of my mind. To those who fought there for whatever cause, was it worth it?

Syria in 1994 was also a time for reflection but of a different order. Syria was important in the context of our Middle Eastern relations because it exercised a great influence on Lebanon. Unfortunately, I was ill in Damascus and late in meeting the government representatives. However, they were very receptive, understanding, and cordial. I was taken to a house where St Paul was said to have been taken after his revelation from God on the road to Damascus. This was in sharp contrast to my experience in Beirut. It was more soothing to the soul and inspiring.

OUR AMERICAN PARTNERS

America is our largest trading partner and the source of many investments, not to mention a getaway destination for thousands of Quebecers during the winter. We pay particular attention to American views. We want them on our side. Premier Lévesque went to New York to appease the US following the election of a PQ government in 1976. Jacques Parizeau felt the need to do the same, to explain his government's position and to get, if not approval, at least a promise not to interfere with his plans for Quebec.

But there were many articles in the American press that gave a negative view of Quebec and its role in a potential breakup of Canada. The Quebec government wanted to alter the bad image. We could not ignore such a powerful neighbour.

Why? Quebec ranked ninth as a United States trading partner worldwide, in the same league as France and Korea. We traded for more than $31 billion worth of goods. Our political situation had to be perceived as stable if we were to maintain our position and attract investments from other countries, especially the US.

Keep in mind the context of the times. The Meech Lake and Charlottetown Accords had been rejected. There had been a referendum and an ongoing wrenching debate in Quebec about its political future. We wanted to make sure that our largest trading partner knew where we stood and how we saw the future of Quebec and Canada. Americans could take punitive measures if they did not agree with what we were doing – boycott Quebec goods, put pressure on investors. We had to get them to understand our position and approve of what we were doing.

In late 1990 I went to New York and Boston to reassure the Americans about our political and economic situation and promote Quebec as a place for investments. I gave a breakfast talk at the Global Action Institute in New York and at a dinner of the New England Council in Boston.

I went twice to Washington in 1991 to speak to Americans in the wake of the failed Meech Lake Accord. I wanted to sensitize politicians, bureaucrats, academics, and media in the American capital to the situation in Quebec and prevent these elites from coming to the conclusion that Quebec's political future was hopeless.

I went to all major US cities and met with political representatives and with the business community. I made more than ten trips to the United States as minister of International Affairs, visiting Washington, New York, Boston, Chicago, Detroit, Miami, Atlanta, and Los Angeles. In New York I visited the Providence Committee on Foreign Relations and the Carnegie Council on Ethics and International Studies. I spoke to the business community and to think tanks. I also spoke to various business groups: the Greater Miami Chamber of Commerce, the Broward Economic Development Council, and the Canadian-American Business Alliance. (I still have the key to the city given to me by the city of Hallendale.) I spoke to a gathering of 250 business people at the Chicago Council on Foreign Relations. I also spoke at the Canadian Club in Chicago and at the Greater Detroit Chamber of Commerce.

In June 1991, I filled in for Robert Bourassa at the New England Conference of Governors and Premiers of Eastern Canada in Newfoundland. I met with the governors of Vermont, New Hampshire, and Maine. In November, I spoke to the Providence Committee on Foreign Relations at a special conference where there were representatives from all regions of the US. I also met with the executive of the American Council for Quebec Studies (which we had supported with financial aid from my department).

In December, I spoke to the Carnegie Council on Ethics and International Trade to explain our constitutional position and rectify a negative image of Quebec, which had appeared in the media. I went back to Rhode Island to participate in the first conference of the Northeast Corridor Initiative, held in Warwick, Rhode Island. There was interest in finding a way to link all of the northeastern states to a proper electric distribution system that would increase access to all concerned. Power was being provided by private companies without central government control. I thought this would offer tremendous opportunities for Hydro-Québec to provide services and equipment.

On my way to a mission to Mexico and Colombia, I stopped in Florida and spoke to the Greater Miami Chamber of Commerce and presided over a seminar organized by the North–South Center of the University of Miami, a group that dealt with relations between North and South America.

When Bill Clinton was elected in 1993, I went to Washington to meet members of the new administration, urging them to support the Free Trade Agreement (which had been agreed upon during the administration of George H.W. Bush but had not yet been signed). I met with Senator Ted Kennedy and spoke to him of the situation in Quebec and our concerns about the reaction in the United States. He was very cordial and receptive. I met with Robert Kennedy Jr. We spoke of Native rights. He had met Matthew Coon Come, a Cree leader who was fighting the Great Whale Project, and had canoed with him and several others to highlight his protest and get support. Robert Kennedy Jr was very respectful, and he had been informed about the James Bay Agreement and my role in it. However, he took the position that the agreement only gave the Natives the same rights that other citizens were entitled to. I did not argue too strongly with him.

THE LOS ANGELES SPEECH – MESSAGES TO AMERICA

The talk I gave in Los Angeles in February 1992 illustrates the message I was giving to Americans in the various cities I visited. There had been much publicity and comment in the American press about the political situation in Quebec and the PQ's demands for independence. Even though we Liberals too were asking for constitutional changes, I did not want the Americans to put us in the same boat as the PQ. We were asking for constitutional changes, not political independence. I wanted to clarify any confusion that may have been in their minds.

My speech in Los Angeles began with a prayer, what I called the Politician's Prayer: "O Lord, grant us the wisdom to utter words that are gentle and tender – for tomorrow we may have to eat them."

I gave them a brief history of what had been going on in Quebec since 1980: the referendum; the promise by Prime Minister Pierre Trudeau to bring changes to the constitution; Meech Lake, where two provinces, representing less than 7 per cent of the Canadian population, did not follow up on the commitment of their premiers, resulting in the failure of the agreement; the failure of the Charlottetown Accord, although approved by 60 per cent of francophone Quebecers. It was very frustrating to suffer all these defeats.

And what was Quebec looking for? I started by explaining the main differences between the American constitution and the Canadian one.

> This was not a constitution similar to yours. Your constitution is based on a vision of society where all men are created equal, with certain inalienable rights. It is a constitution made in America, for the Americans. The British North America Act of 1867 refers to "peace, order, and good government." The BNA, an act of the British parliament that was to be Canada's constitution, was basically a British parliamentary system grafted onto Canada's federal system. Contrary to the American constitution, the Canadian one did not provide for the same checks and balances and did not contain a Bill of Rights.
>
> For French-speaking Canadians who were, and are, a minority in Canada, the lack of adequate constitutional safeguards resulted in the erosion of certain rights. There is a legitimate concern, by a minority, that its identity might not be adequately recognized through the Canadian constitution, and that its evolution might be jeopardized within a constitutional system where some of its fundamental rights could be determined by the majority.
>
> Quebec has changed extensively over the past thirty years. But it has remained different. Because of its language, its culture, and its institutions and other distinctive characteristics, Quebec has always wanted to protect and promote its identity.

I told them the story of my son Mark. When he was five years old, I noticed one day that he had his right hand to his forehead saluting the American flag! He was watching Captain Kangaroo, on television. The American anthem was playing and all the kids in the audience were saluting the flag. Mark did the same. The problems of identity! My Los Angeles audience found this amusing.

I continued by referring to the situation in Quebec, its needs and expectations.

> Even for our closest neighbours we may be perceived differently: rich in natural resources, big producers of hydro-electricity, intent on keeping our culture alive in spite of our size and geography.

We make the news at times as an emotional people attached to its traditions. Come and see for yourself

You'll feel at home with McDonald's, General Motors, Merrill Lynch, and IBM. Then you'll notice that the signs are in French. Still you'll have no problem communicating in English in the streets, stores, museums, government offices, or seeing your favourite Hollywood movies. Montreal is a true metropolis with a vibrant and original cultural life. In fact, in 1990 the population crisis committee in Washington ranked Montreal, Melbourne, and Seattle the top three metropolitan areas in the world in terms of quality of life.

I mentioned the different types of institutions in Quebec.

You'll find a network of original institutions and corporations. Institutions like the Caisse de dépot et placement, Quebec's pension fund manager, which has assets worth more than $36 billion dollars or the Mouvement Desjardins a cooperative financial institution active in industrial loans and insurance as well as consumer banking. We have universities that function in two languages and are therefore connected to both the United States and Europe. And this is a point I'd like to insist on: I sincerely believe that the presence of French and English in Canada is a major plus. It gives us an advantage when we do business elsewhere in the world.

There had been a separatist government in power. There had been a risk of political independence and the break-up of Canada. I suggested that the reaction and acceptance by the rest of Canada of the cultural differences of Quebec would go a long way in convincing the people of Quebec that they belong in the Canadian confederation.

The failure of Meech Lake strengthened the PQ. Even Jacques Parizeau had admitted at the time that its acceptance would have bolstered federalism and reduced the power of his party. History would have taken a different turn – and perhaps would not have given the PQ much later (as I write this) the power to try to impose on Quebec a so-called charter of values that desecrated the notion of individual rights.

My Los Angeles talk was not limited to the constitutional problems of Quebec. I took this opportunity to bring to their attention other major issues that we had with America. I pointed out that Quebec ranked ninth worldwide as a US trading partner – equal to France and Korea. We traded more than $31 billion worth of goods with each other. We did $2 billion dollars with the American West Coast alone.

To illustrate the closeness of our relationship, I gave as an example Quebecor's $31 million investment in San Jose, Quebec's annual participation in the Santa Monica American Film Market, and the triumphant 1990 West Coast tour of Cirque du Soleil. These were concrete examples of the nature and extent of our exchanges with California.

I told them that the Free Trade Agreement would not have come into effect without the active endorsement of the Quebec government, which was its staunchest supporter.

I spoke about America's attempt to reduce its dependence on imported oil through the production of electricity. I gave as an example the contract between Hydro-Québec and NEPOOL, which, over the term of the contract, would save the US from using 130 million barrels of oil. Using electricity from Quebec also translated into consumer savings in the order of $2.5 billion. Both American consumers and American industries benefited.

I also gave some examples of things that shouldn't be happening: "To put it bluntly, it is okay for a US electrical utility like Bonneville Power Administration to have risk-sharing contracts to attract large customers, but it is out of bounds for Hydro-Québec to do the same. It is acceptable for the US government to subsidize corn, a major factor in the raising of hogs, but it is not acceptable for the Canadian government to help stabilize the revenues of its pork producers.

I quoted Earl Warren a famous Californian who became chief justice of the Supreme Court: "What government does for us we call social progress, what it does for others we call socialism."

We had disputes with America, which we were contesting, and I wanted my listeners to know about them. I wanted to plead my case and get support. Our relationship with the United States has always been a very close and friendly one. Geography makes us neighbours, trade makes us partners, and shared beliefs in democratic values makes us friends and allies. I ended by saying that in this age of global trade we are not competitors; we are allies. I thought it important to give these messages to this audience. I wanted America to know the concerns of Quebec. I wanted to show that there were great advantages in working together. And I wanted to bring to their attention our concerns about certain issues, hoping to get their support to resolve them.

AFRICA

The place that had the most impact on me was Africa, which I visited in 1992. It was another world. In South Africa, I remember looking up at the sky, overwhelmed with its vastness. It seemed higher than any sky I had ever seen before and it extended farther. This was a continent like no other, where mankind began. I was overawed by its natural beauty and grandeur. There was an atmosphere of peace and tranquility. Even the storms did not take away that feeling of tranquility. I saw the dark sky speckled with white clouds, the rain plummeting from the rolling clouds. Now I understood why the Afrikaner author Laurens Van der Post found these storms beautiful and enjoyed their grandness.

In Gabon, I went into small villages where the people were open, friendly, unspoiled, and welcoming. People lined the side of a sandy road to greet me. Shabby, small, dull brown, low huts lined the road. Yet, happy mothers came out of these small dwellings, with their smiling children. The smiles were contagious. I smiled back. As a mark of it being a special occasion, people were in the streets, dancing and singing. There was a person on stilts, with a tribal costume and a masked face, holding a stick, walking in the background. People were moving and bowing to the rhythm of their folk dancing. There was jubilance in the air. Visitors had arrived. I was given a drum and banged it to the beat of the music around me. I had never seen such simple joy.

I went to Ye Tsanou, a tourist village. In the distance I could see a herd of buffalos crossing the veld.

Africa represented two different facets of international activities. There was obviously the commercial aspect – opportunities for trade and investment in a changing region with myriad development needs: infrastructure, hospitals, energy, electrification, and related activities. There were also humanistic reasons for working with these countries. It is one thing do deal strictly for commercial reasons, as most of our exchanges were. It is another to do business with a country where you know the benefits will help to improve the life of needy citizens. I was aware of that difference. I couldn't see the poverty in such countries without being profoundly and emotionally affected, and I hoped that we could make a difference. That was in my mind and heart, not in my words. We had to deal with Africans on a commercial basis, not simply as paternalistic do-gooders. Quebec dealt with them as equals.

We gave financial help to assure that Karen Messing, an eminent professor at uqàm, was able to accept her invitation by the University of Witwatersrand in Johannesburg. She had been invited as a speaker at a conference on science that included representatives from the United States and Great Britain. We offered scholarships to South African students and expressed the hope that the political conditions would change so that we could resume trade relations. (This was still the era of apartheid, and sanctions against the South African regime would not end until 1994.)

We followed the events in Africa very closely. We were part of the world rising against the injustices of apartheid and the violence that it spawned. We took an active role. We supported the position of the National Congress in South Africa against apartheid. When the world reacted to apartheid and some countries imposed sanctions (including Canada), the Quebec National Assembly passed a motion of support that prohibited Quebec companies from doing business with South Africa. I made a submission to cabinet to adopt specific measures because of their policy of apartheid. Quebec would not buy any goods or services from South Africa. Furthermore, government ministries and crown corporations would have to meet certain objectives: not to export products and services to South Africa; not to give scholarships or exchange commissions with South Africa for cultural, educational, or other purposes unless those were intended to fight apartheid or to favour the majority black population. There must not be any promotion or organization of events in Quebec involving representatives from South Africa unless it dealt with fighting apartheid or with favouring the black majority.

We stipulated that, to set the example, crown corporations must cease any investments or reinvestments that would benefit any company or business in South Africa. Ministries would not invite representatives from the government of South Africa nor would there be any official missions to that country. The only official relations would be maintained by the ministry of international relations to whom all questions relating to theses matters would be referred.

The government of Quebec would favour the respect of the *droits de la personne* (individual rights) and democracy in support of the black majority of South Africa, paying particular attention to the South African visitors to Quebec who supported the movement against apartheid. Quebec would grant scholarships to the black community of South Africa.

I was authorized by the cabinet to inform my federal counterpart, the minister of external affairs, that these measures had been adopted.

I kept in touch with the consul of South Africa who had an office in Montreal. He informed me of events that were going on in his country – the changes in law that brought about the abolition of apartheid in 1994 and the measures taken to reduce violence as the country made its transition to democracy with the participation of all the major groups in the country. He sent me a twenty-page document, "The Recent Evolution in South Africa," that set forth the objectives of the new governing order – the pursuit of justice and the guarantee of fundamental rights with equality of for all. It referred to the new approach to establish a democratic government and measures that the new government was taking to achieve that end. It pointed out the repeal of the legislation that had enabled the imposition of apartheid, the Group Areas Act and the Population Registration Act as well as the Land Acts of 1913 and 1936. The document stated, "History will remember the year 1991 as the year when South Africa will have finally eliminated from its system any discrimination imposed by the law. Apartheid is now a thing of the past."

They were working on a new constitution that would guarantee the participation and representation of all South Africans in a true democracy that would respect the rights of minorities. Even if we didn't realize its full implications, we were involved in the major transformation of a society.

Nelson Mandela came to Montreal in 1990. Unfortunately either thorough bad planning on my part or a late announcement that he would be coming, I was out of the country and unable to meet him. Prior to Mandela's election as head of the South African government in 1994, he worked with the then president F.W. de Klerk to abolish apartheid, asking the world that sanctions be lifted. I responded immediately by presenting a resolution to cabinet to this effect in October 1993, six months before Mandela assumed power.

Quebec had done more business with South Africa than any other Canadian province prior to the imposition of sanctions. In 1991, sanctions were beginning to be dismantled by some countries, and the ANC softened its position, saying it would support a phasing out of many of South Africa's restrictive laws. At this time, Quebec hosted the African Business Round Table, whose representatives came to Montreal after having met with President George H.R. Bush in Washington. Marcel Côté, of the Group Secor of Montreal, was active in organizing the event. I met with Babacar Ndiaye, the president of the African Development Bank who had initiated the round table.

After sanctions were lifted, in February of 1994, I went to South Africa, Zimbabwe, and Côte d'Ivoire with twenty businessmen from various sectors of the Quebec economy including construction, engineering, and communications. SNC-Lavalin had obtained a large contract for the construction of an aluminum plant in Natal. Bombardier had signed a contract for the sale of sixteen Dash-8 airplanes.

There is a certain feeling of exhilaration and fulfillment, when one is supporting and working for a good cause. I had that feeling with South Africa and other African countries. Many African countries were turning to democracy and, for the first time, electing their leaders. We felt that it was our duty to work with them. We created a program called "Programme d'aide a la democracie" (PAD). My ministry coordinated the preparation of this program with the minister of justice and the Commission of Human Rights.

Those who attended our sessions were pleased that there were exchanges between Quebec and their own countries and left with questions to discuss when they returned to Africa. The Africans were particularly impressed that there was not an atmosphere of paternalism of the sort they often experienced when dealing with western countries. We worked with them as equal partners, sharing with them our experiences, our system of government, and the benefits of democracy.

I went to Zimbabwe, a country where Quebec did more business than any other Canadian province. I met with Robert Mugabe. This was in the early stage of his administration when he seemed to be a reasonable person free of the excesses that later marked his regime. I asked him about Ian Smith who had been the leader of the former Rhodesia. He told me, in a very matter of fact manner, as if nothing unusual had happened, that he had gone back to running his farm. There was another person in the room with us, an aide to Mugabe. He was a tall, robust, heavy-set individual who spoke to me about the role of government – its duties and responsibilities. He spoke as a philosopher. I was impressed. I also met with Dr Bernard Chidzero, the minister of finance and planning.

I thought Zimbabwe was fortunate in many respects. Although the transition from the white regime of Ian Smith to Robert Mugabe's had not proceeded peacefully, there were many institutions remaining from its colonial days. In addition to the usual government buildings and the courthouse, I was shown a building owned by a workers' union. I found this to be a marked contrast with the situation in Côte d'Ivoire where the French were still active. I found it amusing that French officials would follow me to see what I was doing, not realizing I knew of their presence.

I had the impression that the former British colonies had a different inheritance than their French counterparts. They were left with institutions – courts and administrative structures – that seemed absent in the former French colonies. Perhaps this was only a superficial impression.

In 1991 I had gone to Gabon, Benin, and Nigeria with fourteen businesspeople. There were opportunities for Quebec companies in rural electrification, electricity distribution, telecommunications, and in the forestry sector. Gabon had a relatively high per capita income because of its petroleum and timber resources. Quebec companies were on the verge of obtaining contracts, and my presence and support would help them to finalize their efforts. I met Omar Bongo, the president of Gabon. I had hosted him when he had visited Quebec. He went out of his way to make my visit pleasant. He provided me with an airplane with a comfortable luxurious interior, which allowed me to see the beauty of the country with its lush greenery and large meadows. At one point we flew over families of elephants that tried to run away from the noise of the airplane, the small baby elephants following behind. It was a striking scene that I can still visualize.

Benin was an experience of a different nature, more personal, reflective, in the person of its president, of the choices that people made in their lives. I met with Nicéphore Soglo, who was not only the first democratically elected president of Benin but the first of any nation on the African continent. When he had previously met Premier Bourassa, he had asked him to send a Quebec representative to his country. I met him in Cotonou, Benin's largest city. He had a law degree from his studies in Paris. He had been with the International Monetary Fund and was an executive director of the World Bank. He chose to leave these prestigious organizations to devote his time to helping his people and improve the conditions of his country. I respected him for his sense of responsibility and dedication. I thought of myself, in a much more modest way, leaving a lucrative law practice in Montreal to help Native people.

My travel to Nigeria was strange and unsatisfying. I was disappointed by what I saw and what I heard. I was driven by the Canadian consul to various parts of Lagos, Nigeria's largest city. For the first time in my visits with a Canadian official, I was in a bulletproof car. Apparently there was the possibility of violence. The city presented an aspect that was the very definition of poverty. Everywhere you looked there was destitution. Merchants were on the side of the road dispensing their paltry products. At one point I saw a stand with pliers on it and was told that these belonged to a dentist who worked the curbside. To add to my consternation I was taken to a small area of the city that contained the luxurious homes of the wealthy. I wondered how some could have so much while a few streets away people were living in misery.

There was a Nigerian government minister – I don't remember his name – dressed in white and blue flowing robes, with a light blue conical hat – who expressed his concerns to me. "Mr Minister," he said, "we are worried about Quebec – about its separation from Canada." I couldn't believe my ears. Here we were, sitting in the middle of abject poverty, where millions didn't have enough to eat, and he was worried about Quebec separatism. I felt like telling him, "Listen mister, you have a lot more to worry about here," but, obviously, I didn't. My visit to Nigeria was the most dissatisfying trip I made as minister of international affairs.

RETURN TO CHINA

I made a final mission to China in June 1994. Quebec-based Dominion Bridge Company was negotiating substantial contracts with China. We were told that the benefit to Quebec could be more than $800 million.

The company believed that the presence of a senior government minister was essential in persuading the Chinese authorities to finalize the deal. France and Australia were sending their highest officials to support their own bids. The projects dealt with the building of a subway and light rail system in the city of Chengdu as well as a hydro storage power station. There was also the construction of an expressway between Chengdu and nearby Dujiangyan. Chengdu was the capital of Sichuan province and had been designated by Beijing as a centre for international finance and economic development.

I was accompanied by André Dorr the associate deputy minister. The negotiations were successfully concluded and then required the final approval from the central government authorities. I was pleased when the Cedar Group Inc., the parent company of Dominion Bridge, sent a press release that stated,

The Chinese authorities of the city of Chengdu and the province of Sichuan want to acknowledge that the active participation and

solid endorsements by the Canadian authorities and of the province
of Quebec were a major factor that contributed significantly
to the success of the long and comprehensive negotiations.
More particularly, the presence of Mr John Ciaccia, minister of
International Affairs and Immigration from the province of Quebec
and Mr André Dorr, deputy minister and Mr Dominique Bonifacio
from the Quebec delegation in Hong Kong and his Excellency Mr
Fred Bild the Canadian ambassador to China, all contributed their
international experience and expertise.

This all happened with the help of my staff, especially Françoy
Raynauld, a very able member who assisted me in my ministerial functions. He would prepare elaborate position papers and briefing notes
for the various countries I visited and background material on the persons I was to meet. This was a great help in my dealings with other
countries. On many occasions he would also travel with me. His father,
Andre Raynauld, had been the head of the Economic Council of Canada. He was the first and, I think, only person from French-speaking
Quebec to have reached that post.

18

Oka – a Failure of Understanding*

When Robert Bourassa named me minister of International Affairs, he also asked me to be minister of Indian Affairs. While I was in Energy, Indian Affairs had been delegated to the minister responsible for mining, Raymond Savoie, who was under my jurisdiction. Now, even though I had a delegate minister who was in charge of francophonie, I was asked to take direct responsibility for Indian Affairs.

I couldn't refuse, but I soon paid a heavy price for my acceptance.

The problem arose in July 1990, the first full year in the cabinet of the new government, over an issue – the expansion of a golf course over Native burial grounds, considered sacred by Mohawks – that should have been easily settled with a little understanding and respect.

Would we accept that Côte-des-Neiges cemetery on the slopes of Mount Royal be converted into a course for golfers to play eighteen holes on the graves of our ancestors? Would any town, anywhere, allow its cemeteries to be used in such a way? To ask the question is to answer it. And yet that is what all levels of government, from the federal on down to the municipal at Oka, would have allowed developers of the proposed project to do. Ignorance, callousness, insensitivity, stupidity, all fanned by greed – these almost won the day and at a terrible cost.

All the federal government had to do was to buy a small parcel of land adjacent to the golf course, which was owned by a private citizen living in France and who wanted to sell it. This would have prevented the expansion of the golf course and put an end to the affair.

* This can be found in my 2000 book *The Oka Crisis: A Mirror of the Soul* (Maren Publications).

Oka mayor Jean Ouellette had seen the determination of the Natives who had erected barriers on a side road that did not impede traffic but which would have prevented workers from expanding the golf course. He knew that the development was unlikely to happen. In fact, he told me so in my office, and he demanded damages of $2 million representing the tax revenues that the town would not receive. That's when I found out that it was not just a question of the expansion of the course but the construction of an entire real estate development surrounding it. He showed me the plans. The real estate development was never publicized!

I agreed because I knew that the federal government would either pay the claims by the mayor because it had a constitutional responsibility for "Indians and Indian lands," or that it would acquire the land adjacent to the golf course thereby preventing the development and putting an end to the crisis. It would then not be obliged to pay damages to the city. I went to Ottawa to try to persuade the federal government to purchase the land. It refused to act. It too was succumbing to its "political interests." It didn't want to "create a precedent." With that kind of thinking we would still be reading by candlelight.

When I returned from Ottawa, Mayor Ouellette had changed his mind and reneged on his original commitment, presumably because of the pressure put on him by the developers – what other reason could there be?

I was obliged to cancel a scheduled trip to Siberia to deal with the events at Oka. It was also during this period that Nelson Mandela made a short visit to Quebec, which I missed. But these were minor consequences compared with the real damage to Quebec in human terms as well as with lost opportunities for deal making with other countries.

Because the town of Oka did not have a police force, Ouellette could call upon the Sûreté du Québec, the provincial police force, to remove the blockade. The weekend before the sq was asked to do this, I had warned Sam Elkas, the minister of public security responsible for the sq, not to send them in. I said to him, "What will you tell the widow of an officer who is killed – that he gave his life so that a golf course could be expanded?"

My words were prophetic. When the sq did attempt to remove the blockade, Cpl Marcel Lemay was killed, leaving a widow and a child. The Natives claimed he was killed by a bullet fired by the sq that had ricocheted off a tree. No one has been able to prove this supposition to be correct or wrong. Officially, the matter remains unresolved.

Following this day of violence, the Mohawks set up a blockade on the main road blocking all access to Oka. A long row of armed SQ officers was on one side, aiming their weapons at the blockade. On the other side were the Mohawks. It was a standoff.

I tried to negotiate a settlement, going behind the blockade to the Mohawk side under the disapproving and unfriendly gaze of the SQ. On one occasion, I stopped at the SQ line to make the point that I was also doing this for them, in order to arrive at a peaceful settlement that would eliminate the need for violence and the risk of more deaths. But I spoke to deaf ears.

Before the end of the first week of the blockade, I reached a settlement with Ellen Gabriel, who was the spokesperson for the Mohawks. I had to get back to her to finalize all the terms, and I had to get the government to accept. This placed the premier in an uncomfortable position with the SQ who were not disposed to deal with the Natives, especially the more militant Mohawks. By the time that I got back to the Mohawks, behind their lines, late the next day our settlement had fallen apart. Both militant Mohawks and the SQ had succeeded in derailing it. I left the blockade on a Sunday evening under a raining, leaden sky, the weather reflecting the foul turn of events. I was dejected and discouraged knowing that we would be in for a long, uncertain, and difficult time.

Even though the public was screaming for action, Bourassa had the patience to wait – for seventy-six days it turned out – as the blockade at Oka continued and was followed by the barricading of the Mercier Bridge by Kahnawake Mohawks who were acting in solidarity with their Kahnasetake brothers. Detours took four hours for those commuting to Montreal for work. The army was called in, and many of my colleagues in cabinet urged Bourassa to give the order to demolish the barriers. He refused. He did not want to risk other deaths, and, indeed, an SQ officer had said that demolishing the barriers could result in the deaths of twenty to thirty people. In the end the army overran the Native positions at Oka, fortunately without any further loss of life.

The costs in terms of damages, policing, and military intervention was $200 million. The human costs could not be measured. The excesses were not only on the government side, although government decisions encouraged the more radical warriors to reach for their guns.

The reactions to the events at Oka were a reflection of the values and convictions of those involved, a window on their souls. There were many who deplored what was happening, but they did not have the political will or the power to influence decisions. No one saw the light.

All had other interests and groups to satisfy. Respect for Native rights was not a vote getter. So their rights were ignored. Moderates on both sides, as always, were caught in the middle.

The golf course extension was never built. Ouellette was reelected as mayor. It took more than twenty years to establish some kind of rights for Natives over the lands. They still have not been given full ownership, but the sacred lands that held the graves of their ancestors were preserved.

So here's the lesson: go too far and there will be a reaction, sometimes a violent one. Meanwhile, governments have not become more respectful of Native rights. Only more careful.

19

Meech Lake and Charlottetown: Attempts at Constitutional Change

I had other issues to deal with in addition to my international activities.

Quebec did not ratify the Constitution Act of 1982. Pierre Trudeau had successfully manoeuvred around René Lévesque and the PQ government to get the other provinces to accept the new constitution, culminating in a ceremonial signing in Ottawa in the presence of the Queen. Given the political situation in Quebec, with an almost constant threat of separation, it certainly seemed like a good idea to respond to the concerns of Quebecers so as to draw the province into participation in the Canadian constitution. Both Robert Bourassa and Prime Minister Mulroney, a Quebecer, believed the province's nonpresence could not be ignored.

The first attempt was the Meech Lake Accord. Crafted by Mulroney's Conservative government, Robert Bourassa and the nation's other premiers, the accord was meant to resolve the major issues left unfinished when the new constitution was drawn up. Chief among them was the recognition of Quebec as a distinct society as well as a veto power for the provinces over future constitutional changes. Provinces would get greater powers in certain areas like immigration, and they could opt out of future federal programs in areas where there was overlapping provincial jurisdiction.

The agreement was doomed to fail when the premier of Newfoundland, Clyde Wells, who initially supported the accord, decided, at Trudeau's behest, not to submit it to his legislature. This, combined with the filibuster in the Manitoba legislature led by Native MLA Elijah Harper, caused the deal to fail in reaching the June 1990 deadline. What a pity.

Parti Québécois leader Jacques Parizeau at the time warned that a "no" vote meant that Quebec would proceed down the road to independence. They were prophetic words. After the failure of the Meech Lake Accord, support for sovereignty in Quebec rose to 60 per cent. Both Mulroney and Robert Bourassa tried again. They both realized that the issue was far too important to abandon attempts to resolve it. They came up with the Charlottetown agreement, another effort to accommodate Quebec in a modern Canadian constitution and recognize its particular characteristics. At one time, even Trudeau recognized this principle, recorded in his book *Federalism and the French Canadians*. He later changed his mind, but that didn't make the differences disappear in the two distinct societies that called Canada home. It only showed that sometimes certain gods have feet of clay.

When one looks at the main points of the Charlottetown agreement, one wonders why it too was turned down. Essentially, it provided for the recognition of Quebec as a distinct society. The practice that three judges in the Supreme Court would come from Quebec would be enshrined in the new constitution. There would also be recognition of Aboriginal self-government as a third level of government within Canada. The provinces were also given a greater say in vetoing any major constitutional changes.

In 1992, I gave a speech in the National Assembly, and part of it moves me even today when I read it:

In the agreement, we recognize and give guarantees recognizing that Quebec is a distinct society. By this agreement we recognize and we constitutionally enshrine this fundamental aspect of Quebec. Il est important que cet aspect soit reconnu, qu'une personne s'y retrouve, qu'elle puisse être elle-même. Sans crainte pour la reconnaissance de son identité. Et ceci est important. Cela fait partie du besoin humain qu'ont ressenti les différents peuples à travers l'histoire du monde. La reconnaissance de son identité propre est un besoin humain et elle commande un respect fondamental.

This touches on the identity of a people, their pride, their history, their development. It is important that this condition, having been recognized, permits that everyone who is a Quebecer should without fear be able to express their identity. This is primarily important. It is a human requirement, one felt among all peoples around the world. The recognition of one's own identity is a human desire and requires fundamental respect. This need touches us all. The whole of Canada recognizes it in the agreement of 28 August, and it must be accepted.

My past never left me. The need for the recognition and acceptance of my culture and identity was still there.

So much confusion was created by the opponents of the Charlottetown Accord, especially the strident and sometimes vicious attacks of Pierre Trudeau, that it too was turned down in a referendum. But 60 per cent of francophones in Quebec voted "yes," a very significant figure that indicated francophone approval and a way to bring the province into the constitution.

Hindsight shows that the acceptance of the Charlottetown Accord would have been a good move, and it would certainly have steered Canada past the dangerous shoals of the referendum of 1995 when Quebec came within a hair's breadth of breaking away.

Meech Lake and its aftermath also created the Lucien Bouchard phenomenon.

At first Bouchard was upset with changes made to the original proposal after federal hearings led by Jean Charest and, in protest, resigned as federal minister of the environment and sat as an independent. When Meech was rejected he founded the Bloc Québécois and then entered Quebec politics, taking over the leadership of the Parti Québécois from Parizeau. This was followed by the 1995 referendum, which the Yes forces almost won. This was his reaction to what he perceived to be the lack of recognition of the French community. I can understand how he felt. He was sincere. It was ironic that he won the next provincial election for the PQ against his former colleague Jean Charest who had become the leader of the Liberal party – two former Conservative ministers under Mulroney, battling it out for the heart and soul of Quebec. Politics can be stranger than fiction.

In sum, one can say that the failure of Meech Lake and everything to do with constitutional moves that came afterward served to keep the flame of separatism alive.

In 2006, the House of Commons of Canada went further than the Charlottetown agreement when under a Stephen Harper government it passed the Québécois nation motion, recognizing Quebec as a nation within a united Canada. But it was too little, too late. The damage had been done.

CARLYLE SCHOOL AND THE CHARLOTTETOWN ACCORD

The Charlottetown Accord also had some interesting side effects that went all the way down to the riding level. On one occasion, just before the 1992 referendum on the constitution, I was invited to Carlyle Elementary School to meet teachers and speak to children. I was overwhelmed by what I heard. The meaning and possible results of the referendum were totally misunderstood by many, especially the children who were misinformed and alarmed by what their parents said.

"What will happen if Quebec separates? A lot of people will lose jobs. If Quebec separates would taxes be higher? Who started it? Who wants to separate us?"

One of the children sadly said that if Quebec separates he would have to leave "because Grandpa will want to leave. He wants to stay in Canada." As a grandfather myself, I was touched.

"Taxes are going to be raised, people are going to be moving, and there will be more muggings because more people will be poor. And we're going to need to pay $1 million to get out of Canada."[*]

Teachers didn't ask me these questions. Young children – eleven, twelve-year-olds, were expressing these worries. I had tears in my eyes. What were parents telling their children? What were the discussions at home? It wasn't fair to the children to alarm them in this way. I spoke to the *Weekly Post*, the local paper in Mount Royal. "Reassure, don't scare, the kids." This was not an atmosphere for them to live in.

CHARLOTTETOWN: A REPLY TO PIERRE ELLIOTT TRUDEAU

The most noble profession of man is to unite other men.
Antoine de Saint-Exupery

I had always admired Pierre Elliott Trudeau. I saw him as an inspiring figure who kept Canada together in the face of a strong separatist government in Quebec. However, I was surprised when he opposed Meech Lake and fought against the Charlottetown Accord. I could not understand why he opposed them so strongly.

He had given an interview to *Maclean's* magazine denouncing the terms of the proposed agreement. In my mind Charlottetown was too important to let Trudeau's attack go unanswered. On 5 October 1992,

---

[*] Town of Mount Royal *Weekly Post*, 15 October 1992.

three weeks before the referendum on the Charlottetown Accord, I gave a talk to the Canadian Exporters Association at the Queen Elizabeth Hotel in Montreal using the occasion to give my "Reply to Pierre Elliott Trudeau."

I too had been fighting separatism. I was in the trenches in the 1980 referendum. I fought the PQ when they were in power. I too wanted to keep Quebec within Canada and sought every means to make it so. I knew that there were grievances in the French-speaking community that gave rise to separatism, which was the wrong solution to remedy those grievances. I saw the Charlottetown Accord as an answer to those grievances and as an answer to many of the problems that the separatists had raised in pursuing their goals. I was not the only person to think so. The Conservative Party, the Liberals, the NDP, and all of the leaders of the provincial governments supported the accord. It was opposed by the Reform Party, the Bloc Québécois – who knew it would sound the death knell of their movement – and by Pierre Trudeau.

I told the exporter group:

Whenever I lead a trade mission in any part of the world, whether in Europe, Asia, the Middle East, or Africa, the first question that I am asked is, "What is happening to Canada? Will Quebec leave Canada?" It seems that the constitutional issue hangs as a cloud over everything we do and everywhere we go to do business.

The international community, the business community, want political stability, which will help to give us economic stability. There is no doubt that the constitutional question hurts us a great deal.

And if that isn't enough, we have a former prime minister of Canada, who has an international standing and who should know better, making statements that promote confrontation among Canadians and that add to the confusion in the minds of the rest of the world. The world is watching us, and his statements lessen the confidence of the international business community that we can and will settle our problem.

I then went on and described what he had said, criticizing him for it and pointing out what I felt were contradictions with statements that he had previously made in his book *Federalism and the French Canadians*.

I ridiculed his interpretation of the Canada clause in the new agreement. Trudeau had suggested in a *Maclean's* article that the agreement would lead to the disintegration of the federal government and, ultimately, to the end of Canada. I reproached him for using buzz-words that stirred strong emotions against the accord in English Canada, words like "nationalism," "racism," "blackmail." He had no need to convince francophones one way or the other. All he needed was the failure of any one province to approve the agreement and it would come to nothing. I was shocked that the former prime minister of Canada insinuated that Quebec's constitutional proposals had a racist overture. I found this divisive, driving a wedge between English and French speakers. I continued,

> As a Quebecer and Canadian of Italian origin I am proud of my cultural heritage. I have not denied my roots. Because of the circumstances surrounding my studies and my youth I also consider myself an anglophone. But I also feel at home in the francophone community. My two grandsons, Nicholas and Erik, are the great-great grandchildren of the author and poet, Sir Basile Routhier who wrote the French version of "O Canada." There are not many places in the world where someone with the name Nicholas and Erik Ciaccia could be the direct descendants of the authors of the national anthem of their country.

I quoted from *Federalism and the French Canadians*: "I do not accord an absolute and eternal value to the political structures or the constitutional forms of state ... With the exception of a certain number of basic principles which must be safeguarded, such as liberty and democracy, the rest ought to be adapted to the circumstances of history, to traditions, to geography, to cultures and to civilizations."

"Mr Trudeau," I said, "We almost get the impression that the signatories to the Charlottetown Accord took your book and used it as a guideline to draft the agreement. You should be for it, not against it."

Voting "no" would not mean a return to the status quo, as Mr Trudeau asserted. There was a greater danger. I suggested that nationalism was a fact of life. It could no more disappear than the ocean can evaporate. It had only two directions – it could lead to independence or could be channelled constructively into federalism. The Charlottetown Accord offered that channel to those in Quebec who were of nationalist sentiment.

I concluded with an appeal for unity. "The Canada Clause, with all of its provisions, is a reflection of the reality of Canada."* There is a vision of Canada in that clause which confirms the vision that the rest of the world has of Canada – a country that is noted for its tolerance, its attachment to democracy, where persons of different linguistic and cultural backgrounds can work together and thrive together, where we recognize and respond to the Native peoples. That is the country that we want to keep together – the country we want to maintain with the Charlottetown Accord.

"For God's sake, let's come to our senses as a country. At the risk of disappointing lawyers, constitutional experts, and even former prime ministers, let's stop listening to those who would promote confrontation. Let's look at the Charlottetown Accord in a positive fashion. Yes, let's get on with the work of building this country."

The majority of the voters in seven provinces rejected the accord. It was approved by a slim majority in Ontario. Quebec also voted "no," but 60 per cent of francophone Quebecers voted "yes." That says it all. And don't ask now why separatism stays alive.

* The Canada Clause, in brief, put into words the values that defined Canadianism. They included equal rights, recognition of diversity and of Quebec as a distinct society within Canada.

20

Doubts, Uncertainty, and a Referendum

Doubt is something that gnaws at you, that wears you down. In spite of my successes in my missions to other countries, I began to have doubts about what I was doing in Quebec public life and in my relations with my colleagues. I began to question my role in the political process. I didn't seem to have the ability to convince my colleagues. We didn't seem to speak the same language. Either I saw situations different from them, or perhaps I was going through a personal change. Or perhaps it was an accumulation of unattained objectives – the Oka crisis, Meech Lake, the language debates. Perhaps, over time, these conflicts, if you take them to heart, drain you. In any event, I felt that politics no longer had the same appeal for me nor afforded me the same opportunities to help others.

This is how I felt on the eve of my trip to South Africa. In June I was asked to go to China to help Quebec companies finalize certain important contracts. When I came back, I decided to leave politics. I gathered my staff in my office and told them of my decision. I thanked them for their work and expressed my gratefulness for their devotion. They were shocked. Some were on the verge of tears.

I called John Parisella, who had been Premier Bourassa's chief of staff and now had the same role with Premier Daniel Johnson, to tell him of my decision. (Johnson became premier after Robert Bourassa resigned in 1993.) He was very considerate and respectful of my choice. However, without directly asking me to stay, he spoke of the forthcoming elections. If the PQ won – the polls showed them ahead – they would certainly hold a referendum. Parizeau had been speaking about it openly. He asked me in a very considerate and thoughtful way whether I would be more effective in a referendum as a member of the National Assembly rather than as a private citizen. His placid demeanour and genuine concern had their effect on me. I thought about it for a few seconds and told him I would stay. I hadn't lost my sense of responsibility.

ANOTHER REFERENDUM

There are moments in the life of a society that have lasting effects on the future. For me, the failure to support Meech Lake and the Charlottetown Accord were among those moments.

The person who waged the most effective campaign for the independence of Quebec was Jacques Parizeau. His goal was to break off from the rest of Canada by 24 June 1995, the date of the Fête Nationale, Quebec's national holiday, previously known as St Jean Baptiste Day. He almost succeeded by a combination of his own efforts and the mistakes of his opponents (the rest of us).

In a speech to the National Council of his party, in late January of 1993, he said that a majority of French-speaking Quebecers could approve the move toward sovereignty without the support of the non-Francophones. He was right. He had seen the results of the Charlottetown vote. "What it means is that Quebecers can attain the goals they set for themselves even if essentially it's almost entirely old-stock Quebecers who will vote for them," he told the delegates.

I was on a trade mission in Cairo, on my way to Milan and London, when this was said. I reacted immediately. I deplored Parizeau's attempt to create ethnic conflicts. "While the need for harmony between peoples is necessary in many parts of the world to find solutions to racial and ethnic tensions, the statements of the leader of the opposition not only create these divisions within Quebec, but they are also a bad example to give to the rest of the world. Statements provoking interethnic tensions are the last things that the world needs."

I went back as a member of the opposition after the PQ, with Jacques Parizeau as leader, won the election in September of 1994. My heart was no longer in politics and, as someone told me later, when I was a member of the board of directors of Pomerleau Inc., the Montreal-based construction company, it showed. I left after question period when the assembly was sitting and did not participate in any of the debates. I did, however, attend caucus meetings when they were held. This turned out to be important and set the stage for my last hurrah.

I was active in the referendum of 1995. I attended rallies, made speeches, and organized in my own riding. I was enthusiastic. After all, this is why I had decided not to leave politics and to run in elections.

Much has been written about this near tragedy: the misleading question, the tactics of the PQ appointees in rejecting ballots in federalist ridings, the final meagre margin of victory for federalists that nonetheless defeated the expectations of Jacques Parizeau and made him blame the result on money and the ethnic vote. This was not a glorious moment in Quebec politics.

The Cree and Inuit did not accept the position taken by the Quebec government. They did not want to be bound by a possible "yes" vote by the rest of the province. So they had their own referendum and decided that they would remain within Canada.

On election night, as the results were being announced showing, in the early stages, a clear advance by the "yes," pro-Separatist side, there was panic in my committee room. I tried to reassure my volunteers, but I was worried. The owner of the building, Tony Dieni, who had allotted us the committee room, couldn't believe what was happening. At one point I left the room and went to my office in another part of the building to collect my thoughts. I couldn't show that I too was worried. I had to put up a brave front. I kept encouraging my people, telling them to wait for the vote in the federalist ridings to be announced. This would give us a win. Don't panic. Don't worry. I tried to reassure them, but I was not convinced in my own mind. Finally, the total results were announced. The federalist option had won by a margin of less than one per cent. We were all relieved but upset and concerned at the close call.

It was not a happy evening.

The political landscape in Quebec had changed dramatically. Not only was a PQ government back in power, but, as well, the man who recruited me into Quebec politics and made me a minister in his governments was gone. Having been diagnosed with a malignant melanoma, he had resigned in 1993 and would die of the disease three years later. Robert Bourassa's devotion to Quebec and his duties probably came at the cost of his life. During the Oka crisis, he did not take the necessary time to be treated for the melanoma. He believed that it was more important for him to discharge his responsibilities as premier. Politics was his life and, one might say, his death.

21

The Last Hurrah

After the referendum, I continued to be inactive in the National Assembly – until the PQ introduced legislation that would affect the rights of the English speaking community. Then I went back to work.

There had been legislation that abolished confessional school boards and replaced them with language boards, French and English. The PQ government introduced legislation concerning the voters for these boards, providing that only persons who had children at an English school could have the right to vote for the members of the English board. In other words, if you were a member of the English community but did not have school-age children, you had to vote for the French board. This, in my view, took away certain rights of the English-speaking community. All members of the community should have the right to vote for their own boards. This was a community institution and should be controlled by the whole community. Why make this distinction if not to reduce their rights? I could not let this go by – especially since my party was prepared to go along with the proposal.

Legislation requires three readings in the National Assembly. The first is merely a deposit of the legislation and does not require a vote. The second reading is where the battle lines are normally drawn. The Speaker calls for those who are in favour, those against, or those who wish to abstain from voting. This last category is almost perfunctory – there is seldom a response.

When the call was made in second reading, all my colleagues voted with the PQ, accepting the legislation. When the Speaker asked for abstentions, I stood up. Heads turned. This was a very unusual move. Usually if you did not agree with your party, you merely left the room, and your name was not recorded in the "yes" votes. You didn't draw attention to your disagreement. You kept it quiet. My gesture caused surprise – and a little consternation among my colleagues. It was almost unheard of to show publicly that you did not agree with your colleagues and send a message to the public. The press noted it and one journalist wrote that I had given new meaning to the procedure of "abstention."

It should not have come as a surprise to my colleagues. I had already indicated in caucus that I did not agree with stripping away the rights of the English-speaking community in such a petty way. In all fairness to the leaders of the party at the time, the reason they went along with the PQ was not to take rights away from the English community. The change from confessional to language boards had required the tacit consent of Ottawa because confessional boards were guaranteed in the constitution. They feared that the PQ would not accept our position because this could create the possibility of reopening the constitutional question.

The next caucus meeting was very agitated. What happens in caucus is private and there are limits to divulging its proceedings. I made my case, citing the community – you can't divide and weaken it by taking away the right to vote for members of its own school board. You could see that the PQ wanted to reduce the powers of the English-speaking community, giving them fewer rights than Francophones.

As for the constitutional issue, I believed that the PQ didn't want to reopen it any more than anyone else. But I wasn't prepared to sacrifice the rights of a community to avoid a constitutional issue. I would not vote for the law, and on third reading I wouldn't just abstain, I'd vote "no."

If there is one thing that's anathema, it's voting against your party. It shows a split and weakens the party's position. In this case it was even worse. It would send a clear message to the English-speaking community that the party was prepared to sacrifice their rights.

All the caucus members listened. Then one of my colleagues said, "John is right. I'm voting against the law." Then another did the same. After a few others indicated their dissension, the decision was finally made not to accept this provision in the new law. The Liberal Party asked that the terms of the proposed law be changed. English school boards would be elected by all members of the English-speaking community. Period.

What did the PQ government do? They accepted our changes! Mission accomplished – but at the cost of a few bruised egos.

FAREWELL

"I am really changing. Politics no longer has the same fascination for me as it once did. I want to change the way I live. I am changing and as a result, my approach to political life is changing."

I wrote this in 1994 in a small black notebook when I first wanted to leave politics. I decided to stay to fight in the referendum after my conversation with John Parisella, but now the referendum had been won, and after twenty-five years in politics I still felt differently. I had accomplished as much as I could. I was the dean of the National Assembly, the person who had been there longer than any other sitting member. And I was totally exhausted. I no longer felt the need to be in politics.

The Liberal Party had a new leader, Jean Charest. I decided I wouldn't run in the next election, which had been called for 30 November 1998. Instead, I announced my resignation from politics, and on 21 October I gave my farewell speech in the Quebec National Assembly.*

I was graciously introduced by Monique Gagnon-Tremblay, who had become interim leader of the party after the resignation of Daniel Johnson. Gagnon-Tremblay made very complimentary remarks on my career from my time as a lawyer, in the federal civil service, and in Quebec politics. She spoke of my involvement with Natives, my role in the James Bay Agreement, my contribution to the free trade debates, my concern and involvement with minority rights, my efforts at uniting people from all backgrounds.

The premier, Lucien Bouchard, also spoke when I resigned, saying, "On me permettra de noter en particulier, du côté de l'opposition officielle, le départ du doyen de l'Assemblée, le député de Mont-Royal, qui a été un acteur et un témoin du dynamisme et du sens de l'innovation de cette Assemblée au cours des années. Je voudrais le saluer personnellement."

In my farewell speech I spoke of my approach to politics and some of the things that I had learned. First, I had learned humility. Nothing really prepares you for the turmoil and complexity of politics – no matter how much success you might have had in your previous career. When one goes into public service, for that's what politics is, one has to begin anew. Everyone and every situation must be approached with humility and respect.

* Ten other members were leaving at the same time.

Next comes determination. You are placed in situations that you take to heart. You want to change the way things are done. You want new solutions. You want to respond to those you serve. You must be determined to work at it until you have reached a desirable result.

Then comes the most important aspect of political life: You must act according to your convictions. That's where you draw the line in any decision or endeavour. Yes, there can be compromises, grey areas, facilitation on the way, but never at the expense of your convictions. These you must always respect and live up to – no matter what the consequences. There are times when this will put you at odds with your own party, but you cannot stray from principle. You must be able to look at yourself in the mirror and not feel ashamed.

Finally, you must be able to open yourself to others, accept who they are, how they think. Respect differences. Politics is done with heart. Open your heart to the world.

I thanked my colleagues and the members of the government.

I'm using this occasion to warmly thank my colleagues on this side of the House. Thank you for your team spirit, your support over the years on all the legislation, and for your pats on the back and kind words at times when I needed them most.

I want to thank also the opposition members who have been good adversaries, who led me into lively debates, and who – before the Speaker, whom I thank, changed the rules of the Assembly – made me spend many eventful nights in debate.

When I finished all my colleagues came over to my seat to congratulate me. When I saw Premier Lucien Bouchard leaving his seat and coming over to congratulate me, I left my seat and went to meet him. Halfway across the floor of the National Assembly we shook hands and I thanked him.

Then I left the National Assembly and went home.

Index